T. S. ELIOT

A BEGINNER'S GUIDE

T. S. ELIOT

A BEGINNER'S GUIDE

ALISTAIR WISKER

Series Editors
Rob Abbott & Charlie Bell

Hodder & Stoughton

A MEMBER OF THE HODDER HEADLINE GROUP

Orders: please contact Bookpoint Ltd, 130 Milton Park, Abingdon, Oxon OX14 4SB. Telephone: (44) 01235 827720, Fax: (44) 01235 400554. Lines are open from 9.00–6.00, Monday to Saturday, with a 24-hour message answering service. Email address: orders@bookpoint.co.uk

British Library Cataloguing in Publication Data
A catalogue record for this title is available from The British Library

ISBN 0 340 80034 8

First published 2001
Impression number   10 9 8 7 6 5 4 3 2 1
Year 2007 2006 2005 2004 2003 2002 2001

Cover photo from Hulton-Deutsch Collection/Corbis.
Cover illustration by Jacey.
Typeset by Transet Limited, Coventry, England.
Printed in Great Britain for Hodder & Stoughton Educational, a division of Hodder Headline Plc, 338 Euston Road, London NW1 3BH by Cox & Wyman, Reading, Berks.

CONTENTS

How to use this book

The *Beginner's Guide* series aims to introduce readers to major writers of the past 500 years. It is assumed that readers will begin with little or no knowledge and will want to go on to explore the subject in other ways.

BEGIN READING THE AUTHOR

This book is a companion guide to Eliot's major works, it is not a substitute for reading the books themselves. It would be useful if you read some of the works in parallel, so that you can put theory into practice. This book is divided into sections. After considering how to approach the author's work and a brief biography, we go on to explore some of Eliot's main writings and themes before examining some critical approaches to the author. The survey finishes with suggestions for further reading and possible areas of further study.

HOW TO APPROACH UNFAMILIAR OR DIFFICULT TEXTS

Coming across a new writer may seem daunting, but do not be put off. The trick is to persevere. Much good writing is multi-layered and complex. It is precisely this diversity and complexity which makes literature rewarding and exhilarating.

Literary work often needs to be read more than once, and in different ways. These ways can include: a leisurely and superficial reading to get the main ideas and narrative; a slower more detailed reading focusing on the nuances of the text, concentrating on what appear to be key passages; and reading in a random way, moving back and forth through the text to examine such things as themes, or narrative or character.

With complex texts it may be necessary to read in short chunks. When it comes to tackling difficult words or concepts it is often enough to guess in context on the first reading, making a more detailed study using a dictionary or book of critical concepts on later reading. If you prefer to look up unusual words as you go along, be careful that you do not disrupt the flow of the text and your concentration.

VOCABULARY

You will see that keywords and unfamiliar words are set in **bold** text. These words are defined and explained in the glossary to be found at the back of the book.

The book is a tool to help you appreciate a key figure in literature. We hope you enjoy reading it and find it useful.

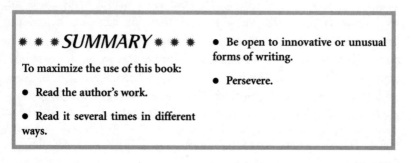

✳ ✳ ✳ *SUMMARY* ✳ ✳ ✳

To maximize the use of this book:

● Read the author's work.

● Read it several times in different ways.

● Be open to innovative or unusual forms of writing.

● Persevere.

Rob Abbott and Charlie Bell

Why Read T. S. Eliot Today?

T. S. Eliot once described a great poet as someone who, in writing of his own experience writes the experience of his time. In exploring the experience of his or her time the poet can also speak to our time and to future generations. Although he was writing about Shakespeare, the thought is relevant to the continuing and growing reputation of Eliot himself. We read Eliot for the richness and newness of his language and the challenge and perception of his ideas and images. No reader or writer can forget his poetry, his critical essays, his drama, his polemic and his thoroughgoing dedication to the production of his audacious and influential works. Such ideas, images, phrases, lines, speeches and paragraphs as Eliot provides us with are not to be forgotten.

ELIOT'S OPENING LINES

Eliot is particularly perceptive in his understanding that his reader must be enticed into his work and caused to read on, as part of a participative activity. Here are the opening lines from four of his greatest works:

* Let us go then, you and I

* April is the cruellest month, breeding

* We are the hollow men

* Time present and time past
  Are both perhaps present in time future

The first is 'The Love Song of J. Alfred Prufrock', the second *The Waste Land*, the third 'The Hollow Men' and the fourth the *Four Quartets*. There is a self-aware contentiousness and questioning here which is characteristic of Eliot. Am 'I' the 'I' in 'Prufrock'? Why is April so cruel, the new spring? What does this mean, 'hollow men'? Is past history connected to present history and both to the future? I think that you will agree that already we have the sense of a poetry which creates effects and asks questions rather than tracing arguments and providing solutions.

UNFORGETTABLE LINES

It is often valuable and instructive to ask ourselves questions about what would make us read on in an author's work based on brief quotations. This is particularly relevant when approaching Eliot's work. He so often seems to compose in unforgettable phrases or lines. Here are just a few:

> I have measured out my life with coffee spoons
>
> ('The Love Song of J. Alfred Prufrock')

An apparently prosaic and yet startling observation about the self of J. Alfred Prufrock, it reveals a state of ennui, the observation of someone who has seen everything and done everything. In context the passage reads:

> For I have known them all already, known them all –
> Have known the evenings, mornings, afternoons,
> I have measured out my life with coffee spoons

The observation of someone who has perhaps seen too much, too often! The words are redolent with repetition and rhyme. Yet how many of us have felt like this! Is this the observation of a lonely, desolate person or of an over-social one?

> What you get married for if you don't want children?
>
> ('A Game of Chess', in *The Waste Land*)

The purpose as well as the experience of marriage has been more and more closely scrutinized during the twentieth and early twenty-first centuries. You don't have to be either for or against the institution of marriage to see that this scrutiny has been a characteristic of the political, religious, social and personal debates of recent years.

In my beginning is my end
        (from 'East Coker' in *The Waste Land*)

One of the central ideas given focus by **modernists** is the importance of the present moment in which may be contained all that has been and is to come. Eliot, opening the second of his *Four Quartets*, 'East Coker', is also thinking of his ancestral connections:

> If one can really penetrate the life of another age, one is penetrating the life of one's own
>
>   ('Introduction' (1928) to
>   *Selected Poems of Ezra Pound*,
>   Faber & Faber, 1959)

As we noted at the beginning of this chapter, Eliot's view was that in exploring the cultural, artistic and emotional life of other ages an artist, any human being, stood a greater chance of comprehending his or her own age:

> Immature poets imitate; mature poets steal; bad poets deface what they take, and good poets make it into something better, or at least something different.

('Philip Massinger' (1920), in *Selected Essays 1917–1932*, p.206)

Ezra Pound provocatively asserted that all poets steal, only the bad ones are found out. It is a truth shared by many writers that imitation is a good way to begin and to learn. In maturity the great poets realize their own style and borrow from others if it suits their purpose.

THE RELATIONSHIPS BETWEEN READING AND WRITING

Eliot is read for the fascination which he reveals in the relationships between reading and writing, tradition and the individual talents of new writers, literature and society, the past, the present and the future.

> **KEYWORD**
>
> Modernist/modernism: Modernism was a movement which affected the arts and sciences between 1885 and 1940 (approximately). Its main elements in its literary form were a reaction against the rather loose conventional poetry and fiction of a previous age and a focus on absolutely accurate presentations of experience, appropriate words to capture feelings and arguments, an attention to trying to capture experience and an awareness that established values and expressions were fragmented and ineffective. Chief writers include T. S. Eliot, Virginia Woolf and James Joyce, and artists Picasso and Brancusi.

It is important to remember that Eliot was growing up as a man, an international citizen, and a writer in a world which was growing more conscious of its development and potential in artistic and scientific terms. At the same time that world was growing more aware of debates and divisions which were so extreme they divided modernity from any past world and societies from each other. The modern world was growing gloomier about its future. There were revolutions in progress in travel, communications, warfare, social and political life, and social, political and religious belief as well as the arts.

Eliot helped to construct a new relationship between poet and reader in a modern world which was growing aware of its own capacity for literacy. The writer was growing more sophisticated, but so also was the reader. Eliot relied on this development of sophistication in the reader very much and gave it a new focus. In a letter to I. A. Richards Eliot wrote:

> A good poem should have a potentiality of evoking feelings and associations in the reader of which the author is wholly ignorant. I am rather inclined to believe, for myself, that my best poems are possibly those which evoke the greatest number and variety of interpretations surprising to myself.

(Library of Magdalene College, Cambridge, 11 November 1931)

He is one of the twentieth- and twenty-first centuries' literary touchstones as author, critic and public figure. His extraordinarily imaginative and versatile early verse was written at a time of political and emotional turmoil, and expresses by diverse means the crisis of identity which the age produced. Consider to what extent our current world has resolved such gender, cultural and racial confrontations as Eliot and others of his generation, Ezra Pound, Virginia Woolf or D. H. Lawrence for instance, present.

RICH VARIETY

It is interesting to explore why the work of some writers survives and that of others doesn't. Eliot's work survives and will continue to survive because of its variety and its recognition of the necessity of experimentation, as well as the richness of his use of language. The variety of the work extends over poetry, drama and a wide range of critical writing engaging with literature and literary traditions, education and faith. Experimentation is a hallmark of Eliot's writing and is especially evident in the poetry. Another and related question to ask is why the work of some writers is rediscovered and revived in different generations. Such an exploration becomes complex and productive, and is helpful in terms of understanding the work.

The factors involved are cultural, political, social, religious and gender related. These complex factors are involved in a study of the production, publication and survival of any literature. And then there is fashion, the suitability of the work of a writer to a new generation. In the modern age we might not have become so closely involved in reading the work of the **metaphysical** poets (in particular, John Donne and Andrew Marvell) if Eliot hadn't written about their work. Eliot himself is read today partly because of his unending freshness as a poet and partly because of his involvement in and understanding of all of these factors.

> **KEYWORD**
>
> Metaphysical: meta-physical poets wrote in the seventeenth century. They include John Donne, Andrew Marvell, Wyatt and George Herbert. Many were courtiers, some political men, some religious. They used wit and metaphor to suggest thoughts and ideas about existence, identity, time, love and other concepts, and they often brought together a variety of references such as astrology, God, travel and science in order to do so. Often their poems turned on a single comparison which was developed into a 'conceit', a complex idea expressed in an image.

IN ADVANCE OF HIS TIME

There are two other important perspectives on reading and responding to T. S. Eliot which are worth thinking about: the first is that Eliot has a reputation for being 'difficult'. That reputation has been modified in our own time largely because readers have become more sophisticated and more at ease with the techniques used by the Modernist writers. Looked at from this point of view we can see that much of Eliot's work was in advance of his own time. He believed that the critic exists to elucidate and not to make judgements of worse against better, that readers will form correct judgements for themselves. The second is that there is a perception of Eliot as someone with a 'secret' life, that there is a mystery about him, forgetting that we all have secret lives of one sort or another.

Eliot has a justified reputation for being brilliant, challenging, humorous and of our modern, urban world. We mustn't ignore the popularity, the public success of *Old Possum's Book of Practical Cats*, first as a book of poems and then as an illustrated book of poems. Public readings of *Old Possum* have been widely successful and more recently Eliot's cat poems have been presented as a stage-show, Andrew Lloyd Webber's *Cats*, which has proved to be one of the most popular ever known. More recently still, Michael Hastings has been highly successful with his *Tom and Viv* both in its stage-play and film versions. Thus there is no apparent end to popular fascination with Eliot's work and life.

In many ways he explores and stands for some of the foremost themes, questions, difficulties and sometimes successes of the modern world in terms of gender, culture, nationality and faith: What is it like to be American? What is it like to be British? What is it like to be male? What is it like to be a poet and author? What is it like to be a great poet and a great author? What is it like to pursue faith and belief in the modern world?

IN SEARCH OF IDENTITY, BELIEF AND THE MODERN

From his beginnings as a writer Eliot was ambitious to express his talent as best and as successfully as he could. He was self-consciously contentious. He was also belligerent, arrogant, opinionated, humble, excited and defeated by modern life as he saw it. Prone to crises, he was someone in search of identity and belief. It is what made him readable in the twentieth century, and what will continue to make him readable in the twenty-first century and beyond. Eliot's search for identity and belief is apparent in his personal life and in his work. As American, British, Christian, male, banker, publisher, writer, teacher, enemy and friend he searched for identity. That same search makes him in many ways characteristic of the century in which he lived. He will be read for as long as reading goes on for that very reason. He will also be read for the challenge, complexity, simplicity and sheer fluency of his work, and the endlessly elaborating possibilities which it offers.

When he arrived in London, in 1914, Eliot had a collection of poetry in the making. He met his fellow American poet, Ezra Pound, and showed him the more serious efforts, including 'Prufrock', 'Rhapsody' and 'Preludes'. Pound instantly recognized a new modern talent. And this is an important point about Eliot. He was 'modern', his work was 'new'.

Eliot played a central role in the project undertaken by a number of writers early in the twentieth century to bring poetry into the modern world, to 'modernize' it as his friend Ezra Pound said. With a few other writers he has dominated modernist and **postmodernist** poetry in terms of both its production and the response to it. Like James Joyce, Ezra Pound, William Faulkner, Virginia Woolf, e. e. cummings and others, Eliot gradually taught his audience how to read his own work. It is worth remembering that the way much present-day poetry looks on a page owes something to the flexibility that Eliot, Pound and cummings introduced, and something to a new sense of the visual. Poetry enters our minds through the eyes and, in an age which

KEYWORD

Postmodernist/postmodernism: a development in the arts, philosophy and science largely taking place from the late 1960s onwards. Its chief characteristics are questioning of order, and of identity or the idea of a continued wholeness of self. Works tend to be fragmented, contradictory, and use paradox, irony and black humour in order to show how any belief structure and any system is a construction, any identity a performance. Postmodernists tend to discuss how works are written, and to see all constructions and values as relative, i.e. depending on the context and the perspective one takes.

was more and more conscious of the visual, the poets were heeding the experimentation and development in painting and film.

In reading Eliot it is quickly apparent that there is a close association between his practice as a poet and his activity as a critic and thinker which highlights the tendency for writers to be both creators and critics. In many ways a **post-colonial** writer – an American who became a British citizen – Eliot also wrote in a range of genres. He was a poet, a dramatist, a literary critic and an editor. Eliot wrote in a range of 'voices': serious, comic, dramatic, religious and historic. He explored ideas about the activity of writing and the activity of reading, and the connections between the two.

The early years of the twentieth century have often been called the modernist years. If this has been helpful then that is because 'modernism' implies that there was an effort to modernize literature. The effort to modernize does not mean that there was one agenda, a focused and agreed list of issues to be resolved. In fact diversity is one of the hallmarks of the first 20 or 30 years of the twentieth century in terms of its literary production.

KEYWORD

Post-colonial: refers to ideas, arguments and writings or other artistic products which have been produced in opposition to the colonial, or the rule and settlement of one people by another. Post-colonial writers react against the kinds of imposition of authority and beliefs made upon one people by another ruling power. The main writers include Achebe, David Dabydeen and Anita Desai. Eliot as a post-colonial writer recognizes the voices and argument and ideas of those who belong to religions of the East, and recognizes other writings of people from the (ex) British Empire.

Eliot will also be read for his unforgettable phrasing. For both readers and writers he provides images which capture the modern world: isolation, identity, searching for beliefs, going to work on the London Underground, the sound of the sea on the east coast of America. His influence on any number of modern and contemporary poets is wide-ranging, even including performance poetry, for Eliot was a great performative reader of his own work in person and on record and 'could do the police in different voices' as well as express modernist angst.

❋ ❋ ❋ SUMMARY ❋ ❋ ❋

● Eliot was a post-colonial writer – an American who became a British citizen.

● He wrote in a range of genres: a poet, a dramatist, a literary critic and an editor.

● He wrote in a range of 'voices': serious, comic, dramatic, religious and historic.

● He was brilliant at wordplay and rhythms.

● He could evoke places and atmospheres in very few words.

● He explored ideas about the activity of writing and the activity of reading, and connections between the two.

● Eliot's concern with identity, with location and with relationships and beliefs remains central to our modern consciousness.

2 How to Approach Eliot's Work

READ IT CAREFULLY SEVERAL TIMES

T. S. Eliot is often considered to be a difficult poet to read largely because of the complex systems of references and the symbols he uses in his major works, particularly in *The Waste Land*. He is actually quite a diverse poet and listening to the sounds and evocations of his words is a good way in, before you work with the references and symbols. Eliot believed that a poem, or a passage of a poem, may tend to realize itself as a particular sound or rhythm before it reaches expression in words.

Some of Eliot's work , such as *The Waste Land* and the *Four Quartets*, is very complex and needs to be read slowly, carefully, several times, listening to the sounds of the words, letting the atmosphere these create suggest mood, argument and theme to you before you try and make sense of them in a more focused manner. Others are very concise and compact, requiring unpicking and exploring – 'The Hollow Men' and 'Gerontion'. Some look at the experiences of ordinary people, often lonely, 'The Love Song of J. Alfred Prufrock', 'Rhapsody on a Windy Night', 'Portrait of a Lady', evoking lives and capturing scenes. Some are amusing and entertaining – *Old Possum's Book of Practical Cats*.

Eliot wrote about his own first reading of Dante that 'it is better to be spurred to acquire scholarship because you enjoy the poetry, than to suppose that you enjoy the poetry because you have acquired the scholarship'. Eliot continues his thoughts about reading Dante by emphasizing that the first response is likely to lead to a desire to explore further. The first deciphering brings on some direct shock of poetic intensity. When that happens 'nothing but laziness can deaden the desire for fuller and fuller knowledge'. The same principle can be applied to reading T. S. Eliot. An aspect of the poetry grabs many readers. It might be the magic and freshness of his imagery or the characters of his cats: The Old Gumbie, Growltiger, The Rum Tum Tigger, Old Deuteronomy, Mr Mistoffelees, Macavity, Skimbleshanks and the others. Or it might be the names of the often strange human characters who inhabit his poetry: Mr. Apollinax, J. Alfred Prufrock, Miss Helen Slingsby, Professor Channing-Cheetah, Mr Silvero, Sweeney, Madame Sosostris and so many more.

ELIOT AS AN INNOVATOR

Eliot was an innovator and he was aware, as were his close literary associates, that what he was producing was new. In fact 'Make it new' was a sort of battle cry for Eliot and his friend Ezra Pound. The battle which had to be fought was to make art in general and poetry in particular viable in the twentieth century. Eliot has sometimes been read as problematic in terms of nationality, history, sexuality, identity and politics. His work is sometimes claimed as difficult, even dangerous. In one of her characteristically athletic sentences Virginia Woolf describes her own experience of reading her American friend:

> I sun myself upon the intense and ravishing beauty of one of his lines, and reflect that I must make a dizzy and dangerous leap to the next, and so on from line to line, like an acrobat flying precariously from bar to bar, I cry out, I confess, for the old decorums, and envy the indolence of my ancestors who, instead of spinning madly through mid-air, dwelt quietly in the shade with a book.

> (*Collected Essays of Virginia Woolf*, vol.1, p.333, quoted in H. Kenner,
> *A Sinking Island: The Modern English Writers*, Barrie & Jenkins,
> 1988, p.173)

It is fun to have Virginia Woolf crying out for the old order, the old indolence and decorums enjoyed by readers of previous generations. Her comment underscores just how much reading as an activity has changed and how, thanks to the efforts of Eliot, Woolf and others, it has become a far more participative activity. If we read Eliot to ourselves we quickly find a level of understanding and empathy, a kaleidoscope of pasts, presents and futures. We know how difficult it is to be here in our modern world, to gather together a sense of identity, to make and keep relationships. Sometimes Eliot's reputation for difficulty derives from a recognition of his determination not to take short cuts or soft options.

To explore the main points about T. S. Eliot, his life and work, any student must consider a number of questions. The following are representative of this exploration:

* What do we know about T. S. Eliot the writer and the influences on him?

* Do we like what we know of his work and what does it mean to us?

* What do we know about Eliot the human being?

* What accounts for the continuing presence of T. S. Eliot in modern literature of the twentieth- and twenty-first centuries?

* Where do I go from here in terms of my own study and development as a reader or student of literature, or a writer of it?

READING 'THE LOVE SONG OF J. ALFRED PRUFROCK'

It is important to have a regard for the richness and newness of the way Eliot uses language and the ideas and themes to which the poetry gives a focus. The early part of 'The Love Song of J. Alfred Prufrock' offers a fine example of these points.

The poem opens with these lines:

> Let us go then, you and I,
> When the evening is spread out against the sky
> Like a patient etherised upon a table;
> Let us go, through certain half-deserted streets,
> The muttering retreats
> Of restless nights in one-night cheap hotels
> And sawdust restaurants with oyster-shells:

Streets that follow like a tedious argument
Of insidious intent
To lead you to an overwhelming question...
Oh, do not ask, 'What is it?'
Let us go and make our visit.

This love song is in a different key to so many that preceded it and so many that have followed it. It surprised the ears of readers which had been dulled by the sonorities of **Georgian** verse in the same way as Fitzgerald's *The Rubáiyát of Omar Khayyám* had surprised the ears of a previous generation of readers. The surprise, colour and energy, the violence and drama of the opening is interesting in the context of the opening of Eliot's poem:

> **KEYWORD**
>
> **Georgian:** these poets included such as the First World War poets Wilfred Owen and Seigfreid Sassoon, and the nature poet Edward Thomas. They wrote with an awareness of nature and humanity, and tended to use conventional rhyme and verse forms, although many were also innovators in their ideas and some expressions. However, by 1920 Georgianism was seen as the last words of a dying nineteenth-century tradition.

Wake! For the sun who scattered into flight
The Stars before him from the Field of Night,
Drives night along with them from Heav'n, and strikes
The Sultan's Turret with a Shaft of Light.

(*The Rubáiyát of Omar Khayyám*, stanza 1)

In *The Use of Poetry and the Use of Criticism* (p.33) Eliot remembers how at 14 he had read the poem and become overwhelmed by the experience of a new world of feeling, 'it was like a sudden conversion; the world appeared anew, painted with bright, delicious and painful colours'.

Reading the opening lines to 'Prufrock' a few times certain features become apparent:

* The deliberate ambiguity of 'you and I'.

* The time in which the poem takes place is evening.

* The sky is like 'a patient etherised upon a table' rather than being illuminated by a shaft of morning sunlight as in the opening of Fitzgerald's poem. This image provides a very dull, draining sense of being.

* It is urban, city poetry set amongst half-deserted streets, one-night cheap hotels and sawdust restaurants, suggesting rootlessness.

* The poem deliberately flaunts convention from its outset.

* There is a challenge here for the reader not to dwell too much on meaning: 'do not ask, "What is it?" Let us go and make our visit'.

The key features of these lines are in many ways characteristic of Eliot's early poetry, which is full of deliberate ambiguity, innovation and challenges. His focus is on urban scenes and the characters who inhabit them. An exploration of this unity of setting helps in approaching Eliot's work. So does an exploration of a certain unity of time. The poems so often take place in the second half of the day, late afternoon, evening or night: in 'Prufrock' the evening is spread out against the sky; in 'Portrait of a Lady' we are among the smoke and fog of a December afternoon; 'Preludes' begins as the winter evening settles down; 'Rhapsody on a Windy Night' opens at midnight. And, of course, the unities of time and setting relate. The working day ends with the afternoon and releases a period of time when the individual may seek for a more intense life. In the evening and night-time the potential is there for the mind to explore inner meanings and images, to reach into, or at least towards, an unconscious life.

READING 'THE FIRE SERMON' FROM *THE WASTE LAND*

His fascination with the new, increased pulse which evening seems to bring continues in Eliot's work and is given vivid expression in 'The Fire Sermon' from *The Waste Land*. Here we read how:

At the violet hour, when the eyes and back
Turn upward from the desk, when the human engine waits
Like a taxi throbbing waiting …

> At the violet hour, the evening hour that strives
> Homeward, and brings the sailor home from sea,
> The typist home at teatime, clears her breakfast, lights
> Her stove, and lays out food in tins.
> Out of the window perilously spread
> Her drying combinations touched by the sun's last rays,
> On the divan are piled (at night her bed)
> Stockings, slippers, camisoles, and stays.
>
> (*The Waste Land*)

This is an evening scene which at the opening is full of anticipation, possibility and even excitement. When work is over and the desk left behind, the human engine is ready like a taxi to transport the typist to a different world. The images are very sharp, new and at the same time pertinent – the evening as the violet hour, the human engine like a taxi. It is an urban scene with the inside view of underclothes and the window view of drying combinations. The human encounter which unfolds in this 'scene' or 'episode' introduces a house agent's clerk with whom the typist has sad and meaningless sex. This is drawn with a distant and fastidious pen which has become even more disillusioned with the possibilities of sexuality than it was in Eliot's earlier poems. The potential of the violet hour is not realized.

The encounter ends with the typist, alone again but hardly aware of her departed lover, thinking 'Well now that's done: and I'm glad it's over.'

IRONY, HUMOUR AND CATS

The quotations in this chapter are characteristic of Eliot and his naturally **ironic** turn of phrase and tone of voice. There may be an unpleasantness and sometimes a bleakness in it, but Eliot's humour is ever present – however quirky!

KEYWORD

Irony: a form of humour which gains its effects by suggesting one set of beliefs or expectations, one set of readings and, in fact, providing the other – often the opposite. A sophisticated and subtle strategy, it allows us to enjoy the gap between what is expected and what things are really like, and so to critique as well as laugh.

His humour is certainly at the heart of a later work, *Old Possum's Book of Practical Cats* in which a clear, narrative, dramatic and humorous voice is not only apparent but crucial. We are introduced to the naming of cats and the heroes amongst cats including the mystery cat, the theatre cat, the cat about town and the railway cat. Any reader of Eliot who hasn't had the opportunity might well listen to the poet reading his own work, and these poems about cats in particular (guidance on this is given in Chapter 7). The audience is rapt in its response to Eliot's sense of story and his sense of humour. The poems about cats represent a fascination with issues of identity, duplicity and character explored in a variety of voices. It might be argued that in focusing on these issues Eliot is characteristic of his century!

It proved possible for his fellow writers and his readers to both love his work and hate it. However, it proved impossible to ignore what he produced as a poet, literary critic and dramatist. In fact, taking a position in regard to Eliot's work became a preoccupation of twentieth-century poets and there are no signs that this will alter during the twenty-first century and beyond.

✳ ✳ ✳ *SUMMARY* ✳ ✳ ✳

● Eliot is a very talented, influential and varied writer – amusing, complex, symbolic – and one who, in his referring to other writing, reminds us of these other works and their arguments.

● He is a critic of the lack of focus and of hope in his period, and of the lies of the past, and he seeks new beliefs in his poems, while doubting that any belief can prove totally satisfactory.

● As a literary 'modernist' his work breaks with tradition, it is experimental in form and it questions old values and ways.

● Eliot uses many voices in his poems; we hear the thoughts and feelings of a variety of people from typists to ancient sightless wanderers, commuters and lonely, shy young men.

Biography and Influences 3

Many literary figures of his generation have written about Eliot and what it was like to meet him. In appearance he was the opposite of the 'romantic' idea of how a poet should look, an idea more obviously exemplified by his great friend Ezra Pound. Eliot was always neatly dressed, elegant, with a perhaps self-conscious suitability and sense of tradition and the fitting. There is an anecdote told to Ezra Pound at the service at Westminster Abbey following the death of Eliot in 1965. 'Remarkable man, Mr Eliot,' said a tailor he patronized. 'Very good taste. Nothing ever quite in excess.' The literary critic Hugh Kenner comments that there has been no more accurate insight (H. Kenner, *The Pound Era*, Faber & Faber, 1975, p.551). His lined face is, in many photographs, serious if not solemn. However, in private there is a lot of evidence that humour and laughter broke through Eliot's formality and primness. Many senior members of the literary world attest that when they were with him they knew they were with a great man and a great writer, although there is little agreement on exactly why this was the case. When he met Eliot, the poet John Pudney found himself tongue-tied. A very fluent and public figure the reputation and stature of Eliot silenced Pudney. After Eliot's death W. H. Auden wrote that to him the proof of a man's goodness is the effect he has upon others. As long as one was in Eliot's presence, Auden explained, you felt it was impossible to say or do anything base.

ANCESTRY

Eliot came from a family which was closely involved in public and religious life, and which, no doubt, influenced his sense of commitment and duty. It is no surprise that Eliot describes himself as bringing together 'a Catholic cast of mind, a Calvinistic heritage, and a Puritanical temperament' (Preface to *For Lancelot Andrewes*, Faber & Faber, 1936, p.3). Neither is it a surprise, bearing these influences in mind, that there is a central focus on sin and guilt in many of his poems. This is often associated with the feelings of disgust which seem to be awoken in him by sex and which he may have inherited from his father. In writing about Charles Baudelaire, another rich vein of influence on him, Eliot approved of the French poet's thought that the unique and supreme pleasure of love lies in the certainty of doing evil and continues:

> having an imperfect, vague romantic conception of Good, he was at least able to understand that the sexual act as evil is more dignified, less boring, than as the 'life-giving' cheery automatism of the modern world.

('Baudelaire' (1930), in *T. S. Eliot: Selected Prose*, Penguin, 1955, p.194)

If you dig further back into his family history, as Eliot himself did, other influences are easy to unearth. Two of these ancestors are especially important influences on the poet. The Reverend Andrew Eliot is the first of these. He came from East Coker in Somerset and emigrated to Salem, Massachusetts, in 1669 seeking religious freedom. Here he played an officiating role in the Salem witch trials which haunted him for the rest of his life. No doubt this family relationship and story underpins the concerns of 'East Coker' the second of *Four Quartets* with its focus on beginnings, endings and futures, its focus also on change and the fragility of structures. All of this is brilliantly recorded in the opening lines of the poem which assert that 'In my beginning is my end' and immediately explore the rise and fall of houses in succession.

The second of these most influential ancestors is Sir Thomas Elyot who was the author of a treatise on kingship, a diplomat in the reign of Henry VIII and a friend of Sir Thomas More. Sir Thomas Elyot provides the phrases quoted in the passage on a marriage dance 20 lines into 'East Coker' which demonstrate how dancing and hand- or arm-holding 'betokeneth concorde'. Concord in marriage is something that seemed to bypass Eliot at the time he was writing 'East Coker'. It was around 1939 and 1940 that Vivien Eliot suffered a final breakdown after years of illness. Eliot's work was always centred on an interrelationship between the personal, the historical, the religious and characteristics of the modern world.

EARLY LIFE

Thomas Stearns Eliot, the youngest of seven children, was born in St Louis, Missouri, USA, on 26 September 1888. Charlotte Champe Stearns, his mother (that is where the name 'Stearns' comes from!) was strictly committed to New England beliefs and was a teacher before she married and wrote moral and didactic poems often on religious subjects. These included a long poem about Savonarola, the fifteenth-century Florentine preacher, the story of whose life his mother read to Eliot as a bedtime treat.

Thus Eliot grew up as a South-westerner but was always aware of and reminded of his New England heritage. So already we have some clues to where Eliot himself came from and what were some major family influences on his life and work. Hugh Kenner commented on Eliot that 'insofar as inheritance can make you Somebody, he was fit to be Somebody' (Kenner, *The Pound Era*, p.275). Through his father, mother and ancestors he had the mixed influences of successful modern business, teaching, creativity in literature, and religion.

THE SEA

Between 1893 and 1910 he summered with his family on the New England coast near to the fishing port of Gloucester, Massachusetts, in a house built for vacations by his father. This experience clearly formed and nurtured his fascination with the sea. Later in life he wrote of his early years:

> In New England I missed the long dark river (the Mississippi), the ailanthus trees, the flaming cardinal birds, the high limestone bluffs where we searched for fossil shell-fish; in Missouri I missed the fir trees, the bay and goldenrod, the song-sparrows, the red granite and the blue sea of Massachusetts.

The New England coast figures prominently in the poetry and particularly in 'The Dry Salvages', which in the real world are rocks on the north-east coast of Cape Ann and north of Gloucester. As for many writers the sea is both a positive and a negative influence in Eliot's work. Any feeling of serenity can always be contrasted to the imagery from 'The Dry Salvages' with its 'drifting wreckage' on 'an ocean littered with wastage' where

> the whine in the rigging,
> The menace and caress of wave that breaks on water
> The distant note in the granite teeth,
> And the wailing warning from the approaching headland
> Are all sea voices

The sea in these images is full of whine and menace, teeth, wailing and warning. These are the sights and sounds of the anxious worried women lying awake and trying to calculate what lies ahead, 'Trying to unweave, unwind, unravel/ And piece together the past and the future'.

But alongside the violent, tragic images and incidents there are balancing and animated images of serenity. The young T. S. Eliot remembered the days sailing with great joy, the presence of the sea always instilled in him feelings of serenity and well-being. Together with his memories of the sea came some beautiful lines on birds. Eliot had the *Handbook of Birds of Eastern North America* and was a fascinated bird-watcher as a child. Out of this come the wonderfully animated lines at the end of 'Ash-Wednesday' in which the weakening, dying spirit quickens and rebels at

> the lost sea smell
> Quickens to recover
> The cry of quail and whirling plover

Readers who go in search of bird-life and some of the wonderful realizations of the natural world in Eliot soon find the palaver of birdsong in the poem 'Cape Ann' from the sequence 'Landscapes'. We are invited to:

> Hear the song-sparrow,
>> Swamp-sparrow, fox-sparrow, vesper-sparrow
> At dawn and dusk.

After following the goldfinch at noon, the shy warbler, the quail, the water-thrush and the bullbat with the poet we resign the Cape Ann land to its true owner, 'the tough one', the seagull.

EARLY STUDIES

The poet's studies had started early, well before his formal education commenced. Between his tenth and seventeenth year he was at school at Smith Academy in St Louis. He studied mostly languages and literature but also physics, chemistry and ancient history. The languages included Greek, Latin, French, German and English. From 1906 to 1909 he was a student at

> **KEYWORD**
>
> **Symbolists:** the French symbolists were a group of late nineteenth-century writers who used symbols to represent ideas arguments, atmospheres and emotions.

Harvard University, Cambridge, Massachusetts. From early on he was fascinated by the **Symbolists**, and Laforgue especially. He learned Italian by reading Dante and introduced himself to the work of Laforgue by reading *The Symbolist Movement in Literature* (1899) by Arthur Symons. From 1909 to 1910 he continued studying as a graduate student at Harvard. Around this time Eliot began the often slow process of writing some early poems including the first two 'Preludes', 'Portrait of a Lady' and steps towards 'The Love Song of J. Alfred Prufrock'.

INFLUENCES: WRITERS AND THINKERS

Eliot's influences range from philosophy, earlier writers, theologians both Eastern and Western, and other contemporary modernist writers such as Ezra Pound. Between 1910 and 1911 he continued his studies in Germany and at the Sorbonne in Paris, and completed 'The Love Song of J. Alfred Prufrock'. From 1911 to 1914 he was back at Harvard continuing his work on the thought and writings of the philosopher F. H. Bradley whilst, at the same time, familiarizing himself with

Sanskrit and Indian metaphysics. He returned to Germany in 1914 with the benefit of a travelling scholarship, but his study there was ended by the outbreak of war. It was at this time that he considered and finally decided against an academic career at Harvard.

After this he took up a fellowship at Merton College, Oxford, where F. H. Bradley was teaching, and continued work towards his doctorate. It was at this time (September 1914) that he met one of the strongest influences on his own writing and creative thinking amongst his contemporaries, Ezra Pound, in London. Of this meeting Pound recalled in his characteristically personal style that Eliot was:

> The only American I know of who has made what I can call adequate preparation for writing. He has actually trained himself *and* modernised himself *on his own*. It's such a comfort to meet a man and not have to tell him to wash his face, wipe his feet, and remember the date (1914) on the calendar.

> (Ezra Pound, *Selected Letters*, Faber & Faber, 1971, p.40)

Eliot read 'The Love Song of J. Alfred Prufrock' to Pound and straightaway and without doubts Ezra Pound recognized the talent that was being revealed to him. Pound was a national and international advocate for so much new writing early in the twentieth century and, in characteristic fashion he persuaded Harriet Monroe to publish the poem in the influential *Poetry* in June 1915. Ezra Pound himself, one of the early writers of **imagist** poetry, was a great influence on Eliot and was asked, by Eliot, to edit *The Waste Land*, which he pared down and made more concise (and complex).

KEYWORD

Imagism: a term coined by modernist poets including T. E. Hulme and Pound (who used it of the poetry of his fiancée, the great modernist woman poet, H.D.). Imagist poetry uses precise images or word pictures to absolutely accurately capture a moment, feeling, event, character or whatever is sought, usually by a direct comparison between that and something else.

WORK AND FIRST MARRIAGE

In 1915 Eliot was living in London and working as a lecturer for adult education classes and as a schoolteacher. One pupil who never forgot the great poet in the classroom was John Betjeman (the former Poet Laureate) who writes about this experience in *Summoned by Bells*. We can see the influences of Eliot on Betjeman in the scenes in the pub in 'A Game of Chess' and other elements of his work where he looks at people in society, a favoured subject of Betjeman's.

In July 1915 T. S. Eliot married Vivien Haigh-Wood, a development which brought strong disapproval from his family who believed he was making a less than advantageous partnership and temporarily withdrew support of Eliot. In 1916 he undertook book reviewing and taught modern French and English literature for extension courses at London and Oxford universities. He also completed his doctoral thesis on Bradley, whose thoughts about the nature of reality influenced Eliot. In 1917 he began working for the Colonial and Foreign Department at Lloyds Bank in London. He also became assistant editor of the *Egoist*, a small magazine which published early work by James Joyce and Eliot's first critical essays. Meanwhile he was teaching courses on Victorian literature, 'The Makers of Nineteenth Century Ideas and Elizabethan Literature', for the University of London Extension Board.

1917–22

The years between 1917 and 1922 are a key to Eliot's life and work. *Prufrock and Other Observations* was published in June 1917, *Poems* appeared in 1920, and in 1918 and 1919 the poet was working on drafts of material which is eventually incorporated in *The Waste Land*. At the same time Eliot was building a reputation as a literary critic, a role which influenced the reception of many writers of his generation, and also influenced how many readers have read critically since. *The Sacred Wood* was published in 1920 and included several critical essays which were seminal both in his development and in the development of studies of his own work, including 'Hamlet' and 'Tradition and the

Individual Talent'. The latter essay sets out Eliot's project to relate to both tradition and his contemporary world, and to educate the audience that was to receive his work.

To readers he has brought insights into, and a love of, Shakespeare, Dante, the **Jacobean revenge tragedy** dramatists such as Webster, and the metaphysical poets such as John Donne and Andrew Marvell, all of whom are renowned for their clever, careful use of language and imagery, and their rather dark views of the shortness of life and the fickleness of love. He has also brought us insights into and a love of a variety of French writers from Paul Verlaine, who writes about the story of the Holy Grail, to Charles Baudelaire, who writes of the darker side of Paris city life.

> **KEYWORD**
>
> Jacobean revenge tragedy: popular during the later years of Shakespeare's life (sixteenth century), Jacobean revenge tragedy was named after the king, James, and more importantly after the sense of decadence and lack of hope and values of the period. The typical revenge tragedy such as Webster's *The Duchess of Malfi* involves revenge taken by monstrous cruel brothers on their sister for her re-marriage.

In 1919 Eliot's father died and in 1921 he was in ill health himself, diagnosed as a nervous breakdown. He went famously to Margate to convalesce producing the lines in Section III, 'The Fire Sermon' of *The Waste Land* which read:

> On Margate Sands
> I can connect
> Nothing with nothing.

Later he went to Lausanne for treatment while still working on the first drafts of *The Waste Land*. The poem was published in 1922, the same year as James Joyce's *Ulysses*. It is worth remembering that the great early poetry of Eliot was written during times of emotional and mental turmoil that gave rise to identity crises and personal re-evaluation. In many ways this personal turmoil and trauma reflected and gave expression to the general turmoil and trauma of the First World War generation which, not at all surprisingly, had growing doubts about the prospects of civilization.

NEW LITERARY RECOGNITION

The first half of the 1920s brought Eliot considerable new literary recognition. He became London correspondent for the journals the *Dial* and *La Nouvelle Revue Française*. In 1922 he became editor of the revered but undersubscribed journal the *Criterion*. Then in 1925 he took up the appointment which made him a substantial influence in the history of twentieth-century publishing, particularly of poetry. Eliot joined the board of directors of the publishers Faber and Gwyer, later to become Faber & Faber, and remained an active member of the board throughout his life. Between 1927 and 1929 he was baptized into the Church of England and formally adopted British citizenship. Between 1932 and 1933 he made his first visit to America since 1915 and delivered the Charles Eliot Norton lectures at Harvard University, later published as *The Use of Poetry and the Use of Criticism* in 1933.

It was at this time that he separated from Vivien Eliot. It had been apparent from early on that the marriage was not a happy one. Vivien Eliot had suffered from ill health with physical and mental aspects from as early as 1915, T. S. Eliot was suffering from acute depression by 1921 and convalesced, from what was described as a nervous breakdown, first at Margate and then at a specialist centre in Lausanne. The consequences of this and their mutual unhappiness are impossible to pinpoint in either case. However, their relationship had clearly not broken down at the time of him writing *The Waste Land*. Vivien wrote 'Wonderful!' in the margin of the draft of the episode with the middle-class couple in 'A Game of Chess' and also suggested the line 'What you get married for if you don't want children?' (*The Waste Land: A Facsimile and Transcript of the Original Draft including the Annotations of Ezra Pound*, ed. V. Eliot, Faber & Faber, 1971, p.21).

The late 1920s and early 1930s constituted a somewhat barren period for the poet Eliot. Then, by invitation, he began writing the religious pageant play, *The Rock*, which was performed in 1934. Later as he reflected on this period he saw that the invitation to write words for this spectacle 'came at a moment when I seemed to myself to have exhausted my meagre poetic gifts, and to have nothing more to say'. Through his work on *The Rock* his creative energy was recharged and Eliot went on to write a great deal, including a number of plays and the *Four Quartets*.

HIS PLAYS AND LATER WORK

Over the following years he turned quite often to drama with the first production of *Murder in the Cathedral* in 1935, *The Family Reunion* in 1939, *The Cocktail Party* in 1949 and *The Confidential Clerk* in 1953. Luckily Eliot was wrong in his feeling early in the 1930s that he had exhausted his poetic gifts. In 1936 he published his *Collected Poems, 1909–1935*, which included 'Burnt Norton.' 'Burnt Norton' was the first of the *Four Quartets*, his final great work. Between 1940 and 1943 he wrote and published the other three: 'East Coker', 'The Dry Salvages' and 'Little Gidding'. The complete volume was published in 1943.

THE DEATH OF T. S. ELIOT

Between 1938 and 1943 Eliot attended meetings of the 'Moot' group (with Middleton Murry, Karl Mannheim and others) to consider political and social issues in relation to Christianity. The poet had a lifelong fascination with culture and Christianity which reaches a temporary culmination in *Notes towards the Definition of Culture* in 1948. So, born in America in 1888, Thomas Stearns Eliot settled in England in the middle of the 1910s and seems to have adopted Englishness as a protective layer, a way of being, a prerequisite for meeting the faces that he met. In 1927, having lived mainly in London for more than a decade, he was baptized and confirmed into the Anglican Church and became a British citizen. Vivien Eliot suffered a final breakdown in 1939 after years of illness and died in 1947. In 1948 Eliot received the Nobel Prize for Literature. In 1957 he married his second wife Valerie Fletcher.

T. S. Eliot died in London on 4 January 1965. About a decade before his death he had arranged for his ashes to be buried in East Coker, to rest in the parish of his ancestors. The place is marked by a simple stone describing him as 'Poet' and his memorial is engraved with the first and last words of his poem 'East Coker':

In my beginning is my end…
In my end is my beginning.

✳ ✳ ✳SUMMARY✳ ✳ ✳

● Eliot was born in St Louis, Missouri on 26 September 1888.

● The period 1917–22 is key to Eliot's life and work including the publication of 'Prufrock' and *The Waste Land*.

● His appointment to the board of Faber and Gwyer in 1925 gave him a position of substantial influence.

● In the 1930s he wrote a number of plays and then, in the early 1940s, his great last work the *Four Quartets*.

4 The Major Works

Eliot is mainly renowned for his great poems and in this chapter we will be exploring 'The Love Song of J. Alfred Prufrock' (1915) and some other early poems, *The Waste Land* (1922) and *Four Quartets* (1943). It is worth reminding ourselves that Eliot produced a significant quantity and quality of literary criticism, a number of successful plays, and some influential essays on education and faith. As Eliot was becoming recognized as a leading new voice in poetry, particularly in the 1920s, he was also gaining recognition as an authoritative new voice in literary criticism. Eliot launched the journal *Criterion* in 1922 under his own editorship, and this, together with publications elsewhere, helped to facilitate the development of his reputation as a critic. Some of Eliot's essays are mentioned or explored elsewhere in this volume. It is particularly helpful and necessary for the further understanding of Eliot to read his essays on 'Tradition and the Individual Talent', Dante, Shakespeare, Donne and 'The Metaphysical Poets'.

Over a period of reading and re-reading many readers find that the *Collected Poems 1909–1962* shape themselves into a coherent whole, and in this context Eliot's own comments on the unity of Shakespeare's work are pertinent – works that have, Eliot believes, continuous development from first to last and are united by one significant, consistent, and developing personality. Much like his own works. A number of readers and critics have observed, for instance, the sense in which Eliot's poetry is united by the image and theme of a journey. Eliot himself, as we have seen, was on a journey to find identity, nationality, belief in religious as well as political terms. His *Collected Poems 1909–1962* begins with the opening words of 'The Love Song of J. Alfred Prufrock'– 'Let us go then, you and I' – and ends with the lines from 'Little Gidding' full of the image of journey as exploration:

We shall not cease from exploration
And the end of all our exploring
Will be to arrive where we started
And know the place for the first time.

It is interesting to trace the journey through 'Prufrock', 'Portrait of a Lady', 'Rhapsody on a Windy Night', 'Gerontion', *The Waste Land*, 'Journey of the Magi', 'Marina', 'Burnt Norton', 'East Coker' and 'Little Gidding'.

The journey is one uniting theme and symbol in Eliot's work which develops into a motif of questing on different planes – psychological, metaphysical and aesthetic. There are other themes and symbols which are worth exploring. Major amongst the symbols are the waste land itself, water, city and stairs. The major themes which develop in the poetry are time, death, rebirth and love.

'THE LOVE SONG OF J. ALFRED PRUFROCK'

This much acclaimed, endlessly fresh and visually innovative poem was Eliot's first major achievement and a key point in the emergence of modernism. Most of the themes and symbols which develop in Eliot's poetry are quite in evidence in this poem which is often presented as the first decidedly modernist poem. 'The Love Song of J. Alfred Prufrock' lays out Eliot's personal programme, something close to a route-guide to the territory ahead. The poet had a number of ideas and offers for a job and a way of life, and the poem reflects or projects his advances and retreats in the person and half-lit world of Prufrock. It is quite apparent, certainly after reading the poem a few times, that Eliot is in close touch with previous writers and their innovations. Uppermost amongst the influences on him at this stage are Alfred, Lord Tennyson, Robert Browning and his development of the dramatic monologue, and the provocative disdain and dramatized self-doubting of Charles Baudelaire. Eliot is ushering in something new in poetry, bringing together his understanding of the traditions of poetry and his individual view of the modern urban world.

His friend Ezra Pound had this to say about Eliot's new work:

> I was jolly well right about Eliot. He has sent in the best poem I have
> yet seen from an American. PRAY GOD IT BE NOT A SINGLE AND
> UNIQUE SUCCESS.

(Letters of Ezra Pound, Faber & Faber, Eliot to Conrad Aiken,
25 July 1914)

'The Love Song of J. Alfred Prufrock' is the dramatic monologue of a man of unspecified age whose life centres on society parties and drawing-rooms. The poem opens in the back streets of a modern city, often taken to be London but sometimes identified as other cities, including Philadelphia and Paris. It is what Stephen Spender described as the universal temporal city of modern Western civilization. The opening lines seem to represent a continuation of the headnote taken from Dante's *Inferno* which explores an epic journey into hell. The seedy atmosphere is compounded by the deliberate ambiguity about who is who in the poem ('Let us go then *you and I* – italics added). The parties and drawing-rooms are approached through the streets which provide **metaphors** for the squalor, the dangers, the mystery and the beauty of the unnamed city.

> **KEYWORD**
>
> Metaphors: used to make imaginative and creative comparisons between different things, comparing one with the other directly (not using 'like' or 'as') in order to better imagine and appreciate each item in the comparison. An example would be 'petrol head' for someone who enjoys car racing (thus suggesting that the petrol is in their minds).

Prufrock's frailty and indecision

The frailty of Prufrock seems to increase as decisions come closer, his introspection becomes paranoid and all he can feel is the eyes of those who see him approach drilling through him:

And indeed there will be time
To wonder, 'Do I dare?' and, 'Do I dare?'
Time to turn back and descend the stair,
With a bald spot in the middle of my hair –
(They will say: 'How his hair is growing thin!')
My morning coat, my collar mounting firmly to the chin,
My necktie rich and modest, but asserted by a simple pin –
They will say: 'But how his arms and legs are thin!'

Prufrock is alarmingly unprepared to meet the faces that he meets even though he has dressed up. The unidentified 'they' see through the garb and discover the thin limbs. He is disturbingly sensitive and vulnerable. His own question for himself serves to undermine the assertion of the clothes and to emphasize self-doubt:

Do I dare
Disturb the universe?
In a minute there is time
For decisions and revisions which a minute will reverse.

J. Alfred Prufrock is aware of an inadequacy in himself, of an inability to take a decision, of a fear of intimacy. In an image which serves as a fulcrum for the poem he comes to see that he 'should have been a pair of ragged claws/Scuttling across the floors of silent seas'. This is often seen by critics as an image continuing a line of crab-like imagery in Eliot's poetry. This interpretation emphasizes a continuity in his work and diminishes the impact of this particular image. The effect is of incompleteness, a pair of ragged claws not even a whole crab. The image is one of nerve-endings without direction, lonely and nervous and buried under silent seas.

As the poem continues, Prufrock continues to misunderstand and to be misunderstood and comes to realize that 'It is impossible to say just what I mean!' He expresses how he feels in a deeply neurotic image of exposure, 'as if a magic lantern threw the nerves in patterns on a screen'. Then he considers whether it is worth doing anything at all when he knows in advance that his action will not be understood:

> Would it have been worth while
> If one, settling a pillow or throwing off a shawl,
> And turning toward the window, should say:
> 'That is not it at all,
> That is not what I meant, at all.'

In one of the final verse paragraphs Prufrock tries to get a clearer image of his own self, deciding that he is not a prince (Hamlet) nor an attendant lord (Pollonius) hanging about at the edge of the action. Indeed he is almost ridiculous, 'Almost, at times the Fool'. In presenting himself as the Shakespearean fool he produces a final irony. The fool was licensed to tell the truth about life, what he has to say should be taken seriously. In this way the poem is an early version of urban sociology, a study in urban alienation. The poet and critic Babette Deutsch wrote very perceptively of Eliot's feelings of the modern city as early as 1935:

He was pre-eminently the poet of the city, not because its tall buildings, its restless surge, its 'million people, surly with traffic' moved him by their greatness or their pathos, but because the crowd, the stench of commerce, the meanness to which life is reduced in the experience of the least common human denominator, exacerbated his nerves.

(Deutsch, B. *This Modern Poetry*, W. W. Norton, 1935, p.120)

SOME OTHER EARLY POEMS: 'THE PRELUDES'

The early poem 'Preludes' was written in fragments and then brought into its final form between 1910 and 1912 and published in Eliot's first book, *Prufrock and Other Observations*, in 1917. In writing about the development of Eliot's work Stephen Spender (1954) declared that nothing in Eliot is so good as 'Preludes'. Readers often find that there are fascinating surface details which attract their attention. Looking closely at the poem you can see these: for instance, the smell of steaks, grimy scraps of withered leaves, broken blinds, the lonely cab-horse. In fact you might list pretty well every phrase here under the heading of interesting detail. At the same time readers find a half-realized reality flickering behind the details and appearances. The poem is cast at a certain, changing time, a winter evening settling down to the lighting of the lamps at the end of the first section. There is also a certain place indicated by, for instance, the smell of steaks in passageways, the newspapers from vacant lots and the broken blinds and chimney pots. There is certainly an atmosphere created out of a kind of cosiness 'scraps of withered leaves' and 'broken blinds and chimney-pots'. Also, the poem is deliberately urban, it is a city poem. And it takes place at a certain time in history during which cab-horses steamed and stamped and lamps were lit.

'GERONTION' AND 'SWEENEY AMONG THE NIGHTINGALES'

The early short poems of Eliot such as 'Portrait of a Lady', 'Rhapsody on a Windy Night', 'Morning at the Window', 'Gerontion' and 'Sweeney Among the Nightingales' repay close reading and are, for many readers and literary critics, a high point in Eliot's achievement.

'Gerontion' anticipates *The Waste Land* with its symbols of dryness and sterility and, indeed, was intended to be a preface to the greater work. The title refers to the Greek word for a little old man and this, together with the epigraph from *Measure for a Measure*, indicates the direction of the poem in which the little declining old man, caught between youth and age, and dreaming of both, remembers and ponders over the images of history.

THE WASTE LAND

The Waste Land is divided into five books, (i) 'The Burial of the Dead', (ii) 'A Game of Chess', (iii) 'The Fire Sermon' (iv) 'Death by Water' and (v) 'What the Thunder Said'. It moves from representing staleness, fear of life, the death in life of the modern world in the first book, through evoking and dramatizing pointless, destructive relationships in the second, a theme which carries into the third book where individual breakdown appears as a theme. In the fourth very short section a drowned figure is mentioned and in the fifth and final section a journey is made to search for spiritual awakening, and new hope and life – but it is not quite found by the end of the poem. This brief summary seems to indicate a narrative, but in fact there is a series of small vignettes, scenes and suggestions. Eliot is exploring and dramatizing for us a spiritual and psychological wasteland which he feels is the state of mind, the everyday experience of people in the first part of the twentieth century. People have lost all spiritual faith and seek some kind of solace, if any at all, in alternative myths and in spiritualism. They live lives which are very mechanised, soulless, dead and pointless. He paints for us a life and a land which has lost all hope and value. This he does in terms of relationships, beliefs, everyday work and hope.

At the end of the poem sequence, there is some hope for a future beginning, starting from almost nothing. This emerges in the Eastern religious image of a boat on water, a disciple being called by Buddha – peace – is what is wanted after all this turmoil. We cannot believe in the old values, which have fallen away, and we just work to revive some value and hope in the spiritual, in faith. That last is one of the main messages of Eliot's poem as it mainly portrays the bleak wasteland of the twentieth century and also a bleak wasteland of humankind's psychological state more generally. But it is not an easy poem to explain in this sense when you read it. The poem is composed of fragments as if to match the fragmentation or lack of beliefs and values felt by the speaker. These fragments 'I have shored against my ruin' says Eliot's speaker Tiresias, the blind seer who wanders through the poem, mourning loss, and bemoaning decay and pointlessness.

The poem uses fragments – of myths, of references to earlier texts such as those from the nineteenth-century decadent poet Charles Baudelaire who wrote about the decay and waste of the city, the sixteenth-century Jacobean revenge tragedy, *The Spanish Tragedy* in which fathers go mad, sons are betrayed and energies are wasted. The decay and rot of civilizations is suggested in seventeenth-century poetry by Marvell and others, the loss of love and hope suggested in operas such *Tristan and Isolda*, lost lovers, the myths and legend we all know and upon which Shakespeare's plays for instance, are based, such as the story of Cleopatra. So readers could find the references to other texts confusing, especially if you have not read the texts in their original. However, the poem itself can be understood without the references because the tone – sombre, decayed, hopeless, magical – can be heard in the words and the descriptions. The references to other texts, **intertextuality**, in the poem adds further to its atmosphere and richness.

> **KEYWORD**
>
> Intertextuality: a strategy for using references to other works. In doing this you suggest similarities or absolute opposites to the reader who thinks about the other text and what goes on in it, its tone, its characters and so on. This set of thoughts influences their reading and appreciation.

'The Burial of the Dead'

The first part of *The Waste Land* begins in spring with the line 'April is the cruellest month', a strange beginning suggesting that there is a reluctance to renew life, that the vitality and new growth of spring is actually feared. The line recalls the opening of Geoffrey Chaucer's

'General Prologue' to *The Canterbury Tales* (Oxford University Press, 1968, p.17) which has a more positive celebratory air about spring. Chaucer says 'when April with his showers sweet the drought of March has pierced to the root…the people long to go on pilgrimage'. In fact this is what Eliot's people are trying to avoid, rebirth – renewal, a search for something to believe in. This reference suggests they need to go on some kind of pilgrimage to find something to believe in, but they can't believe, and everything they invested in before – relationships, God – seems to be letting them down. This partly echoes the inevitable sense of decay and loss in-between the two world wars.

Eliot draws small dramatic scenes. First there is a young woman Marie, who refers to being or speaking Russian, Lithuanian and German; she is rootless, and seeks to escape – to go south in the winter to read. Loss of faith is reflected in the second verse 'A heap of broken images' and the motif of dryness, barrenness which suggests something dead, stale, empty begins at this point. This, as with many other motifs, runs throughout the poem in all five parts, rather like a theme in music. We hear similar words and references and so can relate to the theme or argument which is being developed. Eliot works rather like a symbolist by stringing images or symbols, metaphors or motifs together and relating them, varying them, to make suggestions rather than directly insisting on a point of view. Referring to the hyacinth girl, to flowers, wet hair and then failure, he suggests that love, like belief and a desire for new life, has also proved impossible. The speaker does not seem to be able to focus and summon the energy, the belief, to go into a love relationship.

Spiritualism and superstition

The section which refers to Madame Sosostris looks at alternative religious experiences such as spiritualism and table-tapping, which were common in the late nineteenth and early twentieth centuries. W. B. Yeats, a contemporary of Eliot, joined Madame Blavatsky's Hermetic order of the Golden Dawn, which was a spiritualist group, and Eliot's character is a reference to this. She is telling fortunes, using a tarot pack and the predictions are of death and of deceptive women referred to as 'belladonnas' (beautiful woman/deadly nightshade). The fortune-seeker is told to fear death by water. This is another warning about avoiding the challenge of a new lease of life (water suggests a lease of life) but since Madame Sosostris 'has a terrible cold' her message is blurred and confused. Eliot's characters avoid it, no religion can revive them and their lives.

Death – the city, history and literary echoes

The final section 'unreal city' is set upon London Bridge, with the morning commuters crossing the bridge, but it is also timeless and suggests a moment from Dante's *Divine Comedy*, when the hero is in purgatory, walking across the River of Death with the living dead all around him. So Eliot describes commuters as the living dead and he has been criticized for this. But while on the one hand he is perhaps talking down to those forced to commute for a living, walking across the bridge, their lives numbed and grey, on the other hand he is not necessarily condemning them but pointing out their plight and so signalling that modern life is soul-destroying.

References to dogs digging up bones recalls a play by Webster, *The Duchess of Malfi*, where a widow who is considered dangerously sexually free remarries and is murdered by her powerful brothers, one of whom, Ferdinand, has an illness known as lycanthropia. This (apparently) has led to the condition that myth recognizes in werewolves. He digs up bodies and carries them around. This Gothic rather weird and horrific crime also suggests that any new life in spring, any planting will be dug up, and so suggests any relationship will lead to death. But this image of the 'unreal city' and the dead sprouting up from the ground is also a historical one. Just after the First World War, it recalls the dead in the trenches in Flanders, the loss of a generation of young men. It is not surprising that Eliot's poem is so bleak considering its historical proximity to such horror, sadness and loss. The poem is a rich evocation of modern-day life both in small scenes and, mostly, through patterns of references and images.

'A Game of Chess'

This section of the poem explores stale and neurotic, deceptive and deadly relationships, and has few good words to say about women. The opening 'The chair she sat in like a burnished throne' is a quotation from Shakespeare's play *Antony and Cleopatra* and refers to Enobarbus's speech to Antony which describes the glory, power and beauty of Cleopatra herself. However, the relationship was tragic and deadly for both of them although we also think of them as eternal lovers beyond the grave and their tale has lasted. Here this Cleopatra-like figure is more of a lady of easy virtue. All her perfumes seem like poisons, dangerous 'vials', 'unstoppered', (suggestion of control), 'lured', 'drowns the senses', all of which suggest that a lover or client will be overwhelmed and harmed by relating to her. The reference to Philomela who was a princess raped by King Tereus and turned into a nightingale, 'Philomela, by the barbarous King so rudely forced' makes us think of sordid relationships; 'jug jug' is the sound a nightingale makes, and is an Elizabethan term, as is a nightingale itself, for a prostitute.

Interestingly, Eliot moves from this deadly ancient female figure into a modern neurotic woman preparing to go out, her hair standing up with static as she brushes it because of her nerves. There is dialogue which makes us think how tedious and stressed these lovers are (is it the Eliots going out for the evening?) and while she cries out 'Speak to me, why do you never speak', all he can say is, 'I think we are in rats' alley, where the dead men lost their bones'. Most depressing, theirs is a stale and stressful relationship, with closed cars, rain, and games of chess to pass the time. This scene moves immediately into a London pub in the East End. Eliot's original draft of *The Waste Land*, which was much revised and hugely cut by his friend and editor Ezra Pound, had several dramatic scenes, and this is the main one which was retained. It is a marvellous, overheard conversation between a couple of women talking about their men. They talk about an absent friend, Lil, whose husband Albert is coming back from the army and for whose arrival she is advised to get herself looking better, have her teeth done. The conversation is really rather basic, coarse, linking sex and death (as the previous sections have) and ends with a refrain 'HURRY UP PLEASE ITS TIME', 'Good night, ladies, good night', which is both drinking-up time in the pub and a reference to the end of Ophelia in *Hamlet* who, deceived and threatened, is blamed by Hamlet when it is his mother's sexual infidelities which are upsetting his mind. She drowns herself. Sex, death loss and deceit – it is a very bleak piece.

'The Fire Sermon'

'The Fire Sermon' also reveals Eliot's preoccupation with sex and death. Some critics have commented that he had a problem with women, because frequently his sense of decay and loss, of destitution and lack of faith seem to be expressed through imagery which implicates women in a deceitful destructive, deadly sexual game. The end of autumn in the river is the setting for 'The Fire Sermon', on the banks of a river where the rubbish thrown into it and the detritus of snatched sexual encounters sickens the speaker who thinks of how soon this life ends in death. This he does through references both to the Thames and to the river as represented in the lives of Queen Elizabeth I and her consort Leicester. He also references Andrew Marvell's poem 'To his coy mistress' in 'but at my back in a cold blast I hear/The rattle of the bones, and chuckle spread from ear to ear'. Marvell was a metaphysical poet of the seventeenth century and this great poem is a seduction piece from a speaker to his mistress who is biding her time and refusing to go to bed with him. His argument is that life is far too short for such prevarications and if she does not seize the day by sleeping with him soon, time's chariot will race her away and only worms will enjoy her body. This is a horrible image and Eliot elaborates on it throughout the poem with rats, bones and naked white dead bodies.

No romance

Eliot reminds us of the rape of Philomena (in 'A Game of Chess'), and he also recalls his own Sweeney poems with the coarse lumbering man and his partner, Mrs Porter. The unreal city of the first section of *The Waste Land* also returns, and we are plunged with boredom and lassitude, decay and repetition, into the dull lives of the impoverished typist and the city clerk whose rather stale and limited relationship is played out, as is much of Eliot's work, in an urban setting. Her bedsit is so small that she hangs her washing out of the window. There is no romance here. The mechanical nature of their bored relationship is emphasized by mention of the gramophone or record-player.

Eliot is also being rather snobbish and arrogant in his depictions of ordinary people, the clerk (estate agent in the making) has 'one bold stare' and is one of the ill-at-ease low people on whom 'assurance sits/as a silk hat on a Bradford millionaire'. The image is vivid and in just this description he criticizes the tastelessness of those who have come into money through trade, and the working classes involved in tedious city jobs. She has few feelings. This is not a place or time for death or worth, he suggests to us, 'hardly aware of her departed lover'. The elevated language ironically contrasting with her lack of feeling and value as she thinks, 'I'm glad it's over' and 'smooths her hair with automatic hand', putting a record on. Meanwhile, the whole scene is observed by a classical figure, a prophet, a seer, Tiresias, who has a sense of the agelessness and the repetition of this kind of soulless, valueless existence, yet also has some memory of things being both better and somewhat the same in the past. He is a mythical figure who can see everything. He is part male, part female, blind but able to see more intensely (from inside with sensitivity) as a result.

The section ends with a drifting boat, one in which a seduction has taken place, in the modern world, and which recalls the seduction of Elizabeth I by Leicester. In this comparison it is suggested that corruption and decadence are not the sole prerogative of the twentieth century, they have always been there in even the much idealized past. 'Burning' is the last word and this starts to suggest religious hope, and is taken up again right at the end of *The Waste Land*.

'Death by Water'
This section continues the themes of death and a fear of revival, a possibility that water, although thought in natural terms to bring new life in spring, could actually drown you should you be unready for this revival. The reference also reminds us of Ferdinand, the king's son, in *The Tempest* by Shakespeare. Nobles returning home are shipwrecked in a storm caused by Prospero, wise magician and ex-duke cast out by his deceptive brother. They are punished for their past treachery to Prospero. In the shipwreck he causes for them it is thought Ferdinand is drowned. He is not drowned and out of this near death by drowning comes revival, new unity and harmony, marriage and a return home. The suggestion is hopeful (if slight) that from immersion and even drowning comes something new and beautiful.

'What the Thunder Said'
The fifth section concentrates on searching for faith, for revival, for water, for images of revival. Although there is thunder it does not quite lead to the reviving rain as yet. This section begins with references to

the Garden of Gethsemane where Jesus was betrayed after 'the torchlight red on sweaty faces' and suggests deceit, death and 'he who was living is now dead'. Values in this period are empty, here there is no faith. All the references mention deception and lack, and this is projected through images of rock, stony ground and rotten teeth; although dripping and dropping sounds are heard there is actually no rain. In the middle of the poem Eliot's religious leanings emerge, there are suggestions that a third walks beside you as happens in the Bible where the third is Jesus returned after his death. This suggests revival and hope while the following verse references Europe after the war, with loss, lament and 'murmur of maternal lamentation' from the mothers whose sons have died in the terrible war. Hooded hordes sweeping past suggest invasions in all times and in all places, the destruction we bring to each other in war.

Sums up the whole poem

The section seems to bring together references from the rest of *The Waste Land* as a whole. We have women combing and brushing their hair (from 'A Game of Chess'), bones, the promise or threat of water, and seeking after salvation which seems to be constantly rewarded with emptiness. Eliot uses images of the Grail and the medieval tale of the Knights of the Round Table seeking the original Holy Grail which Jesus drank from before his death. Finding the Grail would mean finding sorts of answers confirming religious belief, achieving all you can. The image of achieving the Holy Grail is such a popular one (think of *Monty Python and the Holy Grail*) that it stands powerfully for a life's quest for meaning. The speaker in this section searches among mountains and in empty deserted chapels but finds no trace. Finally he ends up in a boat – floating, hoping for rain which will bring new life and for recognition and calling from a religious master. Such a call would establish meaning and value in life, give direction. The poem ends on a sense of peace with the word 'shantih', the end to an Upanishad or holy poem.

The empty shell of the modern world

Eliot's evocation of the empty shell of the modern world remains in our imaginations. He gives us a host of images suggesting decay, emptiness, dryness and loss, and he sets up a quest for meaning which relates to historical and mythical quest, a very human need.

The Waste Land is a powerful poem with a whole range of references and more meanings than can be suggested by a brief journey through it. Eliot was aware that this rather condensed cryptic piece would be seen as difficult. His original poem, much changed by his editor and friend Ezra Pound, was filled with more narrative and more drama. The original was less cryptic and less connected together by image, symbol, metaphor, pattern and reference. What we have here we can understand in terms of atmosphere and some of the argument, although Eliot was against a straightforward reading for meaning as such. It is more complex and suggestive, more multi-layered than that.

Looking for patterns of meaning and allowing the sounds and atmosphere to work in your own ear and mind is a safe way to approach the poem. Look for images of dryness, emptiness, decay and some hope just beyond our reach in images of water and faith. Whole industries of writing have grown up around the poem, explaining it bit by bit. The companion books are always several times longer than the poem itself. Eliot was aware of this potential and if we have an idea of his sense of humour we can see the complex notes which he attached to the poem as a bit of a wild goose chase – they are sometimes helpful but are often even more cryptic and inconclusive than the poem itself, occasionally whimsical in what they decide to explain and what to ignore. We have to make our own way through *The Waste Land* and decide what we think it is about, and that is what Eliot wants – remember that he believed the reader will judge!

THE *FOUR QUARTETS*

> Words strain,
> crack and sometimes break, under the burden

There have been many erudite volumes of criticism devoted to this long poem in four parts based on a musical form and a musical metaphor. In order to provide a sense of how you might read this work, we are largely going to concentrate on exploring the first of the quartets 'Burnt Norton'(1935). There are also some suggestions about reading the other three quartets, 'East Coker'(1940), 'The Dry Salvages' (1941) and 'Little Gidding' (1942), often described as the Wartime Quartets. The four of them are very beautiful poems with some memorable lines such as 'humankind cannot bear very much reality' which often have either been quoted from elsewhere (this from Julian of Norwich) or which we have used since in film titles or speeches.

Beliefs and religions

In the *Four Quartets* Eliot seems to be looking at life and death, at time, at values and at faith. There is a sense that he has developed further some of the sense of decay and loss he expressed in the earlier *The Waste Land* but that here he is gradually discovering and establishing a sense of faith, and not merely a Western sense of faith. He had been greatly influenced by Eastern religions, Hinduism and Buddhism, and in this poem sequence he uses the Eastern religious idea of circularity rather than the Western idea of linearity. Life is not about a steady progress to an end, it is turning and channelling, circular, and while we can appreciate and somehow capture the moment, the present, this is not all we have. He upsets the **post-Enlightenment** (the eighteenth-century in the west of Europe) philosophical

> **KEYWORD**
>
> Post-Enlightenment: the Enlightenment is commonly considered to be a period in the eighteenth century when scientific discoveries and rational thought were very important and everything seemed explicable by logic and science. Since those days we have come to realize that science and reason do not and cannot explain everything that happens, particularly in relation to human behaviours and emotions. Post-Enlightenment thinkers and writers recognize emotions, the imagination and diversity.

beliefs which lie behind Western versions of religion, that our lives are a trek towards progress, and towards an end, that, if you like, there is a single Grail or major discovery and solution to be found.

Having seen war in the past and its current approach closer and closer across Europe in the present (Second World War 1939–45), it would probably have been impossible to believe in progress at that time – horror was on the doorstep. While the poem used to be read as a sequence of symbols, motifs and metaphors, in a musical structure, repeating, revisiting and adding to previous versions of expression and ideas, it is now also read as a way of responding to a particularly difficult political period and a questioning of values in the midst of war. Now we tend to read poetry both for its language and symbolism, sound and structure, and also its connections to its own time and ours.

'BURNT NORTON'

Much of the *Four Quartets* is a kind of personal quest for belief and meaning. In this poem Eliot uses Eastern references to indicate that time is both ever present, and circular, not linear. 'Time present and time past/Are both perhaps present in time future,/And time future contained in time past.'

Time is cyclical

These opening lines to 'Burnt Norton' set up the idea of circular time. The present is contained (reflected on, leaves traces, sets up hints) in the past which leads towards it and leads into the future in which it leaves its traces. The past affects the present, the future is somehow predicated upon the past. Of course, this is so – but Eliot moves on from this rather fate-dominated statement. The present is composed of things which did happen in the past and things which we chose not to do, or which did not happen to us. The poem moves through memories of childhood, following the movement of a bird which leads into a rose garden. The image of the rose garden is one of possibilities, love and life, but this youthful period was, he suggests, possibly not so ideal but rather artificial and rather constructed. The garden becomes one in which flowers, 'Had the look of flowers that are looked at', posing and artificial. Experience is restricted, in a 'formal pattern'. Using images of both performance on stage and of restraint he mentions the garden:

So we moved, and they, in a formal pattern,
Along the empty alley, into the box circle,
To look down into the drained pool.
Dry the pool, dry concrete, brown edged
And the pool was filled with water out of sunlight

There are recollections in here of the staleness and dryness in *The Waste Land*, a place, a feeling, a period without hope, suddenly in this case filled with what is probably a mirage of hope and beauty, of lively experience. And then the mirage is gone.

The beautiful garden of our lost youth

The imagery is beautiful and recalls excitement and life, youth, but also the sense that there is a short-lived enjoyment and much of what happens is artificial both at the time and in our memories; 'Go, said the bird, for the leaves were full of children,/Hidden excitedly, containing laughter' is a graphic image of children playing in a garden, of potential. The garden like Eden has lots of hope involved in its depiction. But then comes the learning, that we both need to and cannot entirely face up to the reality of our lives:

Go, go, go, said the bird: humankind
cannot bear very much reality

The second part of the poem is tightly condensed with images and symbols. Eliot is using imagism here to evoke and explore feelings, arguments and ideas. It is a philosophical and a symbolic piece. Mentioning both stars and mud, the present where 'we' are (presumably us the readers, people generally, the speaker, even Eliot himself) and the past, he uses tight patterns of imagery to indicate ways in which wheels, time and life circulate. The moment seems at the centre of this, the specific movement of now, the moment which gives us some fixity. Each individual movement is part of this turning pattern, this circulation and so is part of a circular sense of time and of continuity. By placing the individual moment and the individual in images of time, the circulation of the blood, eternal patterns, Eliot suggests (he does not state) a rather resolved, harmonious, satisfying sense of life as being part of something bigger. Everything is linked to everything else. The argument is expressed in these linked images, the ideas from Eastern religion where everything that happens fits into and affects everything else. As if stuck initially in the mud, our lives of pain and beauty:

> Garlic and sapphires in the mud
> clot the bedded axle-tree

are part of the turning world of cyclical time and eternal patterns:

> We move above the moving tree
> In light upon the figured leaf
> And hear upon the sodden floor
> Below, the boarhound and the boar
> Pursue their pattern as before
> But reconciled among the stars.

The difficulty of finding the right words

Eliot bemoans the difficulty of saying all he needs to, of being interpreted, and bemoans the inaccuracies of language itself – which leads to confusion in which feelings and ideas cannot easily be expressed. But by using symbols and images, patterns and repetitions he gets closer to expression, and there is a belief in the poem that it is important to articulate, suggest, convey these arguments because this articulation in the literary work (although never finally capturing the expression and feeling) is something which lasts. Like Yeats, his contemporary, and Woolf also, Eliot believes that art outlasts its creators, that art can say something to us all for all time. So while:

> Words strain
> crack and sometimes break, under the burden,

nonetheless:

Words after speech, reach
Into the silence. Only by the form, the pattern,
Can words or music reach
The stillness, as a Chinese jar still
Moves perpetually in its stillness.

The moments must be captured because art, pattern rather than the inexplicitness of just words alone, can convey something lasting which links us into existence.

'EAST COKER'

This section of the poem begins with depictions of a village lane, a country road in England in summer which is both here and now and also resonates with death and new life, building and rebuilding:

Houses rise and fall, crumble, are extended,
Are removed, destroyed, restored, or in their place
Is an open field, or a factory, or a by-pass.

He uses biblical images and references, 'a time for living and for generation' and the medieval past, to Sir Thomas Browne and the days of a past where people were more unified, more part of the earth, more community oriented.

The association of man and woman
In daunsinge, signifying matrimonie -
A dignified and commodious sacrament

He indicates continuity and patterning again, refers to his own earlier poetry as rather inexact 'that was a way, a way of putting it – not very satisfactory' and suggests that previous communities have long gone, and are 'dark dark. They all go into the dark'. Which reminds us of the London Underground (referenced in 'Burnt Norton') and commuters earlier in *The Waste Land*. In the central section there is dense symbolism as there was in 'Burnt Norton', and this time there are references to a 'wounded surgeon' which could be taken to mean Christ or God, and the earth is described as a hospital. Some of the elements of belief and the sacrament are evoked, 'The dripping blood our only drink', but this loss of blood also recalls the war.

'THE DRY SALVAGES'

God and belief appear again in 'The Dry Salvages' which is set on the American East Coast where Eliot grew up, bells sound, sails and banks are evoked. The end of the poem brings together in a condensed form the major issues and images of all the quartets. In this, there is a very satisfying, aesthetic sense of resolution and completion which renders a sense of order to the messiness of life. In the *Four Quartets* as a whole, while decay, death and the exactness of language are main issues, the very circularity and patterning of the form itself suggests harmony and resolution. It is in his final masterpiece that Eliot works through the tensions between life and death, the individual, eternity and the present, and suggests a pattern, a resolution into which each element can fit. The poem can be read at any point to influence its whole circular pattern, just as it seems to be arguing that each individual and individual moment is part of a cosmic pattern.

❋ ❋ ❋ *SUMMARY* ❋ ❋ ❋

● Eliot's early work such as 'The Love Song of J. Alfred Prufrock' deals with a lonely, wandering alienated person/viewer in strange cities, looking for a sense of identity and a place in the modern world, seeing some rather sordid everyday experiences, feeling a sense of loss of and personal lack of purpose.

● *The Waste Land* evokes the loss of values, of beliefs and of relationships in the modern world just after the First World War. It uses references to a wealth of earlier literary texts and to a range of religious and philosophical arguments to represent a search for worth, value, belief using myth and journeying, symbolism and dramatic scenes.

● *Four Quartets* is structured on musical patterning and symbols. Images repeat as do themes. It also shows a seeking after belief and values which are suggested in a sense of the circularity of time, the relationship between the individual and individual moment and the whole of existence. It is philosophical and lyrical.

5 Contemporary Critical Approaches

ELIOT AS AN INNOVATOR IN A TIME OF CHANGE

Eliot was an innovator both as poet and literary critic. In exploring the critical response to his work it is important to appreciate that he combined in himself a dedication to help bring about a literary revolution and an impulse to social, political and religious conservatism. He had to abandon his plans for graduate study following the outbreak of war in 1914, and in the August of that year he came to London. He began to publish his poetry in avant-garde magazines and to review for more respectable publications such as the *New Statesman*, the *Athenaeum* and the *Times Literary Supplement*. To some extent, then, Eliot, like others in the modernist generation, is preparing the minds and feelings of those who will receive his work. He is also the first poet of a generation which became used to, if not devoted to, considered, systematic scrutiny of the literature which it produced.

This devotion to studying literature produces what is in effect a whole new area of the higher education curriculum, Literary Studies, which quickly makes its impact at all levels of education. The Cambridge English School was founded in 1917 and became very influential in this development, with I. A. Richards and F. R. Leavis as central to its work. Eliot turned down an invitation to join the Cambridge School although his influence, along with that of Ezra Pound, was manifest in its development.

ELIOT AS CRITIC (OF HIMSELF)

Eliot wasn't only a poet with a growing reputation, he was also a critic with rapidly expanding spheres of influence. In studying his poetry and drama it is always helpful, and often more helpful than any other strategy, to have regard for his own comments on his work. The criticism which Eliot wrote from about 1917 onwards can be viewed as having one coherent purpose: to recognize and explore the relationship between his poetry and his critical thinking. His critical writing is to some extent his personal creative workshop. As he writes in 'The Frontiers of Criticism':

> The best of my *literary* criticism – apart from a few notorious phrases which have had a truly embarrassing success in the world – consists of essays on poets and poetic dramatists who have influenced me. It is a by-product of my private poetry-workshop; or a prolongation of the thinking that went into the formation of my own verse.

> (In *On Poetry and Poets*, Faber & Faber, 1957)

Eliot's critical writing often provides material towards an informed appreciation of his poetry, and always provides information about the sources and styles which influenced him. What is particularly reassuring is that he has the same scepticism about critical exploration of his poetry that some of us sometimes have. He admits in one essay that his own experience as a minor poet (as he puts it) may have jaundiced his outlook. He comments that he is used to having his personal biography reconstructed from passages which he got out of books or *invented* because they sounded good and, ironically, ignored in what he has written from personal experience. 'I am used,' says Eliot 'to having cosmic *significances*, which I never suspected, extracted from my work by enthusiastic persons at a distance.' ('Shakespeare and the Stoicism of Senecca, in *Selected Essays*, 1951, p.127).

THE RESPONSE TO THE EARLY POETRY
Eliot was leading something of a double life as poet and banker at the time of publication of *Prufrock and Other Observations* in an edition of 500 by the Egoist Press. This was June 1917, just four months after he began work for the Colonial and Foreign Department of Lloyds Bank. The work caused a sensation when Katherine Mansfield read it to a gathering at Garsington. However, it caused little response anywhere

else and did not sell out until early 1922. Press reviews were short and dismissive and Peter Ackroyd comments that the major complaint was that this was verse rather than poetry, with no conception of 'the beautiful'. Conrad Aiken commented in the *Dial* (8 November 1917) that Prufrock was the work of a bafflingly peculiar man. On the whole Eliot's first slim volume was greeted initially as quirky and amusing but little more.

EZRA POUND

However, there was one great perceptive voice of acclaim right from the start. Ezra Pound was in many ways the guiding spirit for the project. He had worked with Eliot on many of the poems as he wrote them, tried one publisher and then done a deal with Harriet Shaw Weaver of the Egoist. Not only that, Pound wrote an essay on the Prufrock book which was first published in *Poetry* in 1917. Here he placed Eliot's work clearly on an international stage asserting that it is safe to compare his poetry with anything written in French, English or American since the death of Jules Laforgue.

Pound asks the reader of his work to note how complete is Eliot's depiction of our contemporary condition. The 'lonely men in shirt-sleeves leaning out of windows' are as real as the ladies who 'come and go/Talking of Michelangelo' in 'The Love Song of J. Alfred Prufrock'. The 'one-night cheap hotels' of the same poem are as much 'there' as are the 'four wax candles in the darkened room,/Four rings of light upon the ceiling overhead,/An atmosphere of Juliet's tomb/Prepared for all the things to be said, or left unsaid' in 'Portrait of a Lady'. In his short and still pertinent essay Pound comments on Eliot's uniqueness, his newness, his internationality and his placing of his people in contemporary settings. A quick aside by Pound emphasizes that it is far more difficult to render the contemporary in this way than to render it with medieval romantic trappings – thus indicating a huge flaw that Pound himself and Eliot saw in their immediate predecessors, Browning and the other major Victorian poets. The central point of what Pound has to say is both memorable and relevant today:

Eliot's work rests apart from that of the many new writers who have used the present freedoms to no advantage...His men in shirt-sleeves, and his society ladies, are not a local manifestation; they are the stuff of our modern world, and true of more countries than one. I would praise the work for its fine tone, its humanity, and its realism; for all good art is realism of one sort or another.

(Pound, E., 'T. S. Eliot', *Poetry* (1917), in *Literary Essays of Ezra Pound*, Faber & Faber, 1960, p.420)

What Pound has in mind is that Eliot's poetry, like all great art, does not avoid universals, 'it strikes at them all the harder in that it strikes through particulars'.

WILLIAM CARLOS WILLIAMS

Another critical response to *Prufrock and Other Observations* is important to note because it registers an interesting moment in the direction of poetry for a number of poets and critics in the practice and criticism of twentieth-century poetry. The American poet and practising doctor, William Carlos Williams, admired Eliot's learning but felt the great international poet had in some way betrayed America and the new movement which he believed was developing:

I had a violent feeling that Eliot had betrayed what I believed in. He was looking backward; I was looking forward...I had envisaged a new form of poetic composition, a form for the future. It was a shock to me that he was so tremendously successful; my contemporaries flocked to him – away from what I wanted. It forced me to be successful.

(Williams, W.C., *I Wanted to Write a Poem*, Cape, 1967, p.42)

The society created by poets in every generation has its creative relationships, its oppositions, and allegiances. The intense literary opposition between Eliot and Williams continued throughout their writing lives. Initially Eliot tended to win the skirmishes; however, the work and thought of Williams also grew in stature as did his support amongst innumerable writers and critics. The opposition between them was well put by the critic and academic, Gabriel Pearson, in his essay 'Eliot: An American Use of Symbolism' which appeared in one of the first major retrospective critical volumes on Eliot, *Eliot in Perspective* (Macmillan, 1970) by Graham Martin. Pearson puts it this way:

> (Williams) elected to play it very patient and very cool, to look and to listen, to work and to love among the common noises and sights of his obdurately real city. It is too early to say, but it looks possible that at the end of the game the practising doctor and not the displaced priest may have held the winning card all along.

(Ibid., p.98)

THE RESPONSE TO *THE WASTE LAND*

When *The Waste Land* appeared in the United Kingdom in 1922 (in a version without notes) it was in the first edition of the *Criterion*, the literary periodical which Eliot himself established and edited. Arguably his work as poet and his work as critic had converged. However, the work was at first quite widely considered to be what Hugh Kenner described as a scandalous affair. The reviewer for *The Times* was restrained in commenting that the poem seemed to be very near the limits of coherency. Eliot's great work fared little better at the heavily ironic pen of the *Times Literary Supplement* reviewer who wrote:

> Here is a poet capable of a style more refined than that of any of his generation, parodying without taste or skill. Here is a writer to whom originality is almost an inspiration borrowing the greater number of his best lines, creating hardly any himself.

(20 September 1923)

The hostility of this is only matched by the later response of John Middleton Murry in the *Adelphi* (February 1926) which argued that nobody in 50 or even ten years' time would read *The Waste Land* unless there was 'some liberation into a real spontaneity' in Eliot's work.

These initial adverse comments, described by John Press (in *A Map of Modern English Verse*, Oxford University Press, 1969) as representative of the abusive way in which frothing conservative men of letters saluted Eliot's early verse were soon counteracted by events and other views. The major event was the publication of *The Waste Land* in September 1923 by Virginia and Leonard Woolf under the imprint of the Hogarth Press, this time with the famous notes. With the first publication of the poem in the *Criterion* Eliot had wondered whether it might appear divided between two editions and this clearly indicated his feeling that it did not make a book as it stood. Hence his addition of the notes which Pound believed was a dramatic gesture which paid off because it attracted the attention of the reviewers. Eliot believed that the notes provoked an enormous amount of bogus scholarship and, in some ways, this was true because they provided what Peter Ackroyd has described as 'much needed fodder for academic critics since they seemed to lend thematic or structural coherence to a poem which was otherwise obscure' (*T. S. Eliot*, Abacus, 1985, p.127).

There were many positive views, leading which was that of Harold Monro who wrote that the poem is 'as near to Poetry as our generation is at present capable of reaching. The Waste Land is one metaphor with a multiplicity of interpretations' (in 'Notes for a Study of *The Waste Land*', *Chapbook*, February 1923, p.21). A little later, in 1926, the poem was given an influential and unreserved favourable response in *Principles of Literary Criticism* by I. A. Richards. Those reviewers and literary critics who celebrated the success of the poem saw it as an expression of contemporary malaise which succeeded by virtue of its incoherence not of its plan and by virtue of its ambiguities rather than its certainties or its explanations.

In addition to this *The Waste Land* had considerable popular success with young writers and students who badly needed a new understanding of modern sensibility. The poem with what was understood as its jazz rhythms, its images and understanding of urban life, its fashionable introduction of anthropology and quotations was for Edmund Wilson the great knockout, and a cult grew up round it. Anthony Blanche, the aesthete par excellence in Evelyn Waugh's *Brideshead Revisited* (Penguin Books, 1977, p.34) recites passages of it through a megaphone from the balcony of his Oxford college rooms. He sobs 'I, Tiresias, have foresuffered all' to the sweatered and muffled throng walking past down to the river. *The Waste Land* was imitated by aspiring poets and one editor protested that 'It became such a plague that the moment the eye encountered, in a newly arrived poem, the words "stone", "dust" or "dry" one reached for the waste-paper basket' (*New Statesman*, 8 November 1930).

GROWING REPUTATION AND SUCCESS

Eliot's reputation and success were growing rapidly. Whether he baffled readers and critics or inspired respect he seemed to gain in literary stature. This continued through the publication of the individual quartets in turn, and particularly with the appearance of the 'collected' edition of *Four Quartets* (*Kensington Quartets* as Eliot had previously called them) in October 1944. While reading and studying the work the best aid to have at hand is the lectures which Eliot was giving during and just after its composition, and particularly 'The Music of Poetry' and 'Johnson as Critic and Poet' both reprinted in *On Poetry and Poets* (Faber & Faber, 1957). In these essays Eliot describes a poem which might develop themes instrumentally and be comparable to the different movements of a symphony or a quartet, which would exercise the dramatic, descriptive and narrative talents of its maker. This reminds us that Eliot believed that a poem or part of a poem may be realized first as a particular rhythm before it finds expression in words. We are also reminded just how, and sometimes how desperately, aware Eliot was of exactly what he was doing and how he composed his work.

At this time Eliot was also developing his skills as a dramatist with mixed responses from audiences and critics alike. *Murder in the Cathedral* was performed in the Chapter House of Canterbury Cathedral in June 1935 and was a great success with audiences and reviewers alike. With the impetus of popular interest it was taken on a provincial tour, transferred to the Duchesss Theatre and then the Old Vic, and in January 1936 broadcast by the British Broadcasting Corporation (BBC). Eliot had considerably less success with *The Family Reunion* which opened in March 1939 (an inauspicious year to open a new play!) at the Westminster Theatre and closed after five weeks.

It wasn't until the New York production of *The Cocktail Party* in January 1950 that Eliot had another outstanding popular success as a dramatist and resulting from this, in March that year he was featured on the cover of *Time* magazine. In April of the same year a cartoon in the *New York Times* had a sailor in a tattooing parlour saying 'I have in mind a couple of lines by T. S. Eliot'. Although his health was declining Eliot travelled widely and in 1956 visited the University of Minnesota in Minneapolis. Here he discoursed on 'The Frontiers of Criticism' in the baseball stadium to a massive gathering of 14,000 people. There is plenty of evidence that by this time Eliot had become a popular celebrity as well as a critical success.

Despite, or perhaps with the help of, the adverse criticism that had dogged his work, Eliot's success was clearly demonstrated by the occasions and responses we have recorded already. However, two further occasions must be mentioned. In 1950 he was invited to deliver the Charles Eliot Norton lectures at the University of Harvard. In 1948 he had been awarded the Nobel Prize for Literature and for many years he was an undisputed literary dictator and opinion-maker nationally and internationally. This development of Eliot's popular and critical reputation took him, in literary terms, from nowhere to eminence and this was without any storming of barricades. In devoted support of his journey to eminence were many of the great critical voices of the day. Two of these voices, Ezra Pound and William Empson, describe on several occasions the subtle, intelligent and knowing movement of this journey. In an especially telling comment Empson asserts that he does not know for certain how much of his mind Eliot invented and has no idea how much of his mind was formed as a reaction against Eliot or as a consequence of misreading him. What is not to be doubted is Eliot's great influence on Empson and others, which is penetrating – perhaps not unlike an east wind, as Empson himself put it.

✳ ✳ ✳ *SUMMARY* ✳ ✳ ✳

● Eliot is also important as a critic. Reading his criticism can give important insights into his work.

● Ezra Pound was important to Eliot both as guide and as an exponent of Eliot's work.

● The initial response to *The Waste Land* was not all favourable.

Modern Critical Approaches 6

REASSESSING ELIOT'S WORK

The first and most obvious development in the critical assessment of Eliot's work has unsurprisingly been brought about by the passage of time and the accumulation of understanding of, and sometimes confusion about, it. A number of compendium works were published in the 1960s and 1970s and several of these are still well worth looking up. Graham Martin edited his influential *Eliot in Perspective: A Symposium* (Macmillan, 1970). George Watson wrote of 'The Triumph of T. S. Eliot' in 1965 (*Critical Quarterly*, 4). The triumph, as Watson sees it, was profoundly merited and stemmed from Eliot's ambition to capture the minds of the young intellectuals of creative energy in England and the United States in the 1920s. Watson identified three prongs to Eliot's effort to dominate the world of poetry in English and to influence cultural, religious and educational thinking. Capturing the minds of the new young intellectuals involved, in a very few years:

* attaining a number of seats of literary power

* contributing essays and editorial material to the London literary journals in particular

* associating with the influential younger teachers of literature in the universities.

Whilst being incontestable, Watson's summary of Eliot's achievement does not go far enough for John Press, author of a truly seminal work on twentieth-century poetry, *A Map of Modern English Verse* (Oxford University Press, 1969). Press wants to get closer to the nature of Eliot's literary success and the longevity of his reputation. He points out that Eliot's success was by no means 'total and instantaneous' as Watson claimed. Ivor Brown, for instance, dramatic critic and editor of the *Observer*, was widely read and described *The Waste Land* to his literate audience as balderdash and 'pretentious bungling with the English language'. Press quotes J. B. Priestley as saying that Eliot was donnish, pedantic and cold and that 'it would have been better for contemporary English literature if Eliot had stayed in Louisville, or wherever he came from'. According to John Press, Eliot's early work was often greeted with incomprehension. There was even hostile abuse by representative spokesmen of the middlebrow public, and of the conservative men who occupied leading positions in influential academic and literary circles (J. B. Priestley and Ivor Brown for instance).

So what was the secret of Eliot's relatively early success? According to Press it was the production of *Murder in the Cathedral* at Canterbury, and not his poetic genius, that made Eliot acceptable to the official and ecclesiastical hierarchy of Britain.

ELIOT AND MODERNITY (A SECOND TIME)

Much has changed in more recent times. The earlier focus on Eliot as a high-level phrase-monger and accomplice of the new critics early in the twentieth century has justifiably undergone revision. New generations of students and critics have become disenchanted with the traditional emphases of Literary Studies, and Eliot's work, life and ideas have been the subject of a number of different critical approaches. There is no sign of Eliot's work diminishing as a focus of this new critical attention, in fact quite the reverse is the case and it now seems that postmodern theory is fascinated with his variety and complexity.

The postmodern is partly an outcome of the modernist. One of the threads of argument in Eliot's influential essay, 'Tradition and the Individual Talent', is that the writers, readers and critics of today know more than those of a previous age and those writers are part of what we know today. In other words Eliot, like his co-modernists, helped to train us as today's readers, students and critics.

Eliot left a legacy in which it is difficult to consider him as a writer without considering his complexity, without considering various ambiguities, uncertainties and tensions which arise from his work. The capacity for contradictory interpretation in his work posed a number of difficult questions from the start. The answers which criticism has provided to these questions themselves reveal divided opinion about Eliot and, without doubt, divisions within the author himself. Press on Eliot's sense of the religious and you can easily discover despair and nihilism; press on his classicism and you will find a romantic; press on his influential experimentalism and you find a reactionary; press on his remoteness from it and you discover his deep engagement with history. These divisions in Eliot and his work were well understood by Raymond Williams in his influential study, *Culture and Society*. Williams writes of how an attentive reading of Eliot has the effect of checking the complacencies of liberalism whilst also making complacent conservatism impossible. There are always checks to his arguments.

ELIOT AND THE POSTMODERN

We have noted Eliot's complexity and the debates to which his work gives focus. So perhaps it is not so curious that having had 30 years of postmodern theoretical criticism, from structuralism to Marxism, psychoanalysis, feminism and cultural studies, Eliot's work still thrives in America, the United Kingdom and throughout the world. His complexity may well be the central point in his critical longevity. In this context one of his own essays, 'The Metaphysical Poets', deserves to be read at least as much as any of the others. Here Eliot outlines his thinking about complexity in modern art. His own work reveals a complex, often strange, crowded, mad, fragmented and disconnected world populated by characters of uncertain outline with many layers of emotion. If this doesn't sound a little like the postmodern world then read the following passage with care:

> Our civilization comprehends great variety and complexity, and this variety and complexity, playing upon a refined sensibility, must produce various and complex results. The poet must become more and more comprehensive, more allusive, more indirect, in order to force, to dislocate if necessary, language into his meaning.

('The Metaphysical Poets' (1921), in *Selected Prose*, Penguin, 1955, pp.118–19)

This could certainly be a prompt to a discussion about the origins and characteristics of postmodernism, and the necessity for new and very likely complex theory to be brought into being in order to cope with our changing and complex world. In our time the questions about Eliot tend to be more distinctly ideological, although they still reveal the potential for contradictory interpretations in his work. We will look at some examples of current thinking about Eliot's work.

ELIOT AND IDEOLOGY, SEXUALITY AND NATIONALITY

Ideology

Perhaps the debates about Eliot's **ideology** have been the most forceful in recent years and the questions asked by critics and readers have often concerned the role of prejudice, racism, elitism and misogyny in his private and public, literary worlds.

We have already seen how very often when you think you have found examples of these in Eliot you can also very often find the opposite. Remember we have argued that it is Eliot's very complexity, the possibilities in his work for contrary readings, that has ensured its longevity. Those critics who have written about Eliot and prejudice, for instance, have often simultaneously acknowledged Eliot's

> **KEYWORDS**
>
> Ideology: a strongly held belief by which you live your life, and which drives your decisions. Ideologies include, for example, political beliefs, and cultural values such as feminist beliefs and arguments, Marxism, conservativism and so on.
>
> Marxist criticism: an approach to literature which insists that ideology (particularly social class) has a major influence on both what is written and what is read.

greatness as a poet. Even Anthony Julius's hard-hitting *T. S. Eliot, Anti-Semitism, and Literary Form* (Cambridge University Press, 1996) seems to agree with the thinking of Christopher Ricks in his *T. S. Eliot and Prejudice* (Faber & Faber, 1988). Both confront the ugliness of prejudice whilst agreeing that it is unavoidably part of the poetry.

Marxist criticism tends to give less emphasis to the possibilities of contradictory readings and ambiguities in literature and focuses instead on class ideologies as they seem to be revealed in a particular work.

There is often a focus on close reading of sections of a poem because questions about the larger structure are held to depend on our way of dealing with the poem's micro-structure. This is certainly the case in 'Reading the "Seduction" Fragment' by John Xiros Cooper, from his book *T. S. Eliot and the Politics of Voice: The Argument of The Waste Land*, (UMI Research Press, 1987). Here Xiros looks sensitively at the scene representing the seduction of the typist in 'The Fire Sermon' section of *The Waste Land* which so clearly demonstrates that as an observer of social signals like manners, speech and dress, Eliot is unbeaten.

One of the finest points of this chapter is that whilst Xiros agrees that there can be little doubt about what social types Eliot had in mind in this scene or the attitudes the poet is urging the reader to adopt towards them, these matters are made even more transparent by study of the drafts of the poem. What Xiros does is to reveal how close reading of the detail may persuade the reader of Eliot's global purpose to convince the liberals of Bloomsbury that they are wrong to sympathize with the lower classes and to draw them into his own class prejudices.

A number of factors converge in the production of a work of literature, for instance *The Waste Land*, including the author's class affiliations, ideologies in relation to literary form, techniques of literary production, aesthetic theory, spirituality and philosophy. The Marxist critic, as Terry Eagleton says, searches to understand the unique conjuncture of these factors in a work of literature. Eagleton offers studies of Eliot in his *Criticism and Ideology: A Study in Marxist Literary Theory* (Verso, 1976) and *Marxism and Literary Criticism* (Methuen, 1976). Eagleton's argument is that on leaving his complex 'aristocratic' American upbringing Eliot was spiritually disinherited, like his conservative American expatriate predecessor Henry James, by industrial capitalist America. 'Eliot came to Europe with the historic mission of redefining the organic unity of its cultural traditions, and reinserting a culturally provincial England into that totality' (Eagleton, *Criticism and Ideology*, p.145)

Sexuality

In *Orlando* Virginia Woolf declares that there is much to support the view that it is clothes that wear us and not we them. She adds that clothes may be made to take the mould of arm or breast but in truth they 'mould our hearts, our brains, our tongues, to their liking'. Sandra M. Gilbert quotes Woolf at the opening of an essay titled 'Costumes of the Mind: Transvestism as Metaphor in Modern Literature' (*Critical Inquiry*, Winter 1980, pp.391–404) and develops the comment into a fascinating observation on a distinction between male and female modernists. She argues that whilst even the most theatrical male modernists differentiate between masks and selves, false costumes and true garments, most female modernists and their successors do not. On the contrary, 'many literary women from Woolf to Plath see what literary men call "selves" as costumes and costumes as "selves"'. Gilbert contrasts the fear of sexual ambiguity which she and others perceive in Eliot with Virginia Woolf's embrace of that ambiguity.

Gilbert goes on to argue that behind the unruly sexual behaviour present in *The Waste Land* there is both fear and hatred of women, and a nostalgia for the 'patriarchal sexual rule' of the past, 'that order based upon male dominance/female submission undergoes a process of testing and regeneration in *The Waste Land*. This leads to an analysis of the poem which reveals the possibility that Eliot has sympathy for the androgyny of Tiresias:

> When Tiresias describes himself as an 'Old man with wrinkled female breasts', he is defining his sexuality…But, if as Eliot himself noted, 'what Tiresias *sees*, in fact, is the substance of the poem', we must assume that the vision offered by *The Waste Land* is in some sense a comment on the consciousness through which it is filtered.

> (*Critical Inquiry*, p.391)

With her focus on identity, costume and theatricality Gilbert anticipates an increasing importance of performance in **feminist** studies and a more sympathetic reading of Eliot's work. So it is in part Eliot's theatricality that has kept him interesting. He is, after all, very performative in some postmodern ways and played roles in his life as well as in his work. According to separate observations by the Sitwells, Virginia Woolf and Clive Bell, he wore green face powder, presumably for dramatic effect, and he believed that a very small part of acting is that part which takes place on stage.

There have been a number of feminist studies of Eliot which have concentrated on the question of whether his work is misogynist or not and Sandra Gilbert's essay is a fascinating and sensitive example. Christine Froula in her essay 'Eliot's Grail Quest, or, the Lover, the Police, and *The Waste Land*' (*Yale Review*, September 1989) perceives a transgressive, feminine and homosexual sexuality in *The Waste Land*. The poem reveals in Eliot a strong desire 'not to conquer the woman but to *be* a woman', viewed as the source of creative activity – which is itself subordinated to male authority. There is no resolution between the two in the poem which remains for Froula a debate between desire and law.

Froula goes on to offer fascinating exploration of the manuscript of Eliot's poem in which she discusses the effect of an essay by John Peter in 1952 arguing that *The Waste Land* is

> not an abstract and impersonal report on modernity, it is a dramatic monologue recording the speaker's implacable sadness about a young man with whom he has fallen in love and who has died by drowning.

KEYWORD

Feminist/feminism: feminists argue that women's lives and rights have been excluded or ignored in writings, law, history, art and all cultural formations and expressions, and that this exclusion needs to be changed. Feminism puts women's experiences back into the limelight and has developed arguments about equality, the different ways in which women write, speak, think, paint and so on. Great early feminist thinkers include Simone de Beauvoir, Virginia Woolf and Mary Wollstonecraft.

The essay made it clear that it was the speaker's sadness and not necessarily the poet's but, nevertheless, Eliot and his solicitors invoked libel law to suppress the essay. It appeared again after Eliot's death, in 1969, 'with a postscript in which (Peter) linked the dead beloved with a fellow student, Jean Verdenal, whom Eliot had known in Paris during 1910–11.'

(*Ibid.*)

Verdenal was killed in the First World War and it was to him that Eliot dedicated *Prufrock and Other Observations* in 1917. This subject was developed by James Miller in *T. S. Eliot's Personal Waste Land* (Pennsylvania State University Press, 1977) and again by Wayne Koestenbaum in '*The Waste Land*: T. S. Eliot's and Ezra Pound's Collaboration on Hysteria'. The contentious argument is that the poem longs for and needs a male analyst to cure it – Ezra Pound as editor perhaps! The possibility to which Christine Froula, John Peter, James Miller and Wayne Koestenbaum lead by increments is sensitively and clearly stated by Gregory Woods in his *Articulate Flesh: Male Homo-Eroticism and Modern Poetry* (Yale University Press, 1987):

While I would not seek to claim that T. S. Eliot was, by any significant definition, homosexual – I believe and concede that he probably was not – I am still convinced that *The Waste Land* is, at least in part, a consummate love poem whose object is (most of the time) male. It makes sense to identify this figure as Eliot's beloved friend Jean Verdenal, who was killed in the First World War.

(*Ibid.*, p.4)

Nationality

There is inevitably debate and competing claims about Eliot's nationality, his American-ness versus his British-ness. We have seen that there was critical agreement about the brilliant stylistic, lyric and dramatic qualities of *Four Quartets*. However, there were different tendencies in the American and the English responses. American reviews expressed a distrust of the religious sensibility revealed in the book. And this is indicative of a distinction which entered the later appreciation of Eliot's work and which has grown in recent years. Eliot had growing respect throughout the world but in England this had more to do with his British-ness, the way in which he seemed to adopt English culture and character. American critics were not attracted to Eliot's religion or his politics, which seemed to many to involve a retreat from the continuing newness of American literature. William Carlos Williams had received *The Waste Land* as setting his work back 20 years, and the feeling was the same with the publication of *Four Quartets*.

A new book of critical essays, edited by Harriet Davidson, *T. S. Eliot: A Critical Reader* (Longman, 1999), focuses on distinct contemporary theoretical positions which offer ways to see both some unobserved features of Eliot's work and the links between recent schools of theory and the modernist revolution. Davidson explores the critical trend to view Eliot in the American context. Part of the canonization of Eliot, she explains, was the insistence on his Britishness:

> His adopted nationality, as he well knew, gave him increased authority in the study of literature still routinely called 'English'. Recent critics, working from literary, philosophical and cultural influences, have placed Eliot firmly back in his country of origin, finding not only American themes and allusions, but also American cadences in the music of his verse.

> (*Ibid.*, p.15)

To follow up the theme of Eliot's American-ness it is worth reading the essay we have already mentioned from *Eliot in Perspective* edited by Graham Martin, 'Eliot: An American Use of Symbolism' by Gabriel Pearson. For further and advanced study of Eliot's uniquely American characteristics two other books are worth looking up, *T. S. Eliot and the Poetics of Literary History* by Gregory Jay (LSU Press, 1983) and *The American T. S. Eliot: A Study of the Early Writings* by Eric Sigg (Cambridge University Press, 1989).

In an essay exploring the dialect of modernism Michael North finds the sometimes contentious use of race in Eliot to bear more than one message; there are contradictory elements in the writing which help to produce contradictory readings. Thus, although examples of racism can be found in Eliot's poetry, it is also the case that a number of black writers have been interested in the rhythms and innovations of Eliot's language. Ralph Ellison embraced Eliot while Edward Kamau Brathwaite acknowledges Eliot's influence on writers trying to break away from standard English. Brathwaite acknowledges that despite Eliot himself believing that he had lost his St Louis drawl in Boston in his dry deadpan delivery, 'the riddims of St Louis (though we didn't know the source then) were stark and clear for those of us who at the same time were listening to the dislocations of Bird, Dizzy and Klook' (Brathwaite, E. K., *History of the Voice*, New Beacon Books, 1984, p.31).

What Brathwaite is writing about in his wonderful book (an oral essay lecture first given to students at Harvard University in 1979) is how mainstream anglophone Caribbean poets made the breakthrough from standard English to nation language in the second half of the twentieth century. This process was aided by Eliot who introduced the notion of the speaking voice, the conversational tone, to Caribbean poetry. From Brathwaite's point of view Eliot subverted the establishment through his recorded voice. So the representative of one establishment is also the enemy of another, the writer of so many classroom texts for study is also a highly inflential human voice.

For those who really made the breakthrough, it was Eliot's actual voice – or rather his recorded voice, property of the British Council – reading 'Preludes', 'The Love Song of J. Alfred Prufrock', *The Waste Land* and the *Four Quartets* – not the texts – which turned us on...And it is interesting that on the whole, the Establishment couldn't stand Eliot's voice – far less jazz! Eliot himself, in the sleeve note to *Four Quartets* (HMV) says: 'What a recording of a poem by its author can and should preserve, is the way that poem sounded to the author when he had finished it.'

✹ ✹ ✹SUMMARY✹ ✹ ✹

- Postmodern theory is fascinated by Eliot's variety and complexity.

- Marxist critics focus on the way class ideologies are revealed in particular works.

- Feminist and other critics have found much sexual ambivalence in Eliot's work.

- It is possible to find both racism and multicultural threads in Eliot's work.

7 Where Next?

READ MORE OF ELIOT'S WRITING

This definitely involves reading more of the poetry but don't neglect the essays. The earlier poem 'Portrait of a Lady', which is based on a scenario arising from Henry James's novel of the same name, is a good poem to begin with. Here an older woman with a younger lover is represented as tired, stale and oppressive; the relationship is seen as dated, one which the speaker, the younger lover, wishes to escape from. He is sluggishly climbing her stairs, and feels hemmed in by her friends, her lifestyle. The pressure she feels she puts upon him as she twists flowers represents the way in which she has control over him. Their lack of love represents the tiredness of the age. This is a great evocation both of a period without much hope or many values, a decadent and dreary period, and the end of a relationship.

Eliot's later work, 'Ash-Wednesday' for example, is also worth reading for the beautiful, overwhelming imagery. This poem is based upon the rites and rituals of Ash Wednesday and traces the speaker's tortuous movement towards faith as if it were a climb up an endless staircase with views of life and joy appearing through small windows in the stairwell. There is medieval imagery, and a sense of avoiding the trials of the Devil. Coming between *The Waste Land* and the *Four Quartets*, this poem continues the speaker's straining after belief, values and hope, in the face of deceit and loss.

The very serious side of Eliot's writing is perfectly matched by his humorous side, and further reading must include a closer look at *Old Possum's Book of Practical Cats* in which each cat has a distinctive character. Cats are pirates, private investigators, as well as determined individuals. He has caught their movements, characters, resilience, daring and charm. This is an amusing book for cat lovers, children and adults alike. The antics of the cats also provide asides on those of humans, whom they resemble.

Enthusiastic readers of Eliot will also look at his plays, which most often focus on the limitations and artificiality of social relationships of the kind of upper middle-class society settings which also emerge in novels by Agatha Christie and plays by Noel Coward. Eliot's characters in *The Confidential Clerk* and *The Cocktail Party* are every bit as lonely, aloof and questioning of social constraints and questing after something to believe in in the shallow and oppressive society in which they live as the speakers in his early poems.

There has also been a stage-play which focuses on the relationship between T. S. Eliot and his first, troubled wife, Vivien. *Tom and Viv* dramatizes the rather neurotic, claustrophobic and emotionally charged relationship they developed as her illness grew. The play has been developed more recently into a film.

READ HIS CONTEMPORARIES
It is worth reading contemporaries of Eliot who are also modernist writers, particularly Ezra Pound whose *Selected Poems* include a rich variety of beautiful poems which have grown from translating and rewriting poetry by the medieval French troubadour or wandering minstrel poets who wrote love poems set to music, to woo ladies (usually with the poet/wooer for whom the poem was written standing below the balcony and the lady on the balcony, as in Romeo and Juliet). They tell of sadness and of hope in love. Pound's more complex *Cantos* are also well worth reading, or at least dipping into.

Delicate and articulate, the imagist poems of H.D. are also a delight to read. She explores the constraints of women's lives in, for example, 'The Sheltered garden,' where conventional women's lives seem like plants grown in hothouses, or in neat borders. The speaker wants to smash this constraint. H.D.'s poems also investigate the roles women are consigned to in myths, such as that of Eurydice, whose husband Orpheus, in trying to bring her back up to the world of life, from Hell, foolishly turned round and so condemned her back to an even worse fate than previously (because she had had time to hope). This poem focuses on deception and loss.

READ THOSE WHO INFLUENCED HIM

Poets and dramatists whose work influenced Eliot are also worth reading. After all, he used their work partly to inform his own and partly to encourage readers to rediscover them. The metaphysical poets including John Donne and Andrew Marvell are also poets who focus on the powers, deceits and pressures of love in, for example, Marvell's 'To His Coy Mistress', which features a lover persuading his mistress to come to bed, arguing that she will all too soon lose her looks and youth and so might as well seize the day and have a relationship with him.

Jacobean revenge dramatists such as Shakespeare's contemporary, John Webster, also feature in Eliot's work, and their plays such as *The White Devil*, *The Duchess of Malfi* and Kyd's *The Spanish Tragedy* tell of treachery, poison and love leading to death. Eliot also brought to our notice the city poets of France such as Jules Laforgue and Charles Baudelaire whose 'Le Spleen de Paris' aptly evokes the underside of Paris and the despair and alienation felt by the speaker.

THE INTERNET

There are some useful web sites that enable you to see more about Eliot's background, his writing, and critical thinking about his work. Here are some references and a few notes to get you going.

What the Thunder Said

The 'What the Thunder Said' website (www.deathclock.com/thunder/) is divided into links to four main aspects of Eliot's life: Timeline, Works, Resources and Et Cetera. Definitely one of the most useful of the sites dedicated to Eliot.

Bartleby.com

The T. S. Eliot section of the Bartleby website (www.bartleby.com/people/Eliot-Th.html) begins with some basic biographical information about T. S. Eliot taken from his entry in the *Columbia Encyclopaedia*. The 'poems' link takes you to two collections of his poems. The 'Literary Criticism' section includes *The Sacred Wood*, a collection of essays on poetry and criticism, including 'Hamlet and His Problems'.

The Waste Land

This website can be found at http://eliotswasteland.tripod.com/ It is a split-page affair which has *The Waste Land* on one side and the notes relating to the text on the other. The notes include Eliot's original notes supplemented by additional notations from various sources.

Amy Lozano's website

This website (www.geocities.com/Athens/Acropolis/5616/eliot.html) was created by a student at the University of Southern California during her final semester. It begins with a quote from *The Use of Poetry and the Use of Criticism*. This site has helpful links to a biography of Eliot and details of his works. It also includes a basic bibliography and a link to an e-text of 'The Love Song of J. Alfred Prufrock' with annotations. It also has a page of quotes about Eliot from people such as Ernest Hemingway, F. Scott Fitzgerald, Edith Wharton, Virginia Woolf and Aldous Huxley, amongst others.

✳ ✳ ✳ *SUMMARY* ✳ ✳ ✳

- Read some of Eliot's other works, particularly the essays.

- Read some of his contemporaries' works.

- Read authors who influenced his writing.

- Use the Internet to explore other resources.

Chronology of major works

1917	*Prufrock and Other Observations*
1920	*Ara Vos Prec* (published in New York as *Poems*)
	The Sacred Wood (criticism)
1922	*The Waste Land*, New York; London 1923
1925	*Poems 1909–1925* (including 'The Hollow Men')
1927	*Journey of the Magi*
1928	*For Lancelot Andrewes* (criticism)
1929	'Animula'
1930	'Ash-Wednesday'
1930	'Marina'
1932	*Selected Essays 1917–1932* (criticism)
1932	*John Dryden: The Poet, the Dramatist, the Critic* (criticism), New York
1933	*The Use of Poetry and the Use of Criticism* (criticism)
1934	*After Strange Gods* (criticism)
	The Rock (play)
1935	*Murder in the Cathedral* (play)
1936	*Collected Poems 1909–1935*. This volume included 'Burnt Norton'
1939	*The Family Reunion* (play)
	Old Possum's Book of Practical Cats
	The Idea of a Christian Society (social criticism)
1940	East Coker
1941	The Dry Salvages
1942	Little Gidding
1943	*Four Quartets*, New York, London, 1944
1948	*Notes towards the Definition of Culture* (social criticism)
1950	*The Cocktail Party* (play)
1950	*Poems Written in Early Youth*
1954	*The Confidential Clerk* (play)
1957	*Old Poetry and Poets* (criticism)

GLOSSARY

Feminist/Feminism Feminists argue that women's lives and rights have been excluded or ignored in writings, law, history, art and all cultural formations and expressions, and that this exclusion needs to be changed. Feminism puts women's experiences back into the limelight and has developed arguments about equality, the different ways in which women write, speak, think, paint and so on. Great early feminist thinkers include Simone de Beauvoir, Virginia Woolf and Mary Wollstonecraft.

Georgian Georgian poets included the First World War poets Wilfred Owen and Seigfried Sassoon, and the nature poet Edward Thomas. They wrote with an awareness of nature and humanity, and tended to use conventional rhyme and verse forms, although many were also innovators in their ideas and sometimes in their expression. However, by 1920 Georgian poetry was seen as the last words of a dying nineteenth-century tradition.

Ideology Ideology is a strongly held belief by which you live your life, and which drives your decisions. Ideologies include, for example, political beliefs, and cultural values such as feminist beliefs and arguments, Marxism, conservativism and so on.

Imagism A term coined by Modernist poets including T. E. Hulme and Pound (who used it of the poetry of his fiancée the great modernist woman poet, H.D.). Imagist poetry uses precise images or word pictures to absolutely accurately capture a moment, feeling, event, character or whatever is sought, usually by a direct comparison between that and something else.

Intertextuality A strategy for using references to other of your own works. In doing this you suggest similarities or absolute opposites to the reader who thinks about the other text and what goes on in it, its tone, its characters and so on. This set of thoughts influences their reading and appreciation.

Irony A form of humour which gains its effects by suggesting one set of beliefs or expectations, one set of readings and, in fact, providing the other – often the opposite. A sophisticated and subtle strategy, it allows us to enjoy the gap between what is expected and what things are really like, and so to critique as well as laugh.

Jacobean revenge tragedy
Popular during the later years of Shakespeare's life (sixteenth century) Jacobean revenge tragedy was named after the king, James, and more importantly after the sense of decadence and lack of hope and values of the period. The typical revenge tragedy such as Webster's *The Duchess of Malfi* involves revenge taken by monstrous cruel brothers on their sister for her re-marriage.

Marxist criticism An approach to literature which insists that ideology (particularly social class) has a major influence on both what is written and what is read.

Metaphors Used to make imaginative and creative comparisons between different things, comparing one with the other directly (not using 'like' or 'as') in order to better imagine and appreciate each item in the comparison. An example would be 'petrol head' for someone who enjoys car racing (thus suggesting that the petrol is in their minds).

Metaphysical Metaphysical poets wrote in the seventeenth century. They included John Donne, Andrew Marvell, Wyatt and George Herbert. Many were courtiers, some political men, some religious. They used wit and metaphor to suggest thoughts and ideas about existence, identity, time, love and other concepts, and they often brought together a variety of references such as astrology, God, travel and science in order to do so. Often their poems turned on a single comparison which was developed into a 'conceit', a complex idea expressed in an image.

Modernist/modernism

Modernism was a movement which affected the arts and sciences between 1885 and 1940 (approximately). Its main elements in its literary form were a reaction against the rather loose conventional poetry and fiction of a previous age and a focus on absolutely accurate presentations of experience, appropriate words to capture feelings and arguments, an attention to trying to capture experience and an awareness that established values and expressions were fragmented and ineffective. Chief writers include T. S. Eliot, Virginia Woolf and James Joyce, and artists Picasso and Brancusi.

Post-colonial Refers to ideas, arguments and writings or other artistic products which have been produced in opposition to the colonial, or the rule and settlement of one people by another. Post-colonial writers react against the kinds of imposition of authority and beliefs made upon one people by another ruling power, The main writers include Achebe, David Dabydeen and Anita Desai. Eliot as a post-colonial writer recognizes the voices and argument and ideas of those who belong to religions of the East, and recognizes other writings of people from the (ex) British Empire.

Post-Enlightenment The Enlightenment is commonly considered to be a period in the eighteenth century when scientific discoveries and rational thought were very important and everything seemed explicable by logic and science. Since those days we have come to realize that science and reason do not and cannot explain everything that happens, particularly in relation to human behaviours and emotions. Post-Enlightenment thinkers and writers recognize emotions, the imagination and diversity.

Postmodernist/Post-modernism A development in the arts, philosophy and science largely taking place from the late 1960s onwards. Its chief characteristics are questioning of order, and of identity or the idea of a continued wholeness of self. Works tend to be fragmented, contradictory, and use paradox, irony and black humour in order to show how any belief structure and any system is a construction, any identity a performance. Postmodernists tend to discuss how works are written, and to see all constructions and values as relative, i.e. depending on the context and the perspective you take.

Symbolists The French Symbolists were a group of late nineteenth-century writers who used symbols to represent ideas and argument, atmosphere and emotions. They often used these symbols to provide a critique of the city and its life, knitting together a pattern of symbols to suggest rather than point out, comparing one thing with another and releasing creative imagination as a result. Symbolists whom Eliot appreciated and gained from include Baudelaire and Laforgue.

FURTHER READING

Critical Studies and Collections of Essays

Ackroyd, Peter *T. S. Eliot*, Abacus 1985

Brathwaite, Edward Kamau *History of the Voice*, New Beacon Books 1984

Davidson, Harriet *T. S. Eliot: A Critical Reader*, Longman 1999

Deutsch, Babette *This Modern Poetry*, W. W. Norton 1935

Eagleton, Terry *Criticism and Ideology: A Study in Marxist Literary Theory*, Verso 1976

Eliot, Valerie *The Waste Land: A Facsimile and Transcript of the Original Draft including the Annotations of Ezra Pound*, Faber & Faber 1971

Julius, Anthony *T. S. Eliot, Anti-Semitism, and Literary Form*, Cambridge University Press 1996

Kenner, Hugh *A Sinking Island: The Modern English Writers*, Barrie & Jenkins 1988

Kenner, Hugh *The Pound Era*, Faber & Faber 1975

Martin, Graham *Eliot in Perspective*, Macmillan 1970

Miller, James *T. S. Eliot's Personal Waste Land*, Pennsylvania State University Press 1977

Pound, Ezra *Literary Essays of Ezra* Pound Faber & Faber 1960 (See 'T. S. Eliot' 1917)

Pound, Ezra *Selected Letters*, Faber & Faber 1971

Pound, Ezra *Selected Poems* Faber & Faber 1959 (See 'Introduction' 1928 by T. S. Eliot)

Press, John *A Map of Modern English Verse*, Oxford University Press 1969

Richards, I. A. *Principles of Literary Criticism*, Routledge, 1960

Ricks, Christopher *T. S. Eliot and Prejudice*, Faber & Faber 1988

Sigg, Eric *The American T. S. Eliot: A Study of the Early Writings*, Cambridge University Press 1989

Williams, Raymond *Culture and Society*, Pelican, 1963

Williams, William Carlos *I wanted to Write a Poem*, Cape 1967

Woods, Gregory *Articulate Flesh: Male Homo-Eroticism and Modern Poetry*, Yale University Press 1987

INDEX

BEACH BLANKET HOMICIDE

LUCY MCGUFFIN, PSYCHIC AMATEUR
DETECTIVE 1

MAGGIE MARCH

INTRODUCTION

Everyone agrees that Lucy McGuffin bakes the best muffins in Whispering Bay, but she's got another talent, one that she's tried her whole life to hide. Lucy can always tell when a person is lying or telling the truth. Being a human lie detector isn't all it's cracked up to be. Especially when you don't really want the answer to the universal question, "Does this dress make my butt look too big?"

When Lucy is hired to cater the grand opening celebration of the city's new community center, she stumbles across the dead body of Abby Delgado, a prominent member of the Sunshine Ghost Society. Lucy's brother, Father Sebastian, a local priest, is the last person to have seen Abby alive. Convinced he'll be breaking a confidence, Sebastian refuses to cooperate with the police, forcing Lucy to put her skills to the test to save her brother's good name.

Enter the town's new hotshot deputy, Travis Fontaine. Travis doesn't want an amateur like Lucy snooping around his turf, so he offers her a deal. He'll stay out of her kitchen if she stays away from his crime scenes. But Lucy isn't about to let her brother's fate rest in the hands of an arrogant cop.

Good thing she has her best friend, Will, and her new rescue dog, Paco, to back her up, because it's up to Lucy to figure out what everyone in the quaint little beachside town is hiding.

1

It is a truth universally acknowledged that everyone lies.

I don't say this to be judgmental. Lying is part of the human psyche. Even my perfect, older brother Sebastian, a priest and the pastor at St. Perpetua's Catholic Church here in Whispering Bay resorts to the occasional fib.

"I left the rectory ten minutes ago. The traffic is murder," Sebastian said just the other day when he was late meeting me for dinner.

"You're not even in the car, are you?" I shot back.

Sebastian let out the sort of long-suffering sigh he'd mastered long before he'd thought of becoming a priest. "Cut me some slack, Lucy, I'll be there as soon as I can."

Most people can see through those kinds of lies. Those are the easy ones. The thing is, I can also see through the trickier, more deceptive lies as well, which sounds like a good thing, right?

Not necessarily.

When I was five, a brand-new set of paintbrushes went missing in my kindergarten class. Our teacher, Mrs. Jackson, tore apart our small classroom looking for them. Eventually, she asked us kids if we knew where they were. No one admitted to anything, but there was something odd in Brittany Kelly's demeanor. Some small tell that went unnoticed by everyone. Except me.

After class, I went to Mrs. Jackson and told her that I thought Brittany had taken the brushes.

"How do you know this?" she asked.

My naïve five-year-old self shrugged. "I don't know. I just do."

"Lucille McGuffin," she said, using my full name like she meant business, "It's not nice to accuse someone without proof." She narrowed her eyes at me. "Are you sure you didn't take them?"

A week later, Brittany admitted to taking the brushes.

Now, did Mrs. Jackson ever give me credit for exposing the culprit, or apologize for accusing me? Nope. All I got for my honesty was a letter sent home to my parents telling them that I was a tattletale, and even worse, Brittany Kelly as a life-long enemy (and believe me, over the years she's made me suffer).

By high school, I'd pretty much concluded that despite what people said, no one really wanted to know if their boyfriend was cheating on them or if the real reason they'd been excluded from the math club was because they had bad breath.

How I was chosen to receive this "gift" is a mystery. If someone up there wanted to give me special powers, why couldn't I have been born with the ability to pick winning lottery numbers? Or a perfect nose? I'd kill for a cute little button nose. Or better yet, a metabolism that allows me to eat all the muffins I want without gaining weight.

Lies are a daily occurrence in everyone's life, and I just have to live with them as best I can, which for me, means to smile and ignore them.

Take right now. I'm currently being lied to by Abby Delgado.

"Lucy, you know I didn't order this." She looks with disgust at the sandwich I've just delivered to her table. "When have you known me to like tuna?"

Abby is kind of a character. She's a member of the Sunshine Ghost Society, an organization that communes with the dead. Or so they say. She's a regular customer here at The Bistro by the Beach, the café I own along with my friend, Sarah Powers.

Sarah and I are the perfect team. She makes incredible comfort food and I make the best muffins in town, which might sound like I'm bragging, but everyone says so, and who am I to question them?

A couple of weeks ago I sent an audition tape to the Cooking Channel for a chance to appear on *Muffin Wars*. Think *Cupcake Wars*, but with muffins. I still haven't heard from them, but if they pick me, it would be excellent for business.

But back to Abby. Claiming that I've mistaken her order is a trick she plays once a month, and it always gets her a free lunch. Not that Abby can't afford to pay for her sandwich. Secretly, I think she gets her kicks by thinking she's pulled the wool over my eyes.

"I'm pretty certain you ordered the tuna," I say with as much tact as I can muster.

Abby's blue eyes widen. It's the first time I've ever challenged her, and I think she's shocked.

I'm shocked too. I have a rep for always being upbeat and avoiding confrontation. Typically, on any other day of any other month, I'd apologize and offer to get her the right sandwich. But tomorrow is the grand opening of the town's new rec center. Sarah and I are providing muffins for the event. It's a big job for us, so we stayed up all night baking. I'm tired, my feet hurt, and frankly, enough is enough.

"Maybe Abby is getting dementia," says Betty Jean Collins from the next table.

Betty Jean is a regular here too. She comes in most mornings with the other members of the Gray Flamingos, a local citizens activist group for the retired bunch. Betty Jean is originally from Boston and came to north Florida a few years ago to escape the cold. She's been divorced a bunch of times and is a rabid Red Sox fan, as well as a prepper. She lives for disaster and is not-so-secretly bummed that we haven't had to evacuate for a hurricane this year.

Sitting beside her is the president of the Gray Flamingos, Viola Pantini, and her boyfriend, Gus Pappas. Viola and Gus are two of my favorite customers. Viola is a retired school teacher who now runs a yoga class for the active and mature adult (she hates the word seniors), and Gus owns a plumbing company. He's also a member of the city council. They're both widowed and have been dating for a couple of years. The whole town is hoping they'll get married because not only would that mean a party and free cake, everyone agrees that they're perfect for one another.

"Dementia?" sputters Abby. "My mind is as clear as day, Betty Jean Collins!"

Before Betty Jean says something back that might cause a rumble, Viola intervenes to make peace. "Abby, will you be going to the big grand opening of the rec center tomorrow?" she asks sweetly.

"Naturally. Isn't the whole town?"

A few years ago, the town's old senior center was demolished to make way for a new state of the art twenty-first-century community rec center, making Whispering Bay the envy of every small town in the Florida panhandle. Add to that the beautiful beaches, top-notch schools, and almost non-existent crime rate and Whispering Bay isn't just the Safest City in America (the town's PR slogan), we're just the best place to live. Period.

The big grand opening celebration will include free food, games, tours, and a much-anticipated costume contest. The costume theme is sixties beach movies, which is perfect for Whispering Bay since we're a beach community and the sixties is the decade that half our population considers their heyday.

"Are you going in costume?" I ask Abby.

"I'm going as Annette Funicello."

Rats. "Me too."

Going as the most famous actress from the sixties beach movies era probably isn't the most original idea, but to hear that Abby is also going as Annette is a little depressing. Although to be honest, I can't wait to see how she plans to pull that off because I've never seen her wear anything but tweed skirts and pearls. It's like she dresses as if she lives in the Scottish Highlands instead of a laid-back beach community.

"How about you, Betty Jean?" I ask. "Are you dressing up?"

Before Betty Jean can respond, the door to the café opens and her face lights up faster than a flea on steroids. Since we're not in the throes of a natural disaster, this can only mean one thing. A man has just walked into The Bistro.

Betty Jean is eighty but to call her a cougar would be underwhelming. She's more like a T-Rex, or a raptor. To her, anything male, still breathing, and under the age of sixty is fair game.

I glance over to see who's come in. It's my brother Sebastian and his best friend, Will Cunningham. Sebastian is wearing his collar, but even if he weren't, he'd still give off the priest vibe.

Will, on the other hand, is…

Honestly, I really can't be objective when it comes to Will because I've been in love with him ever since I was seven and he saved me from a pack of ravenous squirrels.

He's handsome in a quiet, smart kind of way (think Henry Cavill playing Clark Kent), loves to read (he's a librarian), and has a great sense of humor. Plus, he always smells delicious. Like the freshly printed pages in a brand new book you want to put up to your face and inhale.

He's also the only person I've never caught in a lie.

Which isn't to say that Will doesn't lie, because I'm sure he does. But I absolutely cannot tell. Which can only mean one thing.

He must be my soul mate.

Too bad he's never gotten on board with that. To Will, I'm nothing more than Sebastian's geeky little sister with the frizzy dark hair and glasses. He wears glasses too, but on him, they look sexy.

Technically, Will is Sebastian's best friend but when Sebastian went away to seminary Will and I started hanging out, and over the years, he's become my best friend too.

Three months ago, Will loaned me the money for my share of the down payment to buy this place. Which was awfully nice of him, but it also means I'm in his debt and I won't feel like things are square between us until I've paid him back every single penny. He's the head librarian at the Whispering Bay Public Library, so he makes a decent living, but he's not rich.

When I asked him where he got the money, he told me a relative left it to him, but the whole thing felt fuzzy. Was it a lie? Maybe. Maybe not. Like I said, I can't tell.

They order their lunch from Sarah, who's working the counter, and I turn my attention back to Abby. "If you don't like the tuna, I'll be happy to get you something else. But I'm pretty sure you did order it. Just sayin'."

She's about to protest when I hear a squeaking sound. I look down at the large tote laying on the seat next to her and I swear, it moves.

She notices my reaction. "The tuna sandwich is fine. No problem. Just move along." To emphasize her point, she shoos me away with her hand.

Apparently, hiding whatever is in the bag is more important to her than the chance for a free sandwich.

I continue staring at the bag and, yes, there is definitely something alive in there. You didn't need any special skills here to figure out that she's lying.

"Hey, Lucy Goosey." Will plunks his tall frame down at the table adjacent from Abby's.

My brother kisses me on the cheek in greeting, and as usual, a solemn hush descends upon the café as the rest of the patrons murmur their hellos. He makes a sweeping gesture to the crowd (I think he's practicing in case he's Pope one day) then spies Abby and nods curtly. "Miss Delgado, how are you?"

"Father McGuffin," Abby replies coldly. "I'd be perfectly fine. If a certain person would only do his job."

Sebastian stiffens. "We've been through this before. I'm not the kind of priest who performs exorcisms."

Exorcisms?

A vision of Linda Blair and all that disgusting pea soup flashes through my brain. Ugh.

"Then maybe St. Perpetua's needs a real priest," she says. "Maybe I should contact the Bishop. I'm sure he'd have a thing or two to say about your behavior."

"I didn't know you were Catholic," I say to Abby.

"Well, there you go. You don't know everything, do you?"

I'm about to give in and ask Abby why on earth she needs an exorcism performed when I hear a yipping sound. Will hears it too because he points to her tote and asks, "You got a dog in there?"

Abby picks up the bag as if to move it, but a little tan head pushes its way out.

"Oh!" I automatically go to pull the dog out of the tote, but Abby snatches up the little pup and presses it against her bosom. He licks her chin and she smiles down at him, which is kind of a miracle because Abby isn't a smiley kind of person.

"He's my...service animal." The dog is maybe fifteen pounds. He looks like a Chihuahua, only bigger.

"Okay, but you know, we allow dogs here at The Bistro. There's no reason to hide him." I scratch his ears and he licks the back of my hand. He's looking at me with soulful brown eyes that smack of intelligence. I nearly melt into the floor, he's so dang cute.

I've always wanted a dog, but I'm allergic to fur, so, there you go.

I notice he's not wearing a collar. "What's his name?"

"His name?" Her eyes get a wild look in them. "His name is…Paco. Yes, that's it. Paco."

"Hey, Paco," I croon, knowing full well that's a lie, but what can I say? "You are one adorable baby."

Paco's tail wags furiously. Abby stuffs him back in her tote.

"I didn't know you had a dog," says Viola. "When did you get him?"

"Not that it's any of your business, Viola," says Abby, "But Taco belongs to my brother. I'm watching him while Derrick's away on vacation."

"I thought you said he was your service animal and that his name was Paco," says Will.

"Paco… Taco… What does it matter?" She gets up, clutching the tote protectively against her chest like she's afraid someone is going to snatch it from her. "I need to find a new place to eat lunch. One where they get your order right," she says, glaring at me. "And where the other customers aren't so dang nosy!"

We all watch as Abby stomps out of the café. The last thing I see is Paco's little face with the shiny bright eyes sticking out of the tote.

Sarah brings Will and Sebastian their food. "What's gotten into her?"

"It's the dementia," Betty Jean says with a sigh. "It'll get us all eventually."

On that happy note, Will starts eating his turkey sandwich, but Sebastian just stares down at his plate.

"What was all that about an exorcism?" I ask.

His dark eyes look troubled. "Nothing."

Betty Jean, who must have the best hearing aids in town, because neither Sebastian nor I are speaking that loudly, says, "I bet it has something to do with her challenging Phoebe Van Cleave as head of the Sunshine Ghost Society. Abby is still convinced that there's a ghost haunting the land that the rec center was built on. Maybe she wants to drive the devil out of it."

Everyone within hearing distance moans.

A few years back there was a rumor circulating town that a spirit was haunting the old senior center. The Sunshine Ghost Society held a séance in hopes of flushing out the ghost, but of course, nothing happened, and the building was torn down to make way for the city's new rec center.

"Let's not talk about ghosts or exorcisms or Abby Delgado anymore," says Viola, "Let's talk about something happy."

Sarah breaks out in a grin. "Then that would include my new niece and nephew." Sarah is a newlywed and her sister-in-law, Whispering Bay's mayor, Mimi Grant, delivered twins a few days ago. Sarah is just a few years older than me. She's blonde and beautiful, and she and her husband Luke make the perfect couple. Sarah also makes the best macaroni and cheese I've ever tasted. She passes around her cell phone so that Viola and Betty Jean can gush over the pictures of the babies. The men all smile politely.

"How are the new parents doing?" Viola asks.

"This isn't their first rodeo," Sarah says, referring to the fact that Mimi and her husband, Zeke Grant, the town's police chief, already have a college-age daughter and a son in middle school, "but it's a bit of a shocker having two at once."

"I'll say." Gus sets down his coffee. "Good thing we voted to let Zeke hire extra help." By we, I can only assume Gus is referring to himself and the rest of the city council.

"*Wait*," says Betty Jean. "Are you telling me there's a new cop in town?"

"Yep. Officer Travis Fontaine. Good guy. Comes to us from Texas. He started this morning."

Betty Jean smirks, and since we all know the way her mind works, we cringe. "Texas, huh?"

Gus nods. "Dallas area. Lots of big city experience. We're lucky to get him. His dad retired here a few months ago. Travis is his only kin."

"James Fontaine," Sebastian adds. "New parishioner."

"Good for Zeke," Viola says, "That'll give him more time to spend with Mimi and the babies." She smiles at me. "Lucy, who will you be dressing up as tomorrow?"

"Annette Funicello."

Viola is too polite to say *you too*? Instead, she says, "I can't wait to see your costume."

"How about you?" I ask my brother, "Are you going to enter the contest?"

"I hadn't thought about it. Probably not."

The little hairs on the back of my neck start to tingle.

Sebastian has the worst tell in the world. He does this funny thing with his right eye that he's not aware of. But there it is. He's absolutely going in costume. Why he's trying to hide it from me, I have no idea.

I smirk. "You should. The prize is a hundred bucks."

He gauges my reaction and sighs because he knows he's gotten caught.

Sebastian knows all about my little "gift," but he has no idea just how talented I am. It's something I try not to talk about. Even with him.

Everyone begins talking about the big grand opening of the rec center tomorrow, and what they're wearing for the costume contest, but I can't help but be distracted by the pensive look on my brother's face.

Something isn't right.

And that something has to do with Abby Delgado.

2

I STARE AT MYSELF IN THE MIRROR AND CRINGE.

My hair looks like:

A) A grenade has gone off inside my head and it didn't have anywhere else to go but straight up.

B) Like it belongs to a character from a Dr. Seuss book.

or

C) Both.

I choose C.

Last week when I was putting together my outfit for the celebration, I needed some visual inspiration, so I rented the old sixties movie *Beach Blanket Bingo,* which is completely false advertising because not once do those wholesome horny teenagers ever play Bingo. I also use the word "teenager" loosely because I don't think any of the actors were a day under thirty.

To get my costume right, I asked Lauren Miller for advice. Lauren is married to Dr. Nate, one of the two practicing physicians in our town and owns Baby Got Bump, the business next door to The Bistro. She designs retro maternity wear, but before that, she ran a retro boutique.

She loaned me a lime green shift with a matching print scarf that I've tied around my neck. Because I'm going to be on my feet all day I opted for white tennis shoes and ankle socks. My dark shoulder-length hair was supposed to be styled to flip up on the ends *ala* Annette, but something went wrong. I must have gone overboard with the teasing because my hair is ginormous. It's so big I don't think I'll be able to fit my head inside the minivan we use for the business.

I've also used so much hairspray that I should probably be wearing a flammable warning label pinned to my chest. Good thing I did all my baking yesterday so I don't have to go near a stove.

My partner Sarah is completely rocking the Sandra Dee look with a crisp white sleeveless button-down blouse, jeans, ponytail and saddle oxfords.

"You look fabulous!" says Sarah.

I could look like a raccoon and Sarah would still think I look good because she's the kind of person who always looks for the positive in any situation. "Thanks. So do you. Do you really think my hair looks okay?"

"Sure! Er, do you want me to try to flatten it some?"

Obviously, I'm not the only one who's afraid I won't fit into the minivan.

Sarah does her best to bring my hair down a few inches, but it's like trying to move a hundred-pound rock. "How much hairspray did you use?"

"I don't know. Half a can maybe?"

She giggles. "Lucy, have you ever used hairspray before in your life?"

"Just all the time."

She looks dubious.

"Okay," I admit. "Once. High school. Senior year prom."

She shrugs, then smiles. "No worries. You look fabulous. No one's hair is going to look this terrific. You might just win the costume contest."

I've caught Sarah in a few fibs before, but this isn't one of them. She honestly believes this, so I smile back at her.

We load up the back of the minivan with over twenty-four dozen carefully packed muffins. There are six varieties—double chocolate chip, banana nut, blueberry (*yawn*), lemon poppy seed, oat bran (remember, we have a large retired population here in town) and my hands down most-popular ever—the apple walnut cream cheese muffin.

I worked on perfecting the recipe for almost a year. It's my signature muffin. Plus, it's Will's favorite, so it holds a special place in my heart. It's also the recipe I used for my *Muffin Wars* audition tape, which, I'm kind of worried about now because if they pick me, I'll have to bake something different, and not to brag or anything but I would totally win with the apple walnut cream cheese.

We finish packing everything up then head to the rec center. The sun peeks over the horizon throwing an orange haze over the crystal-clear blue water of the Gulf of Mexico. It's early November and sixty degrees, with a projected high of only seventy four. A beautiful north Florida fall day, perfect to celebrate the town's new state of the art recreational center. There are indoor and outdoor basketball courts, two swimming pools, tennis courts, classrooms and my favorite feature, a humongous gourmet kitchen. Sarah and I have already been approached about teaching cooking classes. I'm also thinking of heading up a community garden.

Even though it's barely seven a.m. and the festivities don't start for another two hours, the place is swarming. The Gray Flamingos are acting as event "hosts" and will be doing tours. Most of them are in costume, but a few of them are wearing their Gray Power T-shirts. There will be arts and crafts for the kiddies, free food and lots of fun.

Heidi from Heidi's Bakery is setting up her booth right next to ours. Her donuts are legendary. If you're into donuts, that is.

"Yoo-hoo!" Heidi waves and Sarah and I wave back. "Gorgeous day, isn't it?"

"Sure is!" says Sarah.

Viola and Betty Jean come by to check out our booth. Betty Jean is wearing a black wig (which looks better than her regular hair), capris and ballet flats. "Look, Lucy! We're both Annettes!"

I try my best to smile. *Great*. Another Annette Funicello.

Viola is wearing a dress with a cinch belt that flares at the hips. Her chin-length salt and pepper hair is teased and sprayed. She's also wearing a pair of awesome cat style glasses with little rhinestones at the corners. "I'm going as a sixties school teacher. Believe it or not, I used to wear this back in the day."

Gus, who is dressed as a surfer dude (board shorts, Hawaiian shirt, and flip-flops), guides us to the back door of the building. He pulls a set of keys from his pocket. "We're keeping the building locked until the tours start. Don't want anyone jumping the gun and getting a peek inside until after the big ribbon cutting ceremony." He unlocks the door for us. "Never thought this day would come, but here we are."

"What do you mean?" Sarah asks.

"Between us, this building isn't one hundred percent operational yet, but the city council didn't want to delay the opening celebration since we'd advertised it so heavily."

I glance around. "Everything looks good to me."

"It's nothing major. Just some details that need to be ironed out. Security cameras, temperature controls on the swimming pool, basketball equipment that hasn't come in yet, that kind of stuff."

The door leads straight into the kitchen. Gus turns on the lights and helps us place two large industrial coffee makers onto a cart to take out to our food station. Besides doling out muffins, we'll be making coffee.

I catch Gus staring at my hair.

"I know. It's kind of big."

"No, it looks great," he says.

Ouch. That was such a lie.

We wheel the cart back to our food booth. Sarah and I finish putting out the muffins and start the coffee brewing. The volunteer crowd is getting bigger. Jenna Pantini, the city manager, comes by and checks out our display. "Oh my God, you brought the apple walnut cream cheese muffins!" She looks at them longingly, so I offer her one. "I really shouldn't." But she takes it anyway.

Jenna leaves to check on the rest of the food vendors. Soon it's nine a.m., and the celebration is underway. In no time the entire outdoor area is packed with people. I've seen at least a dozen Annettes and Frankies already. It looks like everyone in town got their cue from *Beach Blanket Bingo*.

Sarah and I are giving out muffins and chit chatting with the locals when an entourage from the Sunshine Ghost Society comes sniffing up to our booth. They are minus Abby, which is a relief. After yesterday's scene at The Bistro, I'm not anxious to run into her again. At least, not until Sebastian explains what's going on between them.

Phoebe Van Cleave is the head of their group and a real nutcase, but her brother Roger owns the local paper and he's a total sweetheart, so I try to be nice to her for his sake. She's dressed as a hippie, which I must admit is a fun take on the whole sixties thing, even if it doesn't exactly say beach movie.

I check out the rest of the costumes, then do a double take when my gaze lands on Gloria Hightower. She's the group's medium, and according to Phoebe, she's the best. Gloria's natural blonde hair has lots of gray, but today she's wearing a black wig because of course, she too, is dressed as Annette Funicello.

"What a coincidence!" she says. "We're both Annette!"

I smile wearily. "Yeah, neat, huh? How do you like the festival so far?"

"Oh, everything is just wonderful." Gloria looks over at the main rec center building with shiny eyes. "I can't wait until the tours begin. You know the site is haunted, don't you?"

"If there's a ghost haunting the new building, then Gloria will feel it right away," Phoebe says.

Gloria blushes. "Well, not *right* away. But, I am pretty good, even if I say so myself."

"Have you heard from the people at *Muffin Wars*?" asks Victor Marino. He's in his late sixties and recently retired from a forty-year career at the post office, and yes, he's dressed as Frankie. He's an Atlanta Braves fan, (me too!) and he always leaves a nice chunk of change in my tip jar.

"Not yet," I admit.

"You'll get picked. And when you go on T.V., you need to make your mango coconut muffin. The judges will love it."

I wish I felt as confident as Victor. The mango coconut muffin project is something I've been working on for the past couple of months. Victor was in The Bistro the day I gave out samples of version number three. Everyone raved about it, but it's still not quite right, and I can't put it on the menu until it's perfect.

"We're all keeping our fingers crossed for you," says Phoebe eyeing my muffin display. "They all look delicious! Which one should I try?"

"For you? The oat bran."

The oat bran has been our least popular today, and we need to get rid of them. Plus, I'm sure Phoebe's diet could use the extra roughage.

Phoebe bites into her muffin and makes the yummy face. I offer the rest of her group muffins and they all jump on the boring blueberry.

The morning goes by quickly. We're down to just two muffins when an amused male voice asks, "What's going on with your hair?"

It's Will. And *holy wow* he looks good.

He's wearing a striped bathing suit and a white button-down shirt. His dark hair is slicked back, and he's not wearing his glasses so when he smiles you can see the skin around his blue eyes crinkle, which is completely adorable. He told me a few days ago he'd be dressing as the James Darren character from the *Gidget* movies and he's nailed it. Will puts the moon in Moondoggie like no one else.

I try to act very cool. "So, you like my hair, huh?"

He gives it a hard look. "You're going to need help taking that thing down. You might even need a hammer."

Sarah sniffs. "I think Lucy looks great."

"So do I." This comes from someone I don't recognize. Except…

Oh no.

I try not to laugh. My brother is decked out from head to toe in leather and has a silly cap on his head. No wonder he didn't want to talk about his costume.

"Please don't tell me you're Eric Von Zipper."

"I saw the movie too," Sebastian says dryly.

In *Beach Blanket Bingo* Eric Von Zipper is the head of the motorcycle gang that doesn't like the surfers. The fact that my brother, the priest, is going as a sixties beach movie villain is pretty funny.

Sebastian *aka* Eric takes the last of the apple walnut cream cheese muffins, but I don't begrudge him that because he's my brother and I love him. Plus, he didn't make fun of my hair.

While we're chatting, an older distinguished looking gentleman joins our group. "Hello, Father," he says, nodding at Sebastian. Sebastian introduces him as James Fontaine, the new parishioner he'd mentioned yesterday at lunch. He just bought a house on Seville Street near Viola.

"Call me Jim." He shakes my hand with a firm grip. "Interesting festival. Very, uh, colorful costumes, too." He's a big guy, maybe six foot three with a full head of white hair and sparkly green eyes.

I love green eyes. Green is the color of everything good— grass, lime flavored jelly beans, money… You get my drift. If he's poking fun at my costume, I don't mind, because, yes, I have to admit, my hair does look ridiculous.

"Lucy makes the best muffins in the world," Sebastian boasts. "She's going to be on T.V. and everything."

I flush. I almost wish I'd kept the *Muffin Wars* thing to myself. What if I don't make the cut? Then everyone in town will feel sorry for me, and I'd hate that. "The T.V. thing isn't a done deal yet." I hand Jim my card. "Sarah and I own a little café here in town. The Bistro by the Beach. First muffin is on the house."

He pockets the card and smiles at me, and something in my chest goes fuzzy warm because I know in that instant that Jim is going to become not just one of my favorite customers, but one of my favorite people. This is another gift I have. Call it my Spidey sense. I'm great at reading people and my first impression is *always* spot on.

"Jim used to be a homicide detective with the Dallas Police," says Sebastian.

Will perks up. "Really?"

"It's a lot more boring than it sounds," Jim says.

"Jim is being modest. He's worked on some really big cases and has even been on T.V. Maybe he can give you some pointers when you get picked to be on *Muffin Wars*, Lucy."

"What show were you on, Jim?" I ask.

He shrugs like he's embarrassed by all the attention we're giving him. "*America's Most Vicious Criminals.*"

"*Holy wow*! Will and I watch that show all the time. What episode? I bet we've seen it."

Will is looking at Jim the way I look at chocolate chip muffins. *America's Most Vicious Criminals* is his favorite show. Every Friday night Will comes over to my place with a pizza from Tiny's (best pizza in Whispering Bay), and we watch it together, but last night's episode was a rerun, so we skipped our usual routine.

Jim clears his throat. "I was the lead investigator in a case involving a nurse in the Dallas Fort Worth area who—"

"The media referred to her as the Angel of Death," Will supplies eagerly. "She killed six patients. About…fifteen years ago. Right?"

How Will remembers every episode in such minute detail, I have no idea.

"That's right." A shadow crosses Jim's face. I don't have Will's memory for this stuff, but I'm pretty sure it's one of those cases where they failed to apprehend the murderer.

Before Jim can say anything else, Sebastian changes the subject. "I hear that your son has just joined our local police force."

"Travis is a good kid. Well, he's thirty, so hardly a kid. Just moved out here this week. I guess he thought his old man needed some company in his retirement."

Jim's casual words can't hide the great love I feel this man has for his son. Personally, I think it's really sweet of this Travis guy to move to be close to his father. Since Whispering Bay is such a small town and all the cops get their coffee at my café, I'll meet him eventually. If he's anything like Jim, I'm sure Travis and I will be great friends.

"What made you retire in Whispering Bay?" I ask.

"I came here on my honeymoon thirty-five years ago. My wife loved it. We always talked about moving here, but she passed last year."

I cringe. "I'm so sorry."

He smiles kindly. "Thank you."

Everyone murmurs words of condolences, but now that I've put my size eight sneaker into my mouth, the mood has soured. Sebastian and Jim excuse themselves to explore the rest of the food booths, leaving Sarah and me alone with Will.

"Oh, Lucy, look! We're out of coffee," says Sarah, like this is a national emergency. "You should go to the kitchen for more supplies. I'd help you, but I *hate* to leave the booth without one of us here."

Sarah is only one of the two people that I've told about my Will crush. My face goes hot at her blatant attempt to throw us together.

Luckily, Will seems oblivious to Sarah's machinations. "Want some help?" he asks.

Even though I don't need help, I'm about to say yes, when who pops into my booth? None other than my arch-nemesis, Brittany Kelly.

3

"Hey, Lucy!" she chirps like she's ecstatic to see me, and even this is a lie because Brittany Kelly can't stand my guts. She's still mad that I called her out in kindergarten for stealing the paint brushes. From Girl Scouts to high school, she's made my life miserable. In a completely passive aggressive way, because to the rest of the world, Brittany is the epitome of the beautiful sweet southern deb.

"Hey, Brittany!" I mimic back.

She's wearing a skin-tight sequined gown, and her auburn hair is artfully arranged in a flattering up do. Even though we're outside on the grass, she's wearing four-inch heels. It's like she's reviving her look from prom night when she was crowned queen.

"What an interesting costume," Sarah muses.

"You like it?" Brittany slowly circles around so we can admire her assets (literally).

"Who are you supposed to be?" Will asks. Although Will has never said it aloud, I know he finds Brittany attractive. His whole body practically *hums* whenever she's around.

"The movie star from *Gilligan's Island.* Technically I suppose it's not a *movie* character, but I don't think you can get more sixties beachy than Ginger."

"You look cute," Sarah concedes, because she's honest, and yes, Brittany is killing the Ginger look.

"Thanks, Sarah!" Her eyes get a sparkly look in them. Brittany has brown eyes, but they're not regular brown eyes like mine. They're so light that sometimes you think they're green and other times you aren't sure. They're her best feature. And she knows it. Besides her hair. She also has incredible hair. And an adorable nose and a gorgeous figure and...

The whole thing is so unfair.

"Lucy," Brittany says. "Who are you dressed as?"

I would think it was apparent, but I fake smile and say, "Annette Funicello."

"Oh." She pauses for effect. "You should have told me you were having trouble coming up with something original. We could have coordinated outfits. You would have made an *adorable* Mary Ann!"

Right. Not that Mary Ann wasn't attractive, but the way Brittany emphasizes the word adorable it's like Mary Ann was Ginger's pet hamster. She would have probably insisted I wear baggy overalls and had straw sticking out of my hair.

"By the way, Lucy, I saw your audition tape for *Muffin Wars*. I've got my fingers crossed for you!"

"*What*? I mean…how is that possible?" I sputter.

"Daddy has a friend who works for The Cooking Channel, and when he came across an audition tape from someone local, he called Daddy to find out all about you. Naturally, Daddy put in a good word for you."

Great. Now if I get on the show, I'll have to wonder if it's because they really liked my muffins or if it's because of Brittany's dad pulling strings on my behalf.

Brittany's family owns The Harbor House, Whispering Bay's fanciest restaurant. I worked there washing dishes during the summers while I was in high school. At first, I thought it was cool of Brittany's dad to give me a job, but in hindsight, I think it was just so that Brittany could lord it over me at school. Still, it was a good experience. Even though the work was hard, it's where I discovered my passion for baking.

You'd think growing up in the restaurant business, Brittany would feel the same way too. But not only does she have no interest, her culinary skills amount to zilch. "I can't even boil an egg!" I heard her brag one day as if this is something to be proud of.

Brittany went to Florida State University where she majored in sorority princess and marketing. After graduation, her daddy got her a job on the chamber of commerce doing PR for the city. She's the one who came up with the Safest City in America tagline that everyone thinks is so wonderful. I hate to admit it, but, it's not half bad.

Brittany says in a staged low voice that everyone can still hear, "Lucy, can I give you some pointers? If you get picked to be on T.V., and I mean, *of course,* you'll get picked, you might want to lose a little weight. The camera always adds ten pounds."

"I think Lucy looks really healthy," Will says in my defense.

I study Will carefully for any signs of deception, but there's nothing. These are the times I wish I knew if Will was telling the truth or just lying to be nice. Because if he's telling the truth, maybe it means he finds me attractive. Which means maybe I have a chance with him. On the other hand, "healthy" could also be interpreted to mean something entirely different.

"Oh, Will," Brittany says in a little girl voice that grates on my nerves, "Lucy is so lucky to have you for a friend!" She bats her lashes at him then proceeds to bore us with details of her last vacation. To be fair, the trip was to Paris. But instead of telling us about all the wonderful French food she ate and the interesting places she got to visit, all she talks about is the great shopping.

Ugh. I don't think I can stand much more of this.

"I can get the coffee by myself," I mutter even though no one's paying attention to me.

I search the grounds until I find Gus, who's over by the main stage. He and some of the other Gray Flamingos are in the middle of counting votes for the costume contest. I'm still holding onto hope that I win. I mean, yes, there are a lot of Annettes here, but half of them are wearing wigs. No one's hair is as big as mine. Surely that must count for *something*.

"I hate to bother you, but can you open the kitchen door for me again? I have to replenish the coffee cart."

"Here, you can have the keys." Gus reaches into his pocket and comes up empty. He gazes around the table and frowns. "I know I put them somewhere."

Viola patiently searches until she finds them. "Sorry! Things have been so disorganized. The one for the kitchen door has a red dot on it."

"Thanks!"

I wheel the empty food cart into the building and make my way to the kitchen. I'm almost finished gathering the supplies we'll need to replenish the coffee station when I hear a familiar whimpering sound. I turn and see a little tan dog huddled in the corner.

"Paco! What are you doing here?" I scoop him up and clutch him to my chest. He's trembling. How on earth did Abby's dog get inside the building? She wasn't with the other members of the Sunshine Ghost Society who came by the booth, but she must be here at the festivities.

Maybe she's avoiding me after yesterday's brouhaha over the tuna salad sandwich.

Whatever. She'll just have to get over it.

"Are you okay, little guy?" Paco licks my hand, but he's still trembling. "Let's go find your momma."

I leave the cart inside the kitchen and walk out into the sunshine. There are even more people here now than before.

Combing through the crowd, I see lots of familiar faces, but no sign of Abby.

Sarah is probably wondering what's keeping me. I should take Paco back to the food booth. Maybe Sarah can watch him until Abby shows up. My eyes are itching, and my nose is running. There's absolutely no doubt that I'm allergic to this sweet little dog.

I weave our way through the crowd. I'm almost back to the food pavilion when Paco starts struggling against me. Before I can stop him, he leaps from my arms and runs away.

Blast! What if he takes off for the beach? Or worse, the road? If anything happens to Paco, I'll never forgive myself, so I run after him. Good thing I'm wearing tennis shoes.

He's almost back to the building when I trip over a hibiscus bush and land face first in the dirt. Luckily, the bush cushioned my weight so that I'm not hurt, but there's blood dripping from my elbow. I brush the dirt off my face and feel my hair for any damage. Even though I can't see myself, I'm confident there's not a hair out of place. Maybe all that hairspray wasn't such a bad idea after all.

Paco is waiting for me by a side door to the building. He's panting (yeah, me too, buddy) like he's out of breath and looking at me with those adorable eyes of his like he's trying to tell me something.

"You want to go back inside?" A part of me feels foolish talking to him like he can understand me, but he wags his tail and barks as if he's answering.

"I'll take that as a yes. But this is the wrong door, sweetie."

There must be at least eight keys on this ring. I have no idea which one will open this particular door. On a whim, I place my hand over the knob and Paco yelps in excitement, like he's encouraging me on.

I turn the knob, and the door opens.

Huh. That's weird. I thought Gus said all the doors were supposed to be locked.

I walk into a small room filled with boxes, which leads me to think this is a storage area. Since I'm here, I might as well head back to the kitchen to collect the coffee cart.

Except Paco takes off running. *Again.* Which is really annoying.

At least this time there are no bushes to trip over.

"Paco!" I yell. "Come back this instant!"

I search the kitchen but he's not there, so I make my way into the large main room. There's a table set up with balloons and flyers in anticipation of the tours, but there's no sign of Paco.

Then I hear the sound of his toe nails clicking against the tile floors. "I hear you!" My voice echoes in the vast empty building.

Paco barks in response like we're playing a game.

I follow the sound through a hallway and into an empty classroom.

"Ha! I found you!"

Paco sits there patiently like he's been waiting for me to show up. Then he looks down at something, and it takes me a few seconds to realize what it is.

It's Abby.

She's lying perfectly still like she's asleep, only…there's a little puddle of blood on the floor next to her head.

Oh my God.

I crouch next to her and shake her arm. "Abby, are you all right?"

Paco looks at me with those big eyes like he's begging me to help her. It's been a while since I took a CPR course and I've never had to use it, but I don't think the basics have changed.

I check to make sure Abby is breathing, which, she's not. Then I check the vein in her neck for a pulse and my own pulse goes wildly out of control.

I push up the sleeve of her sweater and check her wrist to make sure I haven't made a mistake.

But I haven't.

It looks as if I don't have to worry about Abby holding the tuna salad sandwich incident over my head because Abby isn't asleep.

She's dead.

4

———

"Lucy, are you sure?" Will asks.

"There's no pulse, and she's not breathing. So yeah, I'm pretty sure she's dead." I shudder. Poor Abby. What was she doing inside the rec center? Since I didn't have my cell phone on me, the only thing I could do was run back to the food pavilion to get help.

Will notifies the cops, then he, Sarah and Brittany all follow me back inside the building.

Why Brittany has to tag along, I have no idea. It's not like she's going to be a big help or anything. She takes one step into the room and stops cold. "Oh my God," she whimpers. "This is my classroom."

"What do you mean, your classroom?" I ask.

"Didn't I tell you? I just got my Pilates teaching certificate. I'm going to be leading the eight-p.m. class on Tuesday and Thursdays." She closes one eye as she peers at Abby. "I've never seen a dead person before. I mean, other than at a wake."

Neither have I.

Other than the puddle of blood by her head, Abby looks like she does on every other normal day that she walks into The Bistro for lunch. The whole thing is eerie. We stand there staring down at her like a bunch of rubberneckers.

Paco's shivering has subsided, but he has to be traumatized. "Poor little guy," I mutter, holding him tightly. "He must have been with Abby when she fell."

"Is that what you think happened?" asks Sarah.

"I guess so. She must have been looking around then slipped and hit her head."

Nobody else says anything until the cops show up. It's Rusty Newton and, thank God, Zeke Grant is with him. Rusty has been on the Whispering Bay police force since forever. He's a good old boy and super sweet, but think Barney Fife from the old Andy Griffith show, and you'll know why I'm happy that Zeke is here too.

"What happened?" Zeke asks in a quiet, authoritative voice.

I explain how I found Abby.

"Rusty," Zeke says, "Tell Jenna to cancel the tours. And call Travis. I left him at the security tent, but I think we're going to need him here."

"Aye-aye, chief!" As morbid as this sounds, Rusty looks more excited than when I put the lemon poppy seed muffins on sale last week. Those are his favorite, and he stops by

The Bistro every morning to get one along with his cup of coffee.

"I thought you'd be home with Mimi and the babies," I say to Zeke while Rusty makes the call.

"I dropped by to make sure the security detail was running smoothly," Zeke explains. "I have a new cop on the force with lots of experience, so I'm going to let him handle this." He asks us all not to touch anything. Then he says his goodbyes.

Rusty walks around Abby making tsking sounds. After a few minutes, a new cop appears on the scene. This must be the infamous Travis Fontaine we've heard so much about.

He's tall, with dark blonde hair and green eyes like his father. He meets my gaze, but there's none of his father's friendliness or warmth. Instead, his eyes cut through me like razor blades. He looks at Abby then back at me. Any second now I expect fire to come snorting out his nose.

"Are you the one who found Miss Delgado?" he asks in a deep voice with a healthy dose of Texas. A little shiver of *something* runs up my spine. Attraction? *No*. That can't be it. Must be leftover tension from finding poor Abby dead.

"Lucy McGuffin. That's me."

"I'm Officer Travis Fontaine." He stares at my hair for a second, blinks, then eyes the rest of the group. "Can I have your names, please?"

Before anyone else can introduce themselves, Brittany begins to whimper. "I thought...that is..." She gasps like she can't catch her breath. "I think I'm going to faint..." And then in a dramatic swoon, she crumbles her way down to the ground in slow motion.

Both Travis and Will lunge for her, but Travis is faster.

Even though she's fainting (or whatever it is she's doing), Brittany manages to collapse gracefully into Travis's arms. I have to give her credit. She's good.

"Miss, are you all right?" Travis looks down at her with concern.

"I'm… Oh, yes! Thank you so much, *Officer*!" Only Brittany could make a mundane word like "officer" sound sexy.

Travis carefully sets her on her feet like she's a delicate piece of china he's afraid will break.

Sarah secures Brittany by the elbow as Will rustles up a folding chair. Her movie star gown is so tight I wonder how she'll manage to sit without splitting a seam. She folds herself into the chair, and nothing pops or bursts. Go, Brittany!

"Can we get her some juice?" Travis asks Rusty.

Rusty makes a disappointed face like this is beneath him, but he does what Travis asks. Frankly, I don't blame Rusty. For one thing, I'm sure he doesn't want to be bossed around by this younger cop, plus, I doubt Brittany needs the juice.

Travis gets all our names and writes everything down in a notebook. A couple of other people show up and introduce themselves. They're from the county coroner's office. One of them takes pictures. The other one scours the area for what, I don't know, but he's taking measurements. Occasionally he'll pick something up off the floor and place it inside a baggie. It occurs to me that they're making a big production over an accident. It's like we've walked straight into an episode of CSI.

"What made you come inside the building?" Travis asks me. "The tours aren't supposed to begin for almost another hour."

"I was in here earlier, well, in the kitchen, that is, to get supplies to make the coffee."

"And that's what you were doing? Getting more supplies?"

"At first, yes. That's how I found Paco."

"Paco?"

"The dog." I lift Paco's paw and move it up and down like he's waving. "Say hello to Officer Fontaine."

The officer in question doesn't crack a smile. Which, under the circumstances is probably appropriate, but *jeez*. Whenever I'm scared or overwhelmed, I find solace in humor, but I can't imagine this guy ever smiling.

"Paco was in here by himself. At least, I thought he was by himself. He belongs to Derrick, that's Abby's brother. She's dog sitting for him. Or, she was." It just occurred to me that I can't use present tense when talking about Abby anymore. I stifle another shudder.

"And that's when you found Ms. Delgado?"

"Not at first. Paco was pretty skittish, so I picked him up to take him outside, but then he ran away from me. That's when he led me back inside the building."

"He led you back?"

I nod.

"How did he do that exactly?"

"He ran this way, and he was barking. You know, like he was talking to me. In dog speak."

There's a pause. "Are you some kind of dog expert?"

I don't like his tone of voice, but since he's a cop and I was raised to respect authority, I'll let it go. *This time.* "Actually, I'm allergic to them."

"But you're familiar with *this* particular dog?"

"Sure. Abby brought Paco to The Bistro yesterday. That's the café Sarah and I own. Only his real name isn't Paco."

He frowns. "What do you mean that's not his real name?"

Rats. Me and my big mouth. I'm not about to explain my special "gift" to Officer Fontaine. First off, I doubt he'd believe me. I've only known him ten minutes, but I can already tell this guy has a stick up his butt.

"Nothing. I must be confused. This is my first dead person, you know?"

Instead of looking concerned that I might be about to faint, he gives me a look that says he doesn't have time for any more of my monkey business. *Just the facts, ma'am.*

"Do you know Derrick's last name?" he asks.

"I've never met him. He lives in Mexico Beach, I think, but I imagine it's Delgado. Abby wasn't married."

Sarah chimes in. "Lucy is right. It's Derrick Delgado. I haven't met him either, but I've heard her mention him a few times."

"Do any of you know how we might reach him?"

We all shake our heads.

He begins to question the rest of the group. The photographer finishes taking pictures. Then a couple of guys come in with a gurney.

"Will that be all, Officer Fontaine?" Sarah asks. "I need to get back to the food pavilion."

"Can I get all of you to write down your contact numbers, please? And your addresses, in case we need them."

Here is where I want to snicker because Travis has no idea that pretty much everyone in Whispering Bay knows everyone else, as well as where to find them. But we all comply and write down our number next to our name.

"I wrote down my cell phone, my home, *and* all my business numbers," Brittany emphasizes. "Just in case you need me. For *anything*."

I cringe. Brittany's blatant flirtation is an embarrassment to womankind.

I glance at Will to gauge his reaction. He looks miserable.

If the object of Will's affection were anyone other than Brittany, I would feel sorry for him. But she's so not worthy of him. Can't he see that?

We're all about to leave, when Travis says, "Miss McGuffin, can you stay a moment? I'd like to speak to you in private."

Brittany makes a pouty face, but she follows Sarah and Will as they go out the door.

Travis stares at my hair again.

"I'm supposed to be Annette Funicello," I explain. "In case you're wondering."

His eyes cut back to mine. "You said you were following the dog back into the building when you discovered the body?"

The way he says *body* puts me on alert. Like something sinister has happened here.

"Yes. But… this was an accident, right?"

"When was the last time you saw Miss Delgado?" he asks, ignoring my question.

"I already told you. She came in yesterday to The Bistro with the little dog."

"Did she seem agitated in any way?"

Yes.

"No," I lie. Because:

A) I really don't want to get into the whole sandwich thing.

B) I still don't know why Abby and Sebastian were out of sorts. Besides, none of that has anything to do with what's happened here.

Thus:

C) It's not relevant.

"You didn't see Miss Delgado at all today?"

He's already asked me this question three different ways. "No," I say again, this time in a firmer tone.

"Did you get in a fight with someone?"

"*What*? Why on earth would you think that?"

He points to the edge of my shift, which I notice has a tear. My left knee is skinned. "I already told you I chased Paco back into the building. I tripped over a bush, and this happened."

He looks at me for a few long seconds. "Okay. Thanks for your cooperation."

The little hairs on the back of my neck tingle.

Oh boy. Officer Fontaine is lying. Well, not lying exactly but he doesn't think I'm cooperating at all. He thinks I'm hiding something. Which, I am since I didn't tell him about Abby being mad at Sebastian.

"By the way," he says. "What door did you use to get inside the building?"

"The kitchen—*oh*." I pull the keys out of my pocket. "Earlier, Sarah and I came in through the kitchen with Gus Pappas, and I used the keys again to get in the second time to refill the coffee cart. But when Paco led me back, and, *yes*," I glare at him, "He did lead me back, we used a side door to get inside."

"And you used one of those keys to unlock that door too?"

"No. It was already open."

He stills. "There was a side door to the building that was open?"

"Not open exactly. Just unlocked."

"Can you show me?"

With Paco still in my arms, I lead him to the door. "Are you sure it was unlocked?" he asks. "Maybe you used one of the keys and forgot?"

I squelch the urge to roll my eyes at him. "It was unlocked," I say firmly.

He unclips his walkie-talkie and asks the technicians to return.

It's clear that Travis doesn't think Abby's death is a simple case of her falling and hitting her head. "Do you think this is how Abby got inside the building?"

"Possibly." He studies the lock. After a few minutes, he remembers that I'm still there. "Thanks, again. You can get back to whatever it was you were doing now."

In other words, *dismissed*.

Except he's not going to get rid of me this easily. Stubborn is my middle name (actually, it's Elizabeth).

"What are you looking for?"

"I really can't discuss that with you."

"Holy wow. You think that maybe someone shoved Abby and then she fell and hit her head? But that would be like...murder."

Before he can respond, the two guys who were taking pictures and collecting evidence in the building arrive.

"Are you going to sweep the place for fingerprints?" I ask one of them. His tag says *G. Cooper, Crime Scene Investigation*. "Because if you do, mine will definitely be there. Maybe you should go ahead and fingerprint me. That way you can compare the prints on the door to mine and rule those out."

G. Cooper looks confused like he's not sure whether to take my advice.

"Miss McGuffin," says Officer Fontaine, "I have to insist that you leave now."

"But—"

"Please, leave this to the professionals."

Boy, this guy sure could use a course in community relations. He's absolutely nothing like his father. And to think, I thought he and I were going to be friends. *Ha*!

I make my way back to the food pavilion. A sad hush has descended over the festivities. News of Abby's death has spread, and no one feels like celebrating anything, but the adults continue for the sake of the kiddies.

Paco has stopped his shaking. I let him down on a patch of grass so he can do his business. When I get back to our booth, Sarah has already cleaned everything up, and she and her husband Luke are loading up the back of the van.

Brittany is still hanging around, probably because of Will. "They're about to announce the winner of the costume contest!" she says.

Funny. Less than an hour ago she'd been so distraught she'd "fainted." Brittany's ability to bounce back from tragedy is impressive.

"May I have your attention!" Gus's voice booms over the loudspeaker system. "First, I want to thank everyone who came out in costume today. Good job, Whispering Bay! It was a tough competition, but there was one person who stood out for their originality. The votes are in, and the winner of the best sixties beach costume is Brittany Kelly!"

Brittany looks around in shock. "*Me*? Did he say me? Oh my God!" She runs toward the stage in her four-inch heels where Gus is waiting for her with a smile and a trophy. Not to mention her hundred-dollar check, which should keep Brittany in lip gloss for about a month.

"Thank you!" she gushes into the mic. "I'm so humbled and proud that y'all have chosen me as the winner!" Images of high school and Brittany's victory prom night speech come flashing back. I swear, I think she used those exact same words then too. It's probably her standard speech. Besides prom queen, Brittany was also Miss Seashell, Miss Walton County and last but not least, Miss Cheese Grits (although since her daddy's restaurant held the contest, I'm sure that was rigged).

"Y'all are too kind, but I simply can't accept this check." Her southern accent rises a couple of notches the way it always does whenever she's doing any public speaking. "Not when there are so many people who need it more than I do. So, if it's all right with y'all, I'd like to donate it to the food pantry at St. Perpetua's which does such a wonderful job of feeding the hungry."

Everyone claps wildly, and Roger Van Cleave takes her picture for the paper.

I'm not disappointed. I'm really not. Because if I'd won, I'd have to go up on stage in front of everyone and right now, I probably look a mess. Plus, whatever her motives, it was nice of Brittany to donate the money.

Will stares at Brittany with a dreamy look on his face.

"Earth to Cunningham," I say.

He shakes his dark head. "Sorry. I was just—"

"Admit it. You like her."

"I know she made your life miserable, Luce, but that was in high school. She's not a bad person. The thing is… I want to ask her out, but not if it's going to come between us."

I still. "Why would it come between us?" Then I laugh, and it sounds fake, but what can I do? "Ask her out! If you like her, then I like her."

The relief on his face makes me want to cry. Will has no skills when it comes to detecting deception. Either that, or he just doesn't want to see it, because this is probably the biggest lie I've ever told.

Paco nudges me with his nose like he wants attention. I'd forgotten I was still holding him.

"What are you going to do with the dog?" Will asks.

"I hate to hand him over to the animal shelter. I know they'll take good care of him until Abby's brother gets back, but he's been through a hard day."

"I'll take him," Will offers. "Since you're allergic."

This is really nice of Will, but I feel a strange kinship with this little dog, and despite my allergy, I'm just not ready to give him up yet.

"One night with him isn't going to kill me." I glance around the crowd. "Have you seen Sebastian?"

"I texted him after we found Abby, but he hasn't texted back. He probably got called away to the rectory." Will studies my face. "Are you sure you're going to be okay?"

"I'm fine."

He nods. "See you later, Lucy." Out of the corner of my eye, I watch him congratulate Brittany.

Even though the temperature is only in the mid-seventies, I'm sweating and itching. All I want right now is to go home, take a hot shower and crawl into bed.

Sarah comes back to the booth. "I don't know about you, but I'm ready to call it a day. Luke is already on his way home."

I hold Paco on my lap as Sarah drives us back to the café. Luckily, I live in the apartment upstairs which is extra convenient because I'm exhausted. I unlock the back door and start to make my way up the stairs with Paco, when Sarah says, "Want some help with your hair? I mean, taking it down?"

"No thanks. I figure I'll just get in the shower and let it fall apart naturally."

She pauses. "I didn't want to say anything before, because there wasn't a point, but…don't freak out."

"What?" I ask, alarmed because naturally when someone tells you not to freak out, your first instinct is to freak out.

She bites her bottom lip, like she's not sure what to do, then sighs. "Okay, here goes." She closes her eyes as she reaches out and tears something out of my hair.

"*Ouch*!"

She winces. "Sorry about that."

"What did you do that for?"

"You had something stuck in your hair, and I wanted to get it out for you." Then she gingerly holds up a dead lizard by the tail.

"*That* was in my hair?"

She makes a pained face and nods.

"How in the world—"

The lizard must have gotten stuck in the cave of hairspray when I tripped and fell over the hibiscus bush.

No wonder Officer Fontaine kept staring at my hair!

All the while he was asking me questions, there was a dead reptile staring right back at him.

5

When Sarah and I bought The Bistro we made a pact that the business wouldn't take over our lives, so we hired extra help and decided to close the café one day a week. Sunday seemed like the most logical day.

When you're used to getting up at four-thirty every morning, six a.m. is technically sleeping in, but today it takes a huge effort to drag out of bed in time to make my regular seven-thirty Sunday mass. It must be the aftereffects of the Benadryl I had to take last night to keep from itching.

The instant mass is over, I dash out to the front of the church hoping to have a word with my brother, but Sebastian is inundated with parishioners wanting to talk to him, so I don't get a chance to ask him about Abby and the exorcism.

"Hello, Lucy!" Jim Fontaine waves, so I wave back, which he takes as a sign to come up to talk to me. Normally, I'd welcome his company, but unfortunately, he's not alone. "Officer" Travis is with him. He's out of uniform and wearing neatly pressed khaki pants and a blue button-down shirt that contrasts with his green eyes, making them look even greener.

I have to admit, Travis isn't bad looking. He's not classically handsome like Will, but he does exude a certain *something*. Too bad he has no personality. On the other hand, that makes him perfect for Brittany.

It was obvious yesterday that she had the hots for him. I wonder if Will had a chance to ask her out. And if she said yes. Maybe if I'm lucky, he changed his mind. And maybe if I'm really lucky, Brittany will channel all her efforts into Officer Fontaine.

Jim turns to his son. "Travis, this is Lucy McGuffin. She's Father Sebastian's sister and I'm told she makes the best muffins in the world."

My cheeks heat up the way they always do whenever someone uses that particular compliment because obviously, that would be impossible to gauge. I mean, I'm sure *someone* in the world makes better muffins than me. Maybe.

Travis takes in my appearance. Today, I'm wearing normal Lucy-goes-to-church clothes. A denim skirt with a peasant blouse and my dark curly hair is pulled back in a low ponytail. More importantly, it's minus the lizard.

"We met yesterday at the rec center opening," I tell Jim. "I was the one who found Abby Delgado."

"Oh, yes, I heard about that. Poor woman. Terrible accident. Finding her must have been awful for you."

Travis observes my expression carefully. He still thinks I'm hiding something. Which, I am. I have to give him credit. He's more than just a broad set of shoulders and a firm chin.

"It was really hard on her little dog. Or rather, her brother's dog. Abby was dog sitting for him."

Poor Paco spent the night having nightmares. I know this because I let him sleep at the end of my bed (hence, the reason I had to take the Benadryl) and he kept twitching and making all kinds of noises. I hated leaving him alone this morning.

"Where is the dog, by the way?" Travis asks.

"He's with me."

"I was finally able to get ahold of Derrick Delgado yesterday evening. To tell him about his sister's death."

"How's he doing?" The words are no sooner out than I flinch. This is a horribly dumb question. If something ever happened to Sebastian, I'd be comatose with grief.

"He's handling it the way you'd expect. Under the circumstances."

Which, doesn't tell me anything.

"Is he back in town?" I don't know Derrick, but I'd like to pay him a visit to tell him how sorry I am about his sister. And to give him his dog back, of course.

"According to him he never left town. He's been in Mexico Beach this whole time."

"I don't understand. Abby told me her brother was away and that's why she was dog sitting."

Travis looks me square in the eye and says, "Derrick Delgado swears he doesn't own a dog."

I'm confused. Why on earth would Abby lie about her brother owning Paco? And just as importantly, why didn't I pick up on that lie?

Probably because it was mixed in with the other lie about the dog's name and that's the lie I focused on. All I know is that if Paco doesn't belong to Derrick, then who does he belong to?

I swing by my place to pick up the dog, and we go to the Whispering Bay Animal Shelter. Lanie Miller manages the place. She's Dr. Nate's sister and a real hoot. She and her girl-friend, Dhara, are Bistro regulars.

I explain the Paco situation to Lanie.

"What a cute little dog. He's definitely a Chihuahua mix, but there's some terrier there too. You said Abby told you he belonged to her brother, but the brother denies it?"

"That's the official story. At least, according to Officer Fontaine."

"I met him a couple of days ago. He came in here looking for a dog. He's pretty cute."

"The dog?"

She snickers. "The man."

"Not my type."

Lanie smiles sympathetically. She's the other person that I've confided in about my feelings for Will. She thinks I should tell him, but if I do that and he doesn't feel the same way, it will ruin our friendship. And my friendship with Will means everything to me, so I can't take that risk.

"Obviously, Travis Fontaine isn't my type either, but if I were into boys, I'd be all over that one. You should have seen the way he was with the dogs. You can tell a lot about a person by how they treat an animal."

"He adopted a dog?"

"Not yet. He's looking for a specific breed. He's going to volunteer here a few hours a week."

"That's...nice of him." *I suppose.*

Lanie picks up a scanner and runs it over Paco's back. "He's been neutered. Let's see if he's been chipped. Mmmm... We're in luck." She heads over to a computer. "According to the records, he belongs to someone named Susan Van Dyke from Destin. Let me give her a call." She picks up the phone and dials.

Destin is a resort town about thirty miles away. How on earth did Abby end up with this dog?

"No answer," Lanie says. She leaves a message with information on how to contact her. Lanie rubs Paco behind the ears, and he practically melts in her hand. "Hopefully, his owner will call back soon. But in the meantime, little guy, what do you say? Want to stay here and play?"

"Stay here?"

"Sure. I mean, you can't take him, on account of your allergies. Right?"

"Right." Last night was miserable. I could keep taking the Benadryl, but I hate how groggy it makes me feel.

"Heard anything from *Muffin Wars*?" Lanie asks.

"Not yet."

"You will. No one makes muffins the way you do." She puts a leash on Paco. "Say good-bye to Lucy, Paco."

"Are you sure he'll be okay? I mean, he's been traumatized. He was with Abby when she…you know, died. Is there a pet psychologist that can come see him?"

Lanie tries to hide her smile. "Don't worry. He'll be fine." She takes a long look at Paco. "I don't know anyone named Susan Van Dyke, but now that I look at him more closely, I swear I've seen this dog before. I'm just not sure where."

"If he needs anything, anything at all just let me know." I wave to him one last time. He looks at me with the saddest eyes. I hope he doesn't think I don't want him. I don't know a lot about dogs, but I can tell he's special. Regardless of Officer Fontaine's skepticism, Paco *did* lead me to find Abby's body.

6

EVERY MONDAY THE "TOP PEOPLE" AS THEY CALL THEMSELVES from the Sunshine Ghost Society meet at The Bistro for breakfast. Phoebe Van Cleave is the first to arrive. It occurs to me that I never saw Phoebe or anyone else from the society after Abby's body was discovered, so I never got a chance to offer my condolences.

I hand her a coffee. "I'm so sorry for your loss. How is the group taking Abby's death?"

"Even though it's just been a couple of days, we all miss her something fierce. She was a valuable member of our society, you know."

The little hairs on my neck rise.

Phoebe isn't going to miss Abby one bit.

Betty Jean told me that Abby and Phoebe were involved in a power struggle within the group. With Abby gone, it looks like Phoebe's position is no longer in jeopardy.

"Do you know when her service is going to be held?" I ask.

"It's all up to the brother. Apparently, he's a real loser, but he was her only living relative, so he's in charge now." She hesitates. "You know, Lucy, there are all sorts of rumors circulating about Abby and a dog. Do you know anything about it?"

Oh boy. The little hairs on my neck are practically dancing now. I'm surprised Phoebe's nose hasn't gotten longer just standing here talking to me.

This last statement of hers is a blatant lie in that she most *definitely* knows something about Paco. And it's a whole lot of something too. The stronger my physical reaction, the bigger the lie.

But I can't very well call her out on it without exposing my gift. I'd love to find out more about Paco, so I'm forced to tell her what I know in hopes that maybe I can glean more info from her.

"The dog is a Chihuahua mix. Abby brought him here to The Bistro on Friday and told everyone that he belonged to her brother, but he denies the dog is his. The dog was with her when she died."

"Do you know where the dog is now?"

"He's at the animal shelter. Lanie Miller is trying to find out who owned him previously. In case they want him back."

"I've always wanted a dog. As Abby's dear friend, I should offer to adopt him."

Oh, hell to the no. Paco is such a smart little thing. He belongs with someone hipper and let's face it, saner than Phoebe Van Cleave.

I make a mental note to call Lanie and tell her that under *no* circumstances is Paco to end up with Phoebe. Before I can quiz her further on the subject of Paco, Gloria and Victor join us.

"Lucy, how have you been, dear?" Gloria's blonde hair is braided down her back today. She's younger than the rest of her group, but she's got streaks of gray in her hair that make her look older than thirty-nine (I asked her age once). If she cut and colored it, she'd probably look great, but then who am I to be giving out beauty advice? I can barely tweeze my eyebrows.

"I'm fine," I say automatically.

Gloria turns to Phoebe. "Have you asked her yet?"

Phoebe suddenly looks nervous. "Not yet."

Gloria reaches across the counter to take my hand in hers. "You know, Lucy, you don't have to pretend with us."

"O-kay. Not pretending, but if I was, what would I be pretending about?"

"When you find a dead body, you become linked to it."

"The spirit needs a conduit to hang on to," says Victor. "Chances are, Abby's spirit is hanging on to you."

"Have you felt different since Saturday?" Gloria asks. She eyes me curiously, and I can't help but feel creeped out. "We're expecting Abby to make an appearance any day now.

She's the first of our group to go over to the other side. I'm hoping she can tell us what happened to her."

Oh, for Pete's sake. These wackadoos think that Abby is going to communicate with them through *me*?

I snatch my hand away. "Nope. I don't feel different at all."

"It's just a matter of time before you do. When it happens, you'll need us." Gloria slips me her business card. It reads **Gloria Hightower, Professional Medium**. "Call anytime. Day or night. If I'm not available, then leave a message."

Victor nods eagerly.

The whole thing is ghoulish. None of them are even sad that Abby has passed. It's as if they like her more now that she's potentially a ghost than when she was alive. How messed up is that?

Thankfully, Sarah comes along and saves me by getting their orders. Which means I take the next customer in line.

It's Rusty. And Travis is with him.

"Morning, Lucy!" says Rusty. "You know what I want."

I hand Rusty his usual—coffee heavy on the cream and sugar and a lemon poppy seed muffin.

"What'll you have, Officer Fontaine?"

"Just coffee. Black. And call me Travis."

"Are you sure you don't want something to eat? Our muffin of the day is pumpkin spice. First one's on the house."

"No, thanks. I'm more of a donut guy."

I knew it! "Then you should try Heidi's Bakery on Main Street. She makes great donuts, and her coffee isn't bad either."

"Thanks. I'll give it a try." Apparently, Officer Clueless doesn't understand sarcasm. "I checked in on Paco this morning," he adds.

This gets my full attention. "How's he doing?"

"He seemed to be doing fine."

Fine? That could mean anything. "Was he eating? How about the shaking?"

"He wasn't shaking."

He doesn't add anything else, so I give him his coffee. "Do you know when Derrick is planning on holding Abby's service?"

"Can't have the service till they finish the autopsy," says Rusty.

"*Autopsy?*"

"It's standard procedure whenever the cause of death is yet to be determined. But between you and me, it looks like that knock on the head did her in."

"What do you think happened? I mean, did she trip or something?"

"Or *something* might be more like it," Rusty says ominously.

Travis looks as if he's about to admonish Rusty when Betty Jean spies him from across the café. Her ability to sniff out testosterone never fails to impress me. She nearly plows down a mother and her toddler in her hurry to get to him.

"You must be the new cop in town," she says breathlessly. "I'm Betty Jean Collins."

Travis shakes her hand. "Nice to meet you, Ms. Collins."

"Call me Betty Jean. Or better yet, Sugar Momma. Whichever you prefer. No one told me you were Ryan Reynold's doppelganger. Ever see that movie *The Proposal*? I could have played the Betty White role, except she's a lot older than me. A *lot*. My favorite scene is the one where Ryan Reynolds catches Sandra Bullock coming out of the shower, and they end up on the floor naked. You can see his butt, and let me tell you, it's mighty fine. If you pause it, you can even—"

"I haven't seen the movie." Travis looks at me with desperation like he needs to be saved, but I'm enjoying this way too much to help him out here.

Betty Jean looks Travis up and down, then growls. "I guess it's true what they say about Texas. Is *all* of you this big?"

"Ah, Betty Jean, cut it out," says Rusty. "Or he'll think you're serious." Rusty playfully elbows Travis. "Betty Jean is like this with all the cops in town."

"No, I'm not. Just the good-looking ones I want to schnocker." She winks and saunters away. Even though I don't think schnocker is a real word, we all know *exactly* what Betty Jean means. The mental picture those words create in my head is more than a little disturbing.

Travis is left with his mouth hanging open.

Welcome to Whispering Bay, Officer Fontaine!

He shakes his head as if to clear it (he must have gotten the same picture I did). "Miss McGuffin, can we speak to you please? In private?"

Rusty makes a face. "Now? But I haven't eaten my muffin yet."

Travis looks at Rusty for a full three seconds like he's patiently counting to himself before saying, "Go ahead and have your breakfast. I can talk to Miss McGuffin."

"Gee, thanks!" Rusty happily takes off for an empty table near the window.

What on earth could Travis Fontaine want to speak to me about? I'm curious, but my Spidey sense warns me that the last thing I should do is go off for a private word with this guy.

"If this has to do with Abby, I told you everything the other day. Plus, I'm kind of busy. Working? You know?"

Sarah, who's just finished serving table three, overhears the last part of our conversation. "Go ahead, Lucy, Jill's in the kitchen, and I can handle the counter." She smiles at Travis who smiles back at her.

It's the first time I've seen him smile and… I hate to admit it, but Betty Jean is right. He does look like Ryan Reynolds. Sarah probably thinks she's doing me a favor. If only she knew how annoying he is.

It looks as if I have no choice but to talk to him.

"If you want to talk in private, then we should go upstairs."

7

THE UPSTAIRS APARTMENT WAS BUILT BY THE BISTRO'S FORMER owners, and it's completely awesome. Dark hardwood floors, creamy colored baseboards, and light gray walls give the place an upscale feel not to mention the breathtaking views of the gulf. I'd feel guilty living here, but Sarah and her husband also live on the beach in a renovated cottage, so it only made sense for me to take this place.

I can tell by Travis's expression that he's impressed. "Does every room up here have a view like this?"

"Yep. Except for the bathroom. The window in there looks out over the back parking lot, but I'm not complaining."

He changes gears and gets down to business. "Miss McGuffin," he says, and I swear I can hear Mrs. Jackson's voice from all those years ago in kindergarten, "I asked you if Miss Delgado seemed agitated last Friday and you said no, however, witnesses claim that the two of you had some words over a tuna salad sandwich."

"*Witnesses*? Who have you been talking to?"

He pulls out that notebook of his. "Gus Pappas, Viola Pantini—"

"Okay, okay." I blow out a breath. "I get it."

I should never have underestimated this guy.

"Sure, Abby and I had a few words, but it was nothing."

"It didn't sound like nothing."

"The tuna salad sandwich ruse is a little game Abby plays about once a month to get a free lunch. She orders it, then when I bring it out to her, she claims that I got the order wrong. Then I bring her what she really wants, a roast beef on rye and we give it to her for free."

"If you know that she's just yanking your chain, then why go along with it? Why not call her out on it?"

"Because I don't want to accuse her of lying."

"How do you know it's a lie? Maybe she's just forgetful."

"Oh, it's a lie, because—" I snap my mouth shut.

"Because what?"

Rats.

"You're right, maybe she has dementia." I try to sound meek even though it's killing me, but the last thing I want to do is admit my gift to Officer Fontaine. "I give her a free sandwich because I don't want to embarrass her and because other than the sandwich game, she's a good customer. Or rather, she *was* a good customer."

I shudder. I still can't believe she's gone. Poor Abby. What she was doing all alone in the rec center?

It's been two days, but I can still see it all so clearly. Abby, lying on the ground like she's asleep, wearing her tan skirt with sensible shoes…

Wait again.

My brain zeroes in on something.

Abby was wearing a tan skirt, sweater, and her brown loafers. It's a variation of what she wears most days when it's cool outside. But she specifically told me that she was going to be dressed as Annette Funicello.

So why wasn't she in costume?

The answer is obvious. I remember feeling her skin. She was cold and stiff. As if she'd been there a while…

Travis's voice cuts through my thoughts. "But last Friday, you did challenge her."

"What?"

"The tuna salad sandwich?" he prompts.

"Oh, right. I was tired. I'd been up late baking, and I was little friskier than usual." *Now it's my turn to ask questions.* "Why all this interest in what happened Friday? Have you figured out what Abby was doing in the rec center? Did she get in through the side door? Did you dust it for prints? Remember, you're going to find mine there."

"First things first." Travis flips through the pages in his note-book until he finds what he's looking for. "On the day of the rec center celebration you and Sarah Powers were working in your food booth, and according to Mrs. Powers, Will Cunningham and your brother Sebastian came by around ten-thirty?"

That's Father McGuffin to you, buddy.

"That's right."

"But your brother wandered off, leaving Will and Brittany Kelly at the booth with you and Sarah Powers for about, what? Twenty minutes or so before you decided to go back into the building? And that's when you found the dog?"

"I already told you this at least four times the other day. And my brother didn't wander off. He and your dad went to go check out the rest of the food booths."

"Did you see him later?"

"Who? Sebastian or your father?"

"Sebastian."

"No. He probably got called away by a parishioner or something."

What's he trying to get at?

"Let's go back to Friday at lunch. Viola Pantini has gone on record as saying that Miss Delgado and Sebastian seemed at odds with one another. Something about an exorcism she wanted him to perform?"

I swallow hard. "I don't remember that."

"Gus Pappas also recalled an exchange between the two of them and it's very similar to Ms. Pantini's version. Apparently, Miss Delgado threatened to go to the Bishop?"

"It was lunchtime, and we were busy, so I really can't... *Hold on*. You don't think Sebastian had anything to do with Abby's death? Just because she was upset with him on Friday and then you're not sure where he was on Saturday during the celebration? Are you *insane*? Did you ask my brother where he was?"

"He says he was hearing a confession, but he won't tell us whose it was."

"You should know he can't tell you that. Besides, Abby wasn't killed during the rec center celebration. She died on Friday night or possibly early Saturday morning before the celebration began."

"How do you know that?"

"It's simple. Abby told me on Friday that she was going to be dressed as Annette Funicello, but she wasn't wearing a costume, which means she never went to the celebration. Plus, her body was cold. I mean, like really cold and stiff. I just didn't put it together until now."

A flicker of admiration flashes across his face. Have I actually managed to impress Officer Know-It-All?

"You're right. The coroner puts her time of death between midnight and two a.m. According to the security footage, Abby entered the building around midnight, but she never came out."

Security footage? I had no idea there were cameras around the building. Then I remember that Gus mentioned something about security issues.

"And your brother was seen entering the building thirty minutes later," Travis adds.

"My brother? Are you sure about that?"

"Positive. He even admits to it. Only he refuses to tell us what he was doing at the rec center in the middle of the night. He only says he saw Abby, stayed in the building a few minutes, then left."

"Okay, well, there you go. He was probably counseling her."

"In under five minutes? Maybe. Except the footage doesn't show anyone else entering or leaving the building. Which means that Sebastian is the last person who saw Abby alive."

The little hairs on my neck start to dance.

Is Officer Fontaine lying to me? I study him closer. His last statement wasn't exactly a lie, but it wasn't the complete truth either. He's hiding something from me, only I'm not sure what purpose it serves.

"I thought Rusty said she fell. Do the police think someone *killed* her?"

"I never said that," Travis says cautiously. "But we need Sebastian to tell us exactly what happened and we're hoping that you can convince him to do that."

"Well, I'll certainly try."

"Can you talk to him today? It's important we wrap this up as soon as possible."

I nod woodenly because even though I've just told him I'll try, I doubt Sebastian will tell me anything. Not if he feels that it will somehow betray a confidence.

I wait till Travis leaves, then I slump into my living room couch. My head is spinning. What on earth was Sebastian doing in the rec center in the middle of the night with Abby Delgado?

Even though a part of me knows it's irrational to blame Travis Fontaine for any of this, I still can't help it. He might not have said it aloud, but he not-so-tactfully accused Sebastian of... who knows what?

As if my brother, the priest, who's never even hurt a fly in his whole life, was guilty of some kind of wrongdoing!

I grab a sweater and my car keys.

This situation calls for immediate action.

8

I EXPLAIN EVERYTHING TO SARAH, AND SINCE JILL HAS CLEAN-UP duty, she tells me to take the rest of the day off. I don't bother calling my brother because I don't want him to find an excuse to avoid me, so I charge over to the rectory.

It takes Sebastian a few minutes to answer the door. He looks surprised to see me in the middle of the day. "What's going on? Are you okay?"

I brush past him and plop myself down on the couch. "What on earth were you doing at the rec center in the middle of the night with Abby Delgado?"

"How did you—" He scrubs a hand down his face. "Never mind. So the cops came to see you, huh?"

"Yep. And I need you to fess up. Now."

He raises a brow at my use of the word 'fess.'

"Sebastian," I say trying to imitate our mother's voice.

"Okay. This is what I can tell you. Abby wanted me to perform an exorcism on someone she thought was possessed. I tried to humor her because she was a nice lady, and even though she belonged to that ghost society, she didn't have any real friends."

My shoulders sag. Abby wasn't one of my favorite people. Not even close. Most days she was a nuisance, but she was a loyal customer, and as kooky as it sounds, I'm going to miss her sneaky free lunch trick. It never occurred to me that she might have been lonely. I wish I'd been nicer to her that last day.

"Who did she think was possessed?"

"It's not relevant."

"Of course it's relevant! The police think that Abby's death wasn't accidental."

He stills. "They said that?"

"No one has to come out and tell me what's right under my nose. You should have seen that crew at the rec center. Taking pictures and fingerprints...and this Travis person running around like he's auditioning for the lead role in a *Law and Order* remake. So I'm going to ask you again. Who did Abby think was possessed? Let me guess, Phoebe Van Cleave?"

"All I'm going to tell you is that Abby had some concerns about a friend of hers and she wanted me to help. When I explained that I couldn't help in the way she wanted, then she became upset. Friday night she called and apologized for her behavior at The Bistro and asked me to meet her in the rec center. She said it was a matter of life or death."

"Didn't you think that was weird?"

"We're talking about Abby here."

"Point taken."

"So against my better judgment, I went. But when I got there, she told me that she didn't need me anymore and that everything had been taken care of."

"As in, taken care of because her friend was all right, or taken care of because she'd found someone else who'd perform her exorcism?"

"She didn't say, and frankly, I didn't ask because it was late and I was tired, and the whole thing was ridiculous."

Neither of us say anything for a few minutes.

"Okay, so you went to the rec center. You saw Abby. And the two of you talked."

He nods. "But don't ask me what we talked about, because that was confidential."

"You were there for about five minutes?"

"I wanted to walk her to her car, but she insisted on staying longer, so I left."

"And you never saw anyone else there?"

He hesitates like he's holding something back and I'm expecting his next words to be a lie. "Just the dog."

Hmmm.... Sebastian is telling the truth.

"One more question. Why did she want to meet inside the rec center? Why not here at the rectory? And how did you get inside the building?"

"That's two questions."

I give him the same look I use on Tony, our flour vendor when he's late on his deliveries. I mean, how am I supposed to make muffins without flour?

It works because Sebastian answers, "I thought the rec center location was odd, not to mention illegal since we didn't have a right to meet there, but she was adamant. She said that since the building was haunted—her words, not mine—that it was the best location. She told me to go in through the side door. It was unlocked when I got there."

"You know they have security cameras? According to Travis Fontaine, you and Abby are the only ones who went into the building that night."

"That's what he told me."

"Sebastian, this all looks really bad."

"In what way?"

"In what way? If the police think that Abby was pushed or was involved in a struggle, then the fall that caused her death isn't accidental. And if you're the only person who was there that night… Do I really have to spell it out for you?"

"Are you saying that the police think I caused Abby's death?" He shuts his eyes for a few long seconds. "Dear God. They're right. This is all my fault. I should never have left her alone. I should have demanded that she allow me to walk her to her car."

"Oh no. You don't get to play the martyr. If someone did cause Abby's death, then that's on them. But don't you see? You have to tell me who she thought was possessed, because obviously whoever it was, might have had a motive to hurt Abby."

"I can tell you positively one hundred percent that the... person she thought was possessed didn't kill her."

"How can you be so sure?"

"Because I just am."

"And I thought I was the stubborn one in the family," I mutter.

"Why don't we let the police do their jobs? If anything sinister happened, then the truth will come out eventually."

"Eventually? You're so trusting of everyone. Zeke, sure, he's on our side. But this new guy? You should have seen the gleam in his eyes. He's practically feral."

"I think you've been watching too many episodes of *America's Most Vicious Criminals*."

"And you haven't seen enough of them. You should see how wonky the evidence can be in these cases! There's plenty of innocent people who've been railroaded by the police, believe you me."

"Lu-cy," he says, mimicking Ricky Ricardo from the old *I Love Lucy* series. "Do you know something I don't?"

Usually, this makes me laugh, but not today.

"I know that Travis Fontaine has it out for you. What? Did you make him say too many Hail Mary's as penance on his last confession?"

Sebastian grunts. "First off, I never give out Hail Mary's as penance. That's old school. And it's called reconciliation now, which you would know if you ever went."

"I go. Sometimes. Just not to you. Now don't change the subject." I decide to pull out the big guns. "I should call mom and dad and tell them what's going on. I bet Mom could make you tell the cops what they want to know."

Sebastian gives me a look that makes me shrink into the sofa. "Don't you dare ruin mom and dad's last week at the cabin."

I have to hand it to my big brother. He probably graduated top of his class in Guilt Infliction 101.

Our parents are what we call reverse snowbirds. After a lifetime of living in the Florida heat and humidity, they bought a cabin in Maine where they spend the summer months. They'll be back home in Whispering Bay sometime next week. Probably just in time to see Sebastian arrested.

He gets up from his chair. "Look, neither of us is going to change the other one's mind, so I suggest we get back to our lives and let our tax money be put to good use. Let the cops take care of it. Now, I have a sermon to work on. See you later, Lucy," he says back in Ricky Ricardo mode.

I go to leave, because what else can I do?

"By the way," he says casually in a way that makes me think he doesn't want to bring this up but feels like he has to, "have you spoken to Will lately?"

"Not since the day of the rec center celebration. Why?"

"It's just that, he and Brittany are going out Friday night. On a date."

My stomach suddenly turns queasy, like I've licked too much raw muffin batter off the spoon (yes, I know it's not good for me but don't judge till you've tried it). This isn't exactly a surprise. Will told me he was going to ask Brittany out. But I must have been hoping that she'd turn him down.

And if that's the case, what kind of friend am I?

I do my best to smile. "That's great! I hope they have a good time."

"Lucy," my brother says gently, "Brittany's not a bad person."

Et tu, Sebastian? Those are the exact same words Will used to describe her.

Technically, I suppose it's true since as far as I know she hasn't been involved in any criminal activity since kindergarten.

"I'm sure you're right." Before he can say anything else, I kiss him goodbye on the cheek.

He gives me a smile meant to reassure me, but it's strained. Whatever happened between Sebastian and Abby has him troubled. He waits by the door until I get in my car and drive off. I might not be able to save Will from Brittany's French manicured clutches, but I can certainly do something to help my brother.

Let the cops take care of things?

Poor innocent, gullible Sebastian.

If he won't help himself out of this mess, then I'll have to do it for him.

Which means it's up to me to figure out what really happened to Abby Delgado.

9

Mexico Beach is about an hour away, so it's after five by the time I get there. Our beautiful cool November weather has fizzled, and it's back into the upper eighties again. I'm hungry, thirsty, and hot, but I'm on a mission.

I'm going to visit Abby's brother Derrick and offer him my condolences, which is the decent thing to do. Plus, I want to see if he knows anything about Paco. Just because Officer Fontaine says that Derrick denied owning the dog doesn't mean I should just take his word for it.

Since I'm assuming he's around the same age Abby was, I keep my fingers crossed that he still has a landline which would mean he's listed in the phone book. But finding a phone book these days is like coming across a winning lottery ticket just lying around on the floor.

After three gas stations, I find one that still has a pay phone and I'm in luck. There's only one Derrick Delgado in the directory, and according to the map app on my smartphone, his address is just a few miles away.

Mexico Beach is one of those communities on the gulf with the picturesque pastel houses, but Derrick's home is nothing like those. His trailer sits on the edge of town on a big isolated lot. The grass is overgrown, and there's trash strewn all over the place. I carefully make my way through the weeds, lest I accidentally step on a snake, because that would totally ruin my day. I should probably have called first, but my Spidey sense told me not to.

I walk up the wooden steps to the rickety porch and knock on the door. After a couple of minutes of nothing, I ring the doorbell just in case Derrick is hard of hearing. I wait for another couple of minutes, then give up. He must not be home.

I consider leaving him a note, when a man's voice says, "Turn around. Nice and slow and keep your hands where I can see 'em."

Definitely not words you want to hear when you're all alone out in the middle of nowhere. I turn around to find myself looking down the barrel of a shotgun.

But worse than that, sitting on the porch ledge next to the man with the shotgun, is a squirrel. And it's staring at me with his beady little eyes like he's ready to attack.

Most people find squirrels adorable, but they've been fooled. To me, squirrels are nothing more than aggressive rats with furry tails.

"Who the hell are you and what are you doing here?" The man is a little older than Abby was, with a gleaming bald head and small brown eyes. His long-sleeved shirt is sweat-stained and stretched across a massive beer belly.

"Please, um, Mr. Delgado? I mean, I assume you must be Mr. Delgado, I don't mean any harm. Can you…can you tell your squirrel to go away?"

"My *what*?"

While still keeping my hands up, I gesture to the monster on the ledge. "Chip, Dale, Killer…whatever you call him. He's kind of freaking me out."

He snickers, then playfully aims the gun at the squirrel, who immediately takes off running across the lawn.

I breathe a massive sigh of relief. "Thank you!"

He turns the gun back on me. "What are you doing sneaking up on my house? Trying to break in?"

"No, of course not! I'm—"

"You from the bank?" The gun stays firmly aimed at my head, so I keep my hands in the air because I really don't want this bozo to shoot me.

"The *bank*? No, no… You have it all wrong. I was a friend of your sister's."

He relaxes a little. "If you're here to ask for something of hers so you can conjure her back up or whatever it is you people do, then you can forget it."

"You think I'm a member of the Sunshine Ghost Society?"

"If you were a friend of Abby's then you were definitely in that spook club of hers. Abby didn't have any other friends."

"I was more of an… acquaintance. Honest. I don't even believe in ghosts. As a matter of fact, I laughed all the way through *Beetlejuice*."

"So you ain't one of those wackos?"

"Nope. I'm completely normal." *Sort of.*

"Then how did you know my sister?" He inspects me closer. Jeans, T-shirt, sneakers, and a ponytail. Not exactly threatening attire.

"She was a customer," I squeak.

He lowers his gun. *Finally!*

"Why didn't you say so?" he grumbles. "I've been waiting for you all day."

"You have?"

"Sure. When the law office said they were sending a courier, I was expectin' a guy, but I guess these days that's politically incorrect or whatever bullshit you want to call it."

Law office?

I know I should identify myself immediately. I came over here today to tell Derrick how sorry I was about his sister, and to see if he knew anything about Paco, but as far as I'm concerned, this little Hee-Haw routine of his changes everything. Plus, I'd really like to find out more about this law firm business.

He walks around me and opens the door. "Let's get this over with."

If this were a scene from a movie, I'd definitely have blonde hair and big boobs. Because as foolish as it seems, I'm going to be the too-stupid-to-live heroine and follow a strange man, who I've just lied to and who seconds ago was pointing a gun at my head, into his house.

Derrick Delgado's home is furnished moderately and is relatively clean compared to the outside. His T.V. is one of those old behemoths encased in a faux wooden box. Either he:

A) Doesn't believe in flat screens.

B) Can't afford to update.

or

C) Is afraid plasma rays will steal whatever brain cells he has left.

I opt for B with a strong possible side of C.

He sits down on a beat-up sofa. I select the chair farthest from him. "I'm really sorry about your sister. Her death must have come as a shock to you."

"Sort of."

He watches me with an expectant gaze that makes me squirm. Or maybe the chair has a flea infestation. Or worse...

Concentrate, Lucy.

It's a total long shot, but maybe there's a chance he knew something about the exorcism. "Did you know that Abby was being counseled by a local priest?"

"She wasn't religious. Unless you call that ghost society she runs around with a religion. More of a cult, if you ask me." He growls under his breath. "Don't tell me she left all her money to the Church."

Boy, this guy is a piece of work all right. His sister hasn't even been buried yet, and all he's worried about is that she might have left him out of her will.

Which means…

My heart begins to race. Then my cell phone goes off.

I glance at the screen.

Rats. It's Travis. This is the second time he's called in the last hour. The first time he left a message asking if I'd had a chance to talk to Sebastian. There's no way I'm going to tell him that I struck out with my own brother. Plus, I'm busy now. *Go away, Officer Fontaine.* I almost wish he could see the grin on my face as I hit the decline button on his call.

"Sorry about that. Now, where we were? Oh, yes, the will. I'm just a messenger so I'm not privy to the contents of Miss Delgado's will, but I heard that she had some dealings with a Father McGuffin from St. Perpetua's in Whispering Bay."

Wow. Not bad if I do say so myself. I'm actually pretty good at making things up on the fly.

"What the hell does that have to do with anything?"

"Nothing. I was just wondering if you wanted him to do the funeral service."

"Nah. I'm just going to have her cremated. Cheapest way to go and she won't care anyway. But I can't do that till they finish the autopsy. At least, that's what the cops told me."

"The police were here?" I ask, knowing full well that Travis has already spoken to him. But now I have to wonder if Travis asked Derrick where he was at the time of Abby's death, because I for one, would sure like to know.

"They were the ones who told me about Abby slipping and hitting her head. Asked me about a dog, too, but I don't know nothing about no dog."

My neck feels like it's been plugged into an electric socket.

I've just caught Derrick Delgado in a whopper.

"Why did they want to know about a dog?" I ask trying to sound innocent.

He scowls. "What do you care? Where are those papers you brought me?"

I rifle through my bag, pretending to look for them. "You're not going to believe this, but, um, I forgot the papers."

He rolls his eyes in disgust. "What's wrong with you people? First, you never return my calls. Now you show up here with no papers? Wouldn't have happened if they'd sent a man."

"I'll see if I can rustle you up one of those," I mutter.

He raises a bushy brow at me.

I clear my throat. "No worries. We'll get those papers back out here pronto."

"You better. Or I'll sue your firm for being a bunch of idiots."

10

AFTER MY VISIT TO DERRICK DELGADO, I NEED TO BLOW OFF some adrenaline, so I go to Will's house. He owns his own home, a cute little one-story bungalow a few blocks from the beach. The living room is minimalistic—just a couple of dark leather couches, a coffee table, a desk, and two big bookshelves overflowing with classic literature.

Will is a reading snob, preferring the classics to popular fiction. He's the only person I know who doesn't own a T.V. That's why we have to watch *America's Most Vicious Criminals* at my place.

I pace around the room and tell him everything I know so far about Abby's death, including the stuff about the video of Sebastian and Abby going into the rec center and my futile attempt to knock some sense into my brother.

"Sebastian refuses to tell me who Abby wanted the exorcism performed on. Only my money lands on Phoebe Van Cleave."

Will ponders this over. "Go on."

"According to Officer Fontaine, Paco doesn't belong to Derrick Delgado. So I went out to see him. He didn't know anything about a dog, but it was a big fat lie. You should meet this guy. He's like a character right out of *Deliverance*. Oh, and the worst part? The guy has a trained squirrel."

The corner of Will's mouth twitches up like he's going to laugh. Only he knows better.

When I turned seven, my parents threw me a pool party. My entire class was there (Mom's rules: everyone in the class is invited, or no one is). To keep him from being bored, Sebastian, who is five years older than me, was allowed to invite a friend, so he asked Will. And thank God for that because who knows what would have happened to me if Will hadn't been there to save me.

We'd just gotten out of the swimming pool. Mom had placed my ballerina cake with the seven pink candles on top of the picnic table, when out of nowhere, a pack of feral squirrels came flying out of the trees (Will and Sebastian like to say that it was only three, but honestly, when your life is flashing before your eyes, who takes the time to count?).

Those squirrels scurried toward my cake with every intention of stealing it.

No way was I going to let that happen, so I grabbed the cake and took off running. I could hear everyone shouting behind me, but all I could think about was those squirrels making off with my beautiful pink ballerina cake that Mom had baked from scratch.

I turned to see if the squirrels were following me (which they were!) when I tripped and began to fall. In one of those slow-motion clips of your life, I could see what would happen next. I was going to land face down on the patio tile, and worse, my cake would be ruined.

But then out of nowhere, a pair of arms grabbed me, holding me (and the cake) steady. "Get out of here, you grubby squirrels!" Will screamed.

Miraculously, they obeyed him.

By that time, Mom and Dad were also there to help. I didn't land on my face and break my nose. My cake was all in one piece. And the squirrels were vanquished back to their evil hiding nests.

If that wasn't a reason to fall in love with Will, (and hate squirrels forever), then I don't know what is.

I tell Will about the rest of my visit to Derrick, omitting the part where he held a gun to my head, because if I tell him, then he'll tell Sebastian and I don't want my brother to flip out. Plus, Sebastian would tell our parents, and then everyone would make a federal case about nothing.

Will crosses his arms over his chest. "The brother sounds like a nut job. I don't like it that you went out there to see this guy alone." *See what I mean*? Good thing I left out the part about the shotgun. "What's going to happen when he calls this law office and they deny knowing anything about you?"

"I never gave him my name, and I live an hour away. How's he going to find me?" Before Will can answer, I say, "Don't worry about Derrick Delgado. We have more important fish to fry, like figuring out the cause of death. We won't know anything more until the autopsy results come back, but—"

"Wait." He sits up. "Are you saying that maybe Abby was *murdered*?"

"Pay attention, Will! Why do you think the cops questioned Sebastian about what he and Abby were doing in the rec center? They didn't come right out and say the M word, but you should see the way this Officer Fontaine character is acting. Someone needs to remind him he's not in Dallas anymore."

"Sounds like you don't like Travis."

"He's a *donut* man."

Will chuckles. "He joined my basketball league last night. He's got an awesome three-point shot."

All of which means is that Travis has completely won Will over because Will goes nutso over basketball. Personally, I've never gotten into the game. It's run down and make a basket, then, run down and make another basket. Wash. Rinse. Repeat. *Yawn*.

I stop pacing and glance around the room. It's suddenly occurred to me that something isn't right. Will's usually neat desk is cluttered with papers, and there's an empty carton of Chinese on the floor next to his trash can like he went to toss it in and missed. Will is obsessively neat. It's his only fault.

"Work been busy?"

"I've been off for a few days. Mini vacation."

On his days off Will goes entirely off grid. No Internet, no newspapers, minimal cell phone contact. He says it helps keep him sane, but it would drive me bananas because I happen to like being around people. I wonder how Brittany would handle that if she and Will ever got together.

Before I can inquire why his desk is so messy, he asks, "Are you sure you can't get Sebastian to tell you anything more about that night?"

"He's stubborn as a goat. He refuses to help himself in any way. But that's okay because I plan to solve this thing on my own."

"How are you going to do that?"

I smile, which makes Will frown uneasily. "Lucy, what are you up to?"

"I haven't told you the best part yet."

"There's a *best* part here?"

"Phoebe Van Cleave also lied to me about knowing that Abby had a dog. Add that to the fact that I'm pretty sure she's who Abby wanted the exorcism performed on, it makes her look mighty suspicious. Right now, she and Derrick are my two prime suspects."

"*Suspects*? I think you've been inhaling too many muffin batter fumes."

I snort because that's actually pretty funny.

"Okay," he concedes, "Let's say Abby's death wasn't accidental. What motive did the brother have for killing her? Or Phoebe Van Cleave for that matter?"

"Derrick has the oldest motive known to man. I think he must be Abby's heir because he was worried about her will, so it's money. As for Phoebe, there was a rumor going around that Abby was challenging her for her position as head of the Sunshine Ghost Society. I'm not sure what role Paco has in all this, but he's involved too."

"The dog?"

I nod. "I think Abby dognapped him and Phoebe definitely knows something about it, but like I said, she's lying."

"And you're sure about that?"

Will knows about my gift, but like Sebastian, he doesn't know the extent of my talent. "Positive."

Will is quiet for a few minutes while he's trying to absorb everything I've just told him. Or maybe he's already figuring out how we can solve this thing together. He's so smart, and—

"Luce, have you thought that maybe finding Abby's body has made you a little more sensitive to this whole situation?"

"What do you mean?"

"Think about it. You found her body, and she was a customer. Someone you saw probably two or three times a week. She might not have been a favorite of yours, but you liked her because you like everyone. Finding her dead like that must have been a huge shock. Maybe you have some form of PTSD here."

"Are you *serious*?"

"I'm just saying that it's perfectly normal for you to still be freaked out about everything. I think Sebastian is right. I think you ought to let the cops handle this."

"You think I'm *freaked out*? Sorry, but you must be confusing me with Brittany." The minute I say it I wish I could take it back because it sounds mean and jealous. "I'm sorry. That was petty."

He sighs. "I told you before, she's not that person from high school."

Even though Sebastian has already told me all about their date, I still want to hear it from Will. "So, did you ask her out?"

He looks at me warily. "I actually wanted to talk to you about that."

"Oh, like you want my permission? I thought we already went through this."

"I know we talked about it some the other day, but if you really dislike her, I'll break the date. You're my best friend, but more than that, you're the best judge of character I know. Be honest. What do you really think of her?"

Oh boy. Will has no idea. He's just handed me the perfect opportunity to shoot Brittany down forever.

A part of me would love to tell him exactly what I think of her.

But the way he's looking at me right now, like he trusts me explicitly, makes me stop and reconsider.

I have to look at this through someone else's eyes. Besides my parents, Sebastian and Will are the two people I love and trust most in this world. If they both think Brittany is okay, then maybe I'm the one with the problem.

The truth is, I can't be objective here.

It kills me to say this, but I have to. "You should definitely go out with Brittany. Who knows? She could be the one. Besides, you don't want to be a shmuck, do you? What kind of guy asks a girl out and then cancels? It shouldn't matter what anyone else thinks. Only what *you* think."

"You're right," he says sheepishly.

"That goes without saying."

Boy, Meryl Streep has nothing on me. I should probably go ahead and book my front row seat at the next Academy Awards presentation.

"I hope you won't mind if we skip our Friday night pizza and T.V. routine again," he says. "It was the only night Brittany was free this week."

"No worries. I can experiment bake. I really need to get this mango coconut muffin recipe worked out. You know, in case they call from *Muffin Wars*."

"You mean when they call."

"Sure, right."

He walks me out to my car, but it feels awkward between us.

"Wear a blue shirt on your date," I say. "It makes your eyes look less shifty."

He laughs, but it's strained. "So... Luce, can you tell when *I'm* lying?"

"Every single time. So watch, it buddy," I say, adding this to all the other lies I've told today because if Will knew that he was the only person I've never caught in a lie, it would sound strange, and somehow, he'd figure out how I feel about him.

He shakes his head as if he's not quite sure he believes me and waves goodbye. I wave back and begin the short drive back to The Bistro.

It's dark, but I always leave the back light on. I put my key in the door and am about to unlock it when an all too familiar whimpering stops me cold.

I whip around to find Paco staring back at me, his tail wagging furiously.

11

I CALL LANIE AND TELL HER ABOUT MY SURPRISE VISITOR.

"Oh, I'm so glad he's with you! Is he all right?"

"He's fine. But how did he get here?" With my cell phone tucked under my chin, I bend down to give Paco a bowl of water. He eagerly laps it up.

"One of my staff went to take the dogs out for the night, but when she put them back in their cages, she noticed Paco was missing, so she called me. We found a hole he must have dug under the fence. Nothing like this has ever happened before. It's lucky that he found his way to you." Lanie pauses. "Or maybe, luck has nothing to do with it. Maybe he was trying to get back to you specifically."

It's almost two miles from The Bistro to the animal shelter with several residential neighborhoods in between. The thought that Paco walked all this way in the dark just to find me is pretty out there. But then, I'm basically a human lie detector, which most people would scoff at, so I suppose anything is possible.

"You make him sound like he's Lassie," I joke.

"Maybe he is. Or maybe he's something even more. Remember when I told you that I thought I'd seen him before? It all came back to me tonight when we were out looking for him."

"Oh yeah?"

"It's a long story. And kind of kooky."

"Try me."

"Not over the phone. I'll be there in a few minutes."

L anie hands me her cell phone where she's got her Facebook app opened to a picture of a dog that's the spitting image of Paco. "I thought he looked familiar, but I didn't make the connection until now. You remember I told you his owner's name was Susan Van Dyke? Susan is, or rather was, this eccentric millionaire who lived in Destin. She claimed that Cornelius—"

"*Wait.* Are you telling me that Paco's real name is *Cornelius*?"

Lanie grins. "Yep. Anyway, she claimed that Cornelius had special powers, so she used to hold séances in her house, that kind of stuff. She passed away last week."

Paco looks between Lanie and me like he's following our conversation. Which, I must admit, is kind of adorable.

"What kind of special powers?"

"She claimed he could commune with the dead."

"As in—" I make air quotes— "*I see dead people*?"

Lanie giggles. "Not sure if Paco, or rather, Cornelius, is familiar with the movie *The Sixth Sense*, but basically, yeah."

No wonder Phoebe was so interested in the dog. She thinks he can talk to the dead. It's yet another motive for Phoebe to get rid of Abby. I mentally shake my head. Not gonna go there. I basically told Will that I'd leave Abby's death to the police.

"What happened to Susan Van Dyke?" I ask.

"She had cancer. Do you think she left Cornelius to Abby?"

"It makes sense since Abby was a member of the Sunshine Ghost Society, but why did Abby lie and tell me his name is Paco? And that he belonged to her brother?"

"Your guess is as good as mine. All I can tell you is that this is Cornelius. See?" She points to the top of the phone screen. "He has his own Facebook page and everything." **Cornelius Van Dyke, Ghost Whisperer**.

"He's got over a hundred thousand likes!"

"Impressive, huh?"

I bring the phone screen down to Paco's eye level. "Is this you, little guy? Are you Cornelius?"

Paco barks and wags his tail.

Lanie pulls a leash from her backpack. "The attorney handling Susan Van Dyke's estate called me saying that they'd gotten my phone message. Apparently, Susan's sister is in charge. I'll call her tomorrow morning and tell her I have Cornelius. Now that Abby is gone maybe the family wants him back."

Paco looks at the leash in Lanie's hand, and his tail stops wagging. He runs and hides beneath a table in the restaurant.

"I've never had a dog run away from me before." Lanie sounds hurt, but instinctively I know that Paco's refusal to go with her isn't because he doesn't like her. It's just that...he likes me more.

"He can stay here tonight. I'll be happy to take him back to Susan's family tomorrow."

"Are you sure? What about your allergies?"

"Another night of Benadryl isn't going to kill me."

Lanie smiles. "Thanks, Lucy!"

"No problem." Lanie gives me the information on Susan Van Dyke and we say goodbye.

I kick off my sneakers and head into the kitchen. Paco follows me. I'm too wired to sleep, so late night baking it is. Even though I still haven't heard back from *Muffin Wars*, I have to keep believing that they'll call. The prize for winning is ten thousand dollars which would go a long way to paying off what I owe Will.

Mango coconut muffin recipe: take four.

I finish putting a batch into the oven when there's a knock on the door to The Bistro. It's almost midnight, so I can't imagine who might be out there. Paco runs in a circle and barks happily like he's expecting something good to happen.

"Who is it, boy? Not a ghost, I hope." I giggle at my own silliness, because really? A ghost whisperer?

Still, I can tell that Paco (because I refuse to call him Cornelius) is an exceptional dog. He walked all the way from the animal shelter to The Bistro to find me. And he undoubtedly led me to Abby's body. I hope that whichever one of Susan's relatives ends up taking him appreciates just how awesome he is.

Through the large glass pane I see a Whispering Bay police cruiser parked in front and Travis Fontaine standing outside. He's wearing his uniform, and he's alone.

I unlock the door and swing it wide to face him. "This is twice in one day, Donut Boy. Maybe you can't read, but we're closed."

If he's offended by my hostility, he doesn't show it. He looks at Paco and frowns. "What's the dog doing here? I thought he was at the animal shelter."

"He ran away."

"And you found him?"

"More like he found me."

He looks at my bare feet, then his gaze slowly sweeps up to take in my jeans and T-shirt that reads **MUFFINS RULE, DONUTS DROOL**. I'm sure my hair has flour in it because

I'm a little messy that way when I'm baking, but it's better than a dead lizard.

I feel antsy under his perusal. "What are you doing here?"

"Your lights were on, and since I was planning on coming to talk to you first thing in the morning, I figured now was as good a time as any." He shrugs, and for the first time, he seems uncertain. Or maybe he realizes how late it is and he's embarrassed.

I usher him into the café. He glances at my empty coffee pot longingly, so I take pity on him and start up a fresh brew.

"Late night patrol?"

"Technically, I'm a rookie on this squad, so yeah, I'm catching all the crap hours."

He doesn't say anything else until the coffee is ready. I pour us both a cup and we migrate to a table in the front of the restaurant. Paco jumps on Travis's lap and instead of shooing him off, he playfully scratches him behind his ear while he takes a long appreciate sip of the coffee. "You remembered I take it black."

"I remember how all my customers like their coffee. If you're here about Sebastian, I couldn't get him to tell me what he was doing in the rec center with Abby."

"That's too bad. But that's only one of the reasons I stopped by. We got a call from the Mexico Beach Police Department to be on the lookout for a possible scam artist. Derrick Delgado called them with a complaint about a woman impersonating a member of the law office handling his sister's will."

"Really? Who would do that?" I don't even blink, I'm that good now. Who knew that lying was one of my many talents?

"He described her as mid-twenties with dark curly hair, big brown eyes, and glasses." He looks at me over the rim of his cup. "You know anyone who might fit that description?"

"Is that all we have to go on? I mean, that could be anyone."

"Apparently she's also afraid of squirrels."

"It's called scuirophobia, and it affects over two hundred and fifty thousand Americans."

He stares at me.

"I must have picked that up playing one of those kinky trivia games."

He continues to stare.

"Not that I have it! No way. I *love* squirrels. I'd have one as a pet if it didn't violate a health code or something."

"Mr. Delgado was also quite impressed by the way she was able to, as he put it, fill out a pair of jeans."

I almost choke on my coffee. "*Yuck*! He must be at least seventy years old!"

"Miss McGuffin, are you seriously going to tell me it wasn't you?"

There's no way I can fudge around this, so I confess. "Okay, it was me. And...call me Lucy." Which is only fair since this morning he asked me to call him by his first name. Plus, Miss McGuffin sounds ridiculous.

"What were you thinking?"

"I thought that I'd offer my condolences."

"So why lie to him and tell him you were from a law firm?"

"That was an accident."

"I bet."

"No, really, he just assumed that I was from the firm."

"And you didn't clear it up." It's a statement, but he wants to know the reason behind my actions.

The oven timer goes off. Talk about being saved by the bell.

"Hold on." I run back to the kitchen to pull the muffins out of the oven. When I turn around, Travis is standing in the doorway, which is a little offsetting. This kitchen is my private place, at least, at night it is. Even though it's a good sized room, he makes it seem small. And *warm*. Must be the heat from the oven.

"Do you always bake this late at night?"

"It's a new recipe I'm trying out for *Muffin Wars*."

He raises an amused brow.

"Get your mind out of the gutter. It's a television baking competition on the Cooking Channel. I sent in an audition tape, and I'm waiting to hear back."

"Whatever that is, it smells good."

"Too bad you don't like muffins, or I'd let you try one."

He leans back against the counter and watches as I putter around the kitchen. Paco raises his nose in the air and sniffs appreciatively.

"You," I say to Paco, "Can have whatever you want." He pants in anticipation.

"It's like he can understand you," Travis says.

Exactly. I mentally debate whether or not to tell him about the dog. Travis is a cop, and for whatever reason, Zeke seems to think highly of him. Maybe if I share everything I know he'll lay off Sebastian.

"Lanie Miller came to see me. The dog's real name is Cornelius." I tell him all about Paco's famous persona and how I think Phoebe Van Cleave is somehow involved too.

"A ghost whisperer?" he says incredulously.

"Susan Van Dyke might have willed the dog to Abby after her death. But it doesn't explain why Abby told me the dog's name was Paco. Or why she told me he belonged to her brother."

Or why the brother lied to me about it. But I can't tell him this last part without revealing my gift.

"Maybe Abby changed the dog's name. A lot of people do that. As for the lie about the brother owning the dog, I have no clue. Unless…"

"Unless the dog wasn't willed to her and maybe she stole him?" I finish.

"Could be."

"I'm taking the dog back to the family tomorrow. I guess I'll find out the truth then."

He glances at the muffins. "Is that coconut?"

"Mango coconut. But I haven't worked out all the kinks in the recipe yet."

I touch the top of a muffin, and it doesn't feel so hot anymore. Gingerly, I ease one out of the tin then cut it in half, let it cool off a bit, and offer it to Paco, who wolfs it down in two gulps.

"Looks like Cornelius approves."

"He's Paco," I automatically correct him. "At least while he's here with me. Cornelius is such a stuffy sounding name."

Travis stares at the other half of the muffin.

Nope. Don't even think about it. Officer Fontaine sealed his culinary fate when he decreed himself a donut man.

"Any word on the autopsy report yet?" I ask.

"Not yet."

"But Abby died when she hit her head, right? Do you think someone knocked her down?"

"I can't discuss that with you."

"Look, you seriously don't think my brother had anything to do with her death. He's a priest, for God's sake."

"Your brother is hindering a police investigation by refusing to tell us what he and Abby were doing in the rec center in the middle of the night. There's also the matter of the unlocked door. Technically they're both guilty of trespassing."

"Well, gee, Abby's dead, so I guess that just leaves Sebastian to arrest. What? Are you trying to fill a quota or something?"

His jaw tightens. I can't help but feel a teeny bit sorry for him. He's basically stuck between a rock and a hard place. I begrudgingly hand him the other half of the muffin. "Try this. It'll make you feel better."

He eats it almost as fast as Paco did.

"This is really good."

"Did you think it wouldn't be?"

"No, I mean, it's *really* good."

"Why, Officer Fontaine, are you flirting with me?" The second I say it, we both freeze because *I'm* the one who sounds like she's flirting. "That didn't come out right." I pull another muffin out of the tin and hand it over like a peace offering. "Here. In case you get hungry later."

"Thanks." He takes it and says casually, "I told you, call me Travis."

Travis. It's a name for a lumberjack. Or an old-time western sheriff. It totally fits him.

"Did you ask Abby's brother where he was at the time of her death?"

He narrows his eyes.

Rats. I've just unwittingly reminded him about my nefarious visit to Derrick Delgado.

"As a matter of fact, I did. He was playing cards with friends."

"And you checked up on that?" I ask.

"I have two people who swear Derrick was with them from midnight till two in the morning. Even if the time of death is off by an hour, it's impossible to make it from Mexico Beach that quickly. It's just too much of a stretch."

That all sounds logical enough.

Except I can't get the niggling feeling that of all people, Derrick had the most to gain by Abby's death. "I'd like to know why he's so anxious to get her will resolved."

"He's her next of kin. No husband. No kids."

"That's what I figured. If Abby has any money, I'm sure Derrick will be appreciative. He looks like he's pretty much living month to month."

Travis doesn't blink. Or say a word.

Which…tells me *everything*.

Holy wow. His face is an open book. Only, I'm pretty sure he hasn't moved a muscle. It's like I just know what he's thinking. A surge of excitement rushes through me. I've never been able to read *anyone* this easily.

"Abby was loaded, wasn't she?"

He frowns. "How did you know that?"

"Lucky guess?"

He shakes his head as if to clear it. "I should be getting back on patrol. Thanks for the coffee and the muffin."

I follow him out of the kitchen and back through The Bistro. He stops at the front door and turns to look at me. Boy, he's tall. His green eyes still radiate snark, but there's something else there too. Something that makes me feel even warmer than when we were in the kitchen.

"Even though it was a bust, thanks for talking to Sebastian. But no more pretending to be someone else. Got it?"

"Got it." I mentally cross my fingers, because how on earth can I make a promise like that?

"And if you don't mind, can you let me know what happens tomorrow with the dog? I'd really like to know if Abby had a legit claim to him."

I bat my lashes at him. "Anything else I can do for you?"

Yikes, that sounded kind of flirty too. *What's wrong with me?* Maybe Will is right. Maybe I have been inhaling too much batter fume.

"As a matter of fact, there is something you can do," he says. "Make sure to lock your door."

"Sure, but you know, that's not really necessary. Whispering Bay is the safest city in America."

We both look at each other for a second, and in that tiny iota of time, I'm struck with the eerie realization that neither of us really believe that.

12

AFTER THE MORNING RUSH SLOWS DOWN, I CALL THE NUMBER Lanie gave me for Susan Van Dyke's lawyer. He isn't available, so I give the receptionist my name and information and ask that he call me back as soon as possible. I have to admit, a part of me is relieved because I'm just not ready to give Paco up.

I don't think he's ready to give me up either. The little minx seems perfectly content in his new surroundings. Last night he slept in my bed again (I should probably nix that). He happily trots up and down the stairs between my apartment and The Bistro (the customers think he's adorable), and right now, he's napping on my living room couch like he doesn't have a care in the world.

Because I stayed up late baking and then had to take Benadryl to keep from itching, I feel like I'm dragging. Combined with the tension of the last few days, I think some exercise is in order. I decide to go to the new rec center and check out the classes.

It's the first time I've been in the building since the opening day celebration. After Abby's body was found the indoor facilities were sealed off for the rest of the day and the tours were rescheduled for Sunday with the center going operational on Monday. Today is Tuesday, and the place is packed.

I check in at the front desk and peruse the schedule. I'm an hour too late for Zumba and two hours too early for Brittany's Pilates class (not in the least bit sorry about that), but there's a yoga class for active and mature adults taught by Viola that starts in two minutes. It probably won't be much of a challenge, but it's better than nothing.

I sneak in through the back door to the room and grab a mat. The rest of the class is made up of the usual suspects—Betty Jean and Gus, Phoebe's brother Roger who co-owns the local paper, and some more of the Gray Flamingos. Out of the corner of my eye, I see Jim Fontaine talking to Gus. I'm glad Jim is making friends.

Everyone looks at me curiously as if I'm in the wrong class. I'll have to tone it down so that I don't stand out.

Viola waves to me from the front of the room. "Lucy! We're so happy to have you join us this afternoon."

"Thanks! Happy to be here!"

Viola proceeds to lead a dozen senior citizens and me through an hour of deep breathing, stretching, and yoga-ass-kicking positions.

I'm about four decades younger than the average student, but I'm the only one who's wheezing at the end of class.

Viola drapes a towel around her neck. Her skin is glowing with vibrant health. I, on the other hand, am sweating. Not perspiring, but drip-all-the-way-to-the-floor sweating like a construction worker in August.

It's embarrassing. Who knew that active and mature are secret senior citizen code words for *really in shape*?

"How did you like the class?" Viola asks.

"It was great," I pant before taking a big swig of my bottled water.

"You're welcome to come back anytime." She goes around to make small talk with the rest of the students.

Betty Jean slaps me on the back. "Look who's having a hard time keeping up with the old folks. Ha-Ha!"

I make a mental note to step up my cardio routine.

"Say, now that you're hanging out with the Geritol crowd, you should join our book club."

"Oh, well, um…"

"This month we're reading J.W. Quicksilver's newest thriller. Four people are assassinated in the opening scene. It's awesome."

"J. W. Quicksilver? I've never heard of her. Or is it a him?"

"It's a him, but that's definitely a pen name. He probably has one of those big top-secret state department jobs because he sure does seem to know a lot of hush hush stuff. And those sex scenes. Whew!" Betty Jean fans herself with her hand. "If he's done even half the stuff he writes about in his books, Mrs. Quicksilver is one lu-cky lady."

"Mmm... I'll think about it."

A really buff guy wearing a black T-shirt walks through the hallway and is immediately picked up by Betty Jean's radar. "There goes one of those yummy personal trainers! I need some help with the elliptical machine, if you know what I mean. See you later, Lucy. And if you're interested in the book club, we're meeting next Thursday at my house. But don't drag your feet. You need to let me know ASAP because technically, there's a waiting list. But if you promise to bring muffins, I'll shoot your name up to the top." She sprints across the room to catch up to the trainer.

I stuff my water bottle back inside my work out bag and turn to leave, when Jim comes over to say hi. "Good class, huh?"

"I'll be honest, I didn't think it would be this challenging."

His gaze lingers on Viola, who's still talking to a few of the ladies. "She really knows her stuff." The way Jim looks at her makes me nervous for him. I hope he realizes that Viola and Gus are an item. "Want to get a smoothie?" he asks. "My treat."

"Sounds good. Thanks."

The fresh juice bar is located near the back of the rec center and has an outdoor patio facing the water. Jim hands me my pineapple mango vitamin enhanced smoothie, and we sit at the lone empty table.

"How are you liking retirement?" I ask.

"More than I thought I would. There's always something that needs doing. And this new center is great. I signed up for a pottery class that Viola recommended."

I glance back toward the building and shiver.

He notices my reaction. "Are you all right?"

I don't have to ask what he means by that. "Will, that's my best friend, thinks I have PTSD."

"In my experience as a homicide detective, I've seen a lot of people go through a myriad of emotions when they encounter a dead person."

I tell Jim all about Abby's connection with Sebastian, the bit about Phoebe and Abby vying for control of the Sunshine Ghost Society, Paco, my visit to Derrick Delgado, everything. He's so easy to talk to it all just spills out. Every now and then he nods his head encouraging me to continue. I can see why he was such a good detective. He's the kind of person other people want to tell things.

"So what do you think?" I ask.

"I'm not a psychologist, but I don't think you have PTSD."

"Neither do I." We both smile. "Can I ask, how you'd solve this case?"

"Well, like my son, I'd like to know what Abby was doing inside this building late at night. And I'd like to know who she wanted an exorcism performed on, and why she lied about the dog. But unless Father Sebastian opens up..." His brow puckers in concern. "I'll be honest, Lucy, once that autopsy report comes back, I wouldn't be surprised if your brother is brought down to police headquarters for questioning."

"But he didn't do anything wrong!"

"Then he doesn't have anything to worry about."

"That's what he says, but you and I both know that if Abby told him anything in confidence, he won't reveal it."

He sighs. "Maybe we'll never know exactly what happened. Maybe some cases just aren't meant to be solved."

"Like your Angel of Death case?" I ask.

"That case is one of the reasons I put off retirement. I wanted so badly to be able to look at the families of the victims in the eye and tell them that I'd caught their loved one's killer. But after all these years it's all gone cold."

"Weren't most of the victims terminally ill?"

His eyes harden. "Yes, but that didn't give her the right to take their lives."

"I agree." I don't want to bring up bad memories for him, but I really am curious, so I ask as delicately as possible, "What made the case so difficult to solve?"

"There were six known victims, but the FBI and my department think the number might have been almost double that. Most of the time the clue to finding a serial killer is the information we get from the first victim, and we simply don't know who he or she was."

Even though this is all a little ghoulish, I can't help but be fascinated.

"I watched the episode when it was featured on *America's Most Vicious Criminals*, but I have to admit, I've forgotten the details."

"The first victim was probably someone important to her. A patient or family member she cared about and didn't want to see suffer anymore, so she slipped them a little extra morphine. Since the victim was probably very close to dying anyway, no one would have thought to do an autopsy or check their blood for the presence of excessive drugs."

It's coming back to me now. "The victims all died of narcotic overdoses, right?"

He nods. "Easy enough to do fifteen years ago when hospitals didn't have the kind of security measures they do now. She could have easily upped their dose through a drug pump and then recalibrated the machine back to the normal dose before anyone checked."

"But you do know that the murderer was a she?"

"The truth is, the murderer could be a man for all we know. The only thing I'm certain of is that he or she had enough medical knowledge to be able to manipulate a narcotics pump. They might have worked for the hospital, or one of the temp agencies, or hell...they could have even come in as a visitor. And it wasn't limited to one area of town. The murders occurred in multiple hospitals."

"What was the motive?"

"Most likely, in her delusional mind, she probably thought she was helping them. Unless we're lucky enough after all these years to catch a break in the case, we'll never know the exact motive. We interviewed hundreds of people, watched hours and hours of surveillance tapes, but we never had enough evidence to arrest anyone. Our *Angel*," he says mocking the nickname, "was clever. We know very little about him or her."

"How do you even know it was the same person?"

He hesitates. "This was never released to the press or featured in the T.V. show, but our Angel left a note each time they struck."

I swallow hard. "What did it say?"

"R.I.P."

"Rest in Peace?"

"Yep. Always written in pencil on a paper towel from the victim's hospital room in block style letters."

I fidget with the straw on my drink. "In your experience, Jim, what would you say the number one motive for killing someone usually is?"

He shrugs. "Depends. Money, anger, jealousy, power. Every murder is unique."

"But money is a big one?"

"Oh yeah. It's straight out of the Detective 101 handbook. Follow the money trail and chances are, you'll find the killer."

Which would make Derrick Delgado the most logical suspect.

"Can I ask you a few questions? As a professional?"

Jim's green eyes sparkle with humor. "Shoot."

"According to Travis, Abby died sometime between midnight and two a.m. The surveillance cameras caught Sebastian leaving the building a little after twelve-thirty, and since he left Abby very much alive, that would narrow the time of death to sometime between twelve-thirty and two."

"Go on."

"Abby's brother, Derrick Delgado is her heir, and according to Travis, she left him a bundle."

Jim's eyes narrow. "He told you that too?"

"Not in so many words. I sort of…inferred it."

No one except my family and Will knows that I'm a human lie detector. Not Lanie. Not Sarah. But what the heck. Like I said, Jim is really easy to talk to, but more than that, even though I barely know him, something deep in my gut tells me to trust him. If anyone will believe me, it's him.

I take a deep breath. "This might sound odd, but I can always tell when someone is lying. Or hiding something."

He doesn't say anything for a few seconds. "That must prove interesting."

"You think I'm strange."

"Not at all. I believe that some people are very adept at reading others."

"It's more than that. I can see through the most benign lies. Go ahead. Try and lie to me."

"You want me to lie to you?"

"In a way you already did. When you called my gift interesting when what you really meant was something else."

He grins sheepishly. "Okay, I'll play along. Let's see, I got married when I was twenty-four."

"That's the truth."

"My wife's name was Julie."

"True."

"Our anniversary is May thirteen."

"None of those were lies, Jim."

He frowns. "I made that too easy. Let's go again. This time I'll tell you three things in a row." He pauses to think. "Got it. Here you go: Travis's middle name is James." He pauses. "Julie was a schoolteacher." Another pause. "Our first home was on Spring Street."

"Your wife wasn't a schoolteacher."

He blinks. "What?"

"Your wife wasn't a teacher," I repeat.

"What made you pick that one?"

"All three statements were important to you because they're about your family. I can't explain it because it's different for everyone, but with you, there's a hitch in your voice when you talk about your family, but the bit about your late wife being a teacher, it was devoid of any emotion. Like it didn't matter to you because it wasn't real."

He looks stunned. "I thought I was careful to keep my voice the same."

I shrug.

"How long have you been able to do this?"

"Ever since I can remember. And, I'm kind of sensitive about it, so I'd appreciate it if you keep what I've just told you between us."

"Of course," he says, but I can tell he's still not sold. "Have you ever thought of going to Vegas? You'd make a killing at the poker tables."

I laugh. "Not my thing."

He raises a brow playfully. "You never know."

"So, back to Abby." I glance around the building. "Let's say, someone wanted to get inside this building without being seen. How do you think they'd do it?"

"You mean how would they avoid the security cameras? From what I can tell, almost every door has one, so it would be almost impossible."

Not what I wanted to hear since according to Travis, the only people seen on tape entering the building that night were Abby and Sebastian.

He must sense my frustration because he gets up and tosses the rest of his avocado shake into a nearby trashcan. "Want to show me the door you came through?"

"For real?"

"Why not? I have to admit, Lucy, you've intrigued me."

We walk around to the side of the building. Everything appears the same as the day of the rec center opening, except this time the door is locked.

He glances up at the security camera, then back at the door. "The way the camera is angled, it would be impossible to get through this door without getting caught on tape. Except…" He looks at me. "What was the time frame on the security footage?"

"I'm not sure. I just know that Travis said that—wait. Are you saying that maybe someone came in this door *earlier* and was waiting inside the building? Gus told me on the day of the celebration that not everything was a hundred percent operational, including the security. At the time it didn't mean anything to me, but maybe he was talking about the cameras."

"It certainly sounds like something that should be checked out."

"So maybe Derrick snuck in the building earlier. He could have waited until Sebastian left and confronted Abby. Maybe they argued, and he pushed her."

"Does he have an alibi for the time of Abby's death?"

"He claims to have been playing poker in Mexico Beach. And Travis said it checked out."

"Well, there you go. Sounds like the brother is off the hook."

As much as I hate to admit it, Jim is right. But I still can't shake the feeling that Derrick Delgado is hiding something big.

My cell phone pings. It's Susan Van Dyke's attorney. He tells me that technically the dog now belongs to Susan's sister, Deborah, so I make arrangements through him to drop Paco off at Susan's home this afternoon.

I thank Jim for the smoothie and the conversation and reluctantly head back to The Bistro. It's time to return Paco to his family.

13

Susan Van Dyke's home is in an upscale neighborhood with a privacy gate. To get inside, I have to pick up a security phone.

"Can I help you?" asks a crusty sounding male voice

"This is Lucy McGuffin. I spoke to Ms. Van Dyke's attorney about returning Pa—, I mean Cornelius."

The gate slowly opens which is my cue to come through. As I guide my car into the circular driveway, the house comes into view. It's a two-story red brick mansion that seems out of place with the more coastal Mediterranean architecture of the other homes on the street.

Paco and I get out of the car and are greeted by an older gentleman wearing a black tie and jacket. It's like he's just stepped off the set of *Downton Abbey*.

"I'm Anthony," he says, "Ms. Susan's former butler."

Paco barks and wags his tail. Anthony bends down and pats him on the head affectionately. "Cornelius. It's so good to see you, sir. And in such good health! I must say, this is a huge relief."

Sir? I try not to giggle. "So this is… I mean, this was Susan Van Dyke's dog?"

"Oh, yes, this is definitely our Cornelius. I'd recognize him anywhere."

Even though I'm glad that Paco is being reunited with his family, a part of me is sad too. Which is utterly selfish because it's not like I could adopt him myself.

Paco trots into the house like he owns it, which, I suppose, he kind of does.

"Miss Deborah is in the study." Anthony ushers me into a good-sized room with wall-to-wall shelves filled with books. My first thought is that Will would love this place. A woman, maybe in her late seventies, thin and fashionably dressed, is wrapping up books and placing them into a packing box.

Paco catches sight of her and freezes.

"I see the little mongrel has found his way back home." She studies me with cool blue eyes. "You must be Miss. McGuffin. The lawyer said you would be by today. Let's get this over with. How much do you want?"

"I'm not sure what you mean."

"Aren't you looking for a reward for returning Cornelius?"

My spine stiffens. "No reward necessary. I just want to see him returned to his family."

"Unfortunately his family, as you put it, is dead."

"I'm sorry for your loss."

"Thank you." She goes back to packing up the books, which I suppose is my cue to slink off, but there's no way I'm leaving Paco with this cold fish until I know for certain he'll be well taken care of.

"Does he belong to you now?"

"I live half the year in Manhattan and the other half in Paris. My lifestyle isn't suited for a dog."

I frown. "What sort of provisions did your sister make for Cornelius?"

"You mean, in her will?" She laughs like I've just said something funny. "Susan would never leave me her precious Cornelius. She knew how much I detested him. Unfortunately, my sister didn't make any provisions for the dog. I suppose it simply never occurred to her that the dog would outlive her. She was very egotistical that way."

"Oh. I thought…that is, I thought she had cancer."

"She did. But she'd been in remission for a while now. Her death came as a surprise." She narrows her eyes at me. "How did you end up with the dog?"

"He was a with a woman named Abby Delgado. Does that name ring a bell?"

"No, but I didn't know a lot of my sister's friends. Like I said, I don't live here. I just came down to clear up her estate and put the house up for sale."

"Abby, that's the woman who had Cornelius, died unexpect-edly a few days ago. I'd assumed that Susan had given her the dog."

"I had no idea Florida was so dangerous," she deadpans. She looks down her nose at Paco. "Or perhaps you're the bad omen."

I *really* don't like this woman. Although, she has a point. How strange that both Susan and Abby died just days apart from one another. "Do you know how Abby might have gotten possession of Cornelius?"

"A few days after Susan died, the little beast needed to go outside to do his business." She shudders in disgust. "Natu-rally I put him out in the yard to give him his privacy like I'd done before. Only this time, when I went to let him back inside, he was gone."

In other words, Deborah put him out, forgot all about him, and Paco ran away. Not that I blame him. I catch Paco's gaze. I swear he's looking at her with the same disgust that I feel.

"Can I ask what you plan to do with him?"

"Find him a good home, I suppose." She looks at me with renewed interest. "Do you want him?"

"Absolutely."

With my allergy getting in the way, I can't keep him. But no way am I going to let Paco's fate rest in Cruella deVil's spiny fingers. I'll find him a good home of my own choosing. Maybe Lanie will take him.

"Wonderful. Anthony will show you and Cornelius out now."

She can't get rid of us fast enough which is just as well because (and I think I can speak for Paco) neither of us want to stay a minute longer than necessary.

I don't need anyone to show me out. I scoop Paco up in my arms, and just as I'm about to open the door on my own, Anthony shows up.

"I'm good—"

He motions with his hand for me to be quiet. "If you don't mind, miss," he whispers, waving me off to the side.

The butler wants a private word with me. The whole thing is deliciously creepy, so, naturally, I go along.

He guides me through a hallway that leads into a large kitchen. Compared to the rest of the house which is dark and overly formal, this room is bright and sunny.

A middle-aged woman with caramel colored skin dressed in black pants and a white shirt breaks out into a smile at the sight of us. "Cornelius! I'm so glad you're back!" She bends down and scratches Paco behind the ears. "We've been so worried about you!"

I introduce myself to the woman. Her name is Aurelia. She's Anthony's wife and the cook for the estate. "You'll join us for tea?" She pours me a cup without waiting for an answer.

It would be rude to decline, plus she's just set a yummy looking plate of scones in the center of the table. She gives Paco a scone and lays down a bowl of water for him.

I'm not a huge tea drinker, but the scones are delicious. I should probably get her recipe. "I love your accent. Jamaica?" I ask.

"Ya mon," Aurelia says, doing a Bob Marley imitation that makes me laugh. "How did Cornelius end up in your care?"

I tell them about Abby.

"How interesting," Anthony says carefully in a way that makes me think he wants to say more.

"How long did the two of you work for Ms. Van Dyke?"

"I've been with her for thirty years." He smiles tenderly at Aurelia. "And the missus here joined us almost fifteen years ago. I took one bite of her scones and fell instantly in love."

"I don't blame you."

Aurelia blushes prettily. "Susan was like family. We would take Cornelius ourselves, but now that the estate is going up for sale, we plan to do some traveling. We're starting with a world cruise."

"A world cruise? That sounds fabulous. And, kind of expensive, huh?"

"Susan was very generous in her will," Aurelia says primly.

"She had cancer?" I ask.

Aurelia nods. "Yes, poor lamb." She makes the sign of the cross. "May her soul rest in peace."

"Her death still came as a bit of a shock," says Anthony. "She'd been in remission for so long. Up until the end she was very active with her charities and of course, with her special projects."

I have a pretty good idea just what those special projects might be.

"Was Susan involved with the Sunshine Ghost Society?" I ask delicately.

"Oh yes," Anthony says, "Susan was very involved with those kinds of groups. She used to host séances here at the house all the time. They came because of Cornelius. He's extremely talented."

Right. Cornelius, the Ghost Whisperer. I glance at Paco who's struggling to lick a fleck of raspberry jam off his nose. More like the Scone Whisperer, if you ask me.

"Did the two of you, um…did you—"

"Did we participate in the séances?" Anthony finished. "Naturally. Miss Susan only hired staff who shared in her beliefs. It would have been too awkward otherwise."

"Do you have any idea how Abby Delgado might have gotten Cornelius? Is it possible that Susan might have left the dog to her?"

Anthony and Aurelia exchange a telling look. "Susan definitely did *not* leave Cornelius with that Delgado woman. Or with the other one either."

The other one?

"You mean, Phoebe Van Cleave?"

Aurelia makes a face. "Pushy woman, that one. Susan wasn't dead a day that she came sniffing around here trying to take Cornelius. She said that they *belonged* together. But Cornelius didn't like her."

"And he liked Abby?"

"He didn't dislike her, but we would never have given Cornelius away without Miss Deborah's consent. It wouldn't have been right."

"Then how did he end up with Abby? Deborah says that he ran away."

Anthony sets down his teacup. "Hardly. Corneluis would have never run away. He was dognapped."

I knew it! "For real?"

"We have security footage showing the culprit. But…Miss Deborah didn't want to involve the police."

So the whole story of Paco running away was just that. A story.

"Do you have proof that Abby Delgado stole Cornelius?"

"No," Anthony says firmly, "Not Miss Delgado. It was a man who took Cornelius."

"A man?" My heart speeds up. "Anthony, is there any way I can take a look at that footage?"

14

HOLY WOW. IT'S JUST AS I SUSPECTED. PACO WAS DOGNAPPED BY my favorite sociopath, Derrick Delgado.

After viewing the tape and promising Aurelia and Anthony that I'll keep in touch to let them know Cornelius' fate, I get in my car and head back to Whispering Bay.

PTSD, my butt. Wait till Will hears about this.

He sits on his living room couch with Paco on his lap listening to my story.

"I knew he was lying to the police, but now we have him on tape."

"You lied to the police, too. When you didn't tell Travis about how Abby was upset with Sebastian. But that doesn't mean you had anything to do with Abby's death."

I give Will the stink eye. "Whose side are you on?"

"I won't dignify that with an answer. So the brother kidnapped the dog for Abby. All that proves is that they were in sync. He was probably doing her a favor."

"Then why lie about not knowing anything about the dog?"

"Maybe because what he did was illegal?"

"Which means that he's capable of doing *other* illegal activities. Like breaking and entering into the rec center."

"What's all this leading to?"

"We need to confront Derrick Delgado."

"*We*?"

"Yes, we. I can't just show up there on my own when he's already reported me to the police, can I?"

"The police?"

Oops.

"I forgot to tell you that part. When Derrick realized I didn't work for the law firm, he called the police. But only because he thought I was a scam artist, which goes to prove how unstable he is. I mean, really? *Me*? A scam artist?"

"I don't like this, Lucy."

"Does that mean you're out? Because I'm going to confront him with or without you."

"That's blackmail."

"So sue me."

He shakes his head as if he can't believe he's going to help me, then goes to the hall closet to pull out a jacket. "I'm driving."

"Awesome! Oh...and, just so you know, Derrick has a shotgun."

Me and my big mouth. If I hadn't told Will about Derrick's shotgun, he wouldn't have involved Travis.

"You were right to call me," Travis says to Will as we all pile into Will's car. He glares at me. "I thought you were going to update me on the dog?"

"I was. Eventually."

Travis is off duty, but the second he heard about my plans to confront Derrick he practically ran all the way to Will's house to join us. "For the record, I'm against this."

"Then go home," I say in a fake sweet voice.

"Believe me I would if I didn't think you were going to high-tail it over there no matter what Will or I say."

Will chuckles. "It's amazing how well you've come to know her in so little time."

"Sweet. I have two knights in shining armor." Despite my sarcasm, the truth is I'm glad that both Will and Travis are coming with me. I have no idea what Derrick Delgado is capable of, and I really don't want to find out on my own. Plus, you know, he does have that squirrel in his arsenal.

It's past eight p.m. by the time we get to Derrick's and it's full on dark. Since he lives on the edge of town on a dirt road, there aren't any street lights. Weeds cover the narrow path leading to the trailer. Luckily, Will keeps a couple of flashlights in the trunk of his car.

"Are you sure this is the address?" Will asks, aiming his light on the dented steel mailbox. The peel-on street numbers are faded from the sun making them difficult to read. I'm confident this is it, but I want to make sure, so I move the red side flag out of the way to get a better look at the numbers. It's so rusty and old that it falls off in my hands.

"This is the place, all right," I confirm.

"I can't believe you came out here all alone," Will says like a disapproving older brother. "Sebastian would have a cow if he knew you were running around confronting strange men with guns."

"How was I to know he'd pull a gun on me? Besides, all's well that ends well, right?"

Before Will can answer, the porch light snaps on.

"Who's out there?" asks a gruff male voice.

"Mr. Delgado, it's Officer Travis Fontaine from the Whispering Bay police department. I'd like to ask you a couple of questions."

The front door opens, and Derrick steps out. He's holding the infamous shotgun, but this time it's not aimed at anyone's head.

"Whoa." Travis points to the gun. "No need for that, sir."

Derrick's eyes go wide as he spots me. "That's her! That's the gal who tried to rob me."

"Rob you?" I sputter. "I admit, I *might* have misrepresented myself the other day, but believe me there is absolutely nothing you have that I'd want to rob you of."

He scowls at Will. "Who are you?"

"I'm a friend of Lucy's."

"So you're her accomplice."

Travis clears his throat. "About those questions, Mr. Delgado?"

"I ain't got nothing to hide, so ask away. But make it quick. I got a pot pie in the microwave."

"Miss McGuffin says she saw a surveillance tape that shows you jumping over a fence at Susan Van Dyke's house and stealing her dog. Do you know anything about that?"

Derrick's face registers shock for a second before he masks it with a sneer. "That's nuts. I don't know any Susan Van Dyke. And what the hell would I want with her dog?"

"Abby had Cornelius with her when she died. You dognapped him for her, didn't you?" I demand.

"Don't know what you're talking about, lady. Unless you're going to arrest me for something, then you bozos better get off my property."

Travis nods sternly. "Thank you for your cooperation, Mr. Delgado."

"*Cooperation*?" I turn to Travis. "That's *it*? You're aren't going to take him down to the police station? What kind of cop are you?"

A muscle on the side of Travis's jaw twitches. "Lucy, I told you before, leave this to the professionals."

Derrick grins like he knows he's got the upper hand. "Yeah, listen to the nice cop, *Lucy*."

The way he says my name gives me the heebie-jeebies.

Will takes me by the elbow. "Let's go," he says quietly. "We're not going to get anywhere by antagonizing him."

The last thing I want to do is leave. Not when I know that Derrick is guilty of taking Paco and who knows what else. But I don't have any choice.

I start to follow Will down the steps, then I remember that I'm still holding onto the mail flag. I hand Derrick the rusty red flag. "By the way, this fell off your mailbox."

He looks at it a second, then tosses it into his yard. "I should sue you for the destruction of personal property, but I'm feelin' generous, so I'll just tell you to go on and get." He slams the door in our faces with a loud whack. A few seconds later the porch light goes out.

"Guess he wants to save on his electric bill," Will mutters.

"I really wish you'd let me ask the questions here," Travis says to me. "You forget this dognapping didn't happen in Whispering Bay. If Deborah Van Dyke doesn't want to press charges or get the Destin police involved, then there's not much I can do about it. I can't haul him down to the police station unless I have some evidence that he committed a crime in Whispering Bay. Got it?"

"So is breaking and entering into a public building considered a crime?"

"I'm not going to arrest Sebastian for that."

"Not yet anyway. What about Derrick? What if *he* broke into the building? What if he…what if he stole a key to the building and left it unlocked for some nefarious purpose?"

Travis looks at me like I've grown another head. "Where do you get this stuff?"

"I don't know, but if it did go down that way, then he was definitely up to no good, and it's your responsibility as a police officer to get to the bottom of it."

"Okay, yeah. If that's the case, then, yeah, I'll arrest him. But good luck getting your proof. " He catches up to Will who's already halfway to the car.

I hang back, slowly walking through the weedy yard, aiming the flashlight on the ground, until—*Bingo!*

I really can't believe our good luck.

I gingerly pick up the mailbox flag.

Will turns around and aims his light at me. "Lucy? What are you doing?" He winces when he sees the flag in my hand. "Unless your tetanus shot is up to date, I'd drop that."

"Yeah, I'd—" Travis stops when he sees the expression on my face. His frown is replaced with a grudging look of admiration.

"Oh," says Will, catching on as well.

"Yep," I say, grinning, "We just got Derrick Delgado's fingerprints."

15

"HA!" I SHOUT GLEEFULLY FROM THE BACKSEAT OF THE CAR. "Now all you have to do is match the fingerprints on that mail flag to the prints on the door knob, and you'll have the proof you need. I can't wait to see the look on Derrick Delgado's face when you arrest him for breaking into the rec center."

Travis turns around in his seat to face me. "That's *if* the prints match. And even if they do that doesn't mean he entered the building illegally."

"Have you always had such a negative attitude? Good thing I was there when the technicians were dusting the door knob. Don't forget my prints are going to be there too. Do you think I should be reprinted? So that the lab can tell whose prints belong to who?"

"The lab is perfectly capable of making that distinction," Travis says testily.

"Anyone want to stop for a burger and a shake?" Will asks. "I didn't have dinner so—"

"You're just mad because you didn't think to get Derrick's fingerprints," I say to Travis.

"Hardly. Like I said, even if his fingerprints are there, it doesn't necessarily mean anything."

"I know. I know. I should leave it to the *professionals.*"

Travis makes a growling sound deep in his throat. "I admit, getting his fingerprints was pretty clever. Happy now?"

"Extremely."

Will catches my gaze in the rearview mirror. He looks confused.

"What?" I say to him. "Oh. The burger and shake. I'm good either way."

"Yeah," says Travis. "Stop if you want, or don't. It doesn't matter to me."

Will doesn't say anything, and he doesn't stop for food either. Instead, he drives back to his house in silence. Once there, Travis heads to the police station with the evidence I'm pretty sure is going to get Derrick in a lot of hot water. Or at least I hope so.

"Luce," Will says, stopping me as I'm about to get in my car, "What was all that about?"

"All what about?"

He pushes his glasses up his nose. "Between you and Travis. I know you don't like the guy, but that was a little extreme, don't you think?"

"Oh, *that*." I chuckle. "That was just some good-natured ribbing. Travis is…all right. A little stuffy, maybe, but we made our peace last night."

"Last night?"

"He came by my place after hours to talk about the case. He even ate one of my muffins. *And* he liked it. I was working on my newest batch of the mango coconut recipe. I think I'm really close to perfecting it."

Will nods thoughtfully, but I can tell something's bothering him. Only I have no idea what it might be, and he doesn't seem inclined to tell me, so we say our goodbyes, and I head to The Bistro.

Back home in my apartment, I settle in for my third night (and second in a row) with Paco, who insists on sleeping at the foot of my bed. I think I'm going to have to double my dose of Benadryl.

Even though I've basically taken enough medication to put me in a coma, I have trouble sleeping. I lay awake with Paco snuggled next to me, and I can't help but think about Susan Van Dyke. Anthony and Aurelia made her sound like she was a nice person. I really need to do right by this little dog of hers.

The next morning, I drag myself out of bed because once again I didn't fall asleep until after two. Paco, on the other hand, looks chirpy and refreshed. Currently, he's trotting back and forth between the apartment upstairs and the restaurant. He goes up to the patrons happily accepting their pats on his head and never begs or makes a pest of himself.

It's as if he's on his best behavior, showing me what a great addition he'd make to The Bistro. Unfortunately, his nice dog routine isn't going to work with me because I can't live on Benadryl forever.

Just as I think that I need to call Lanie to update her on the dog situation, she and Dharma walk through the door. Paco immediately runs up to be petted.

"Hey, little guy!" Lanie scoops him up and kisses him on the nose. "Isn't he adorable?" she asks Dharma.

Dharma gazes at Paco warily.

"I thought you were bringing him back to Susan Van Dyke's family," says Lanie.

I fill them in on what happened yesterday, including the fact that Paco was dognapped by Derrick Delgado.

"Wow. That's crazy. So he needs a permanent home, huh?"

"Babe," Dharma says firmly like she knows where this is headed, "we already have four dogs. You promised. Not one more."

"But—" The look on Dharma's face stops Lanie mid-sentence. "Dharma is right. It wouldn't be fair to Paco if we took him. Between our jobs, we barely have time for the four we have." She reluctantly places Paco down on the floor.

"I understand." *Rats*. I was really hoping that Lanie would take him. "Will you be on the look out for a good family?

Someone who'll really appreciate him? I don't mind keeping him until you find the right person."

"Sure thing, Lucy."

I hate taking medication, but it's just temporary until Paco finds his forever home. Maybe Dr. Nate can prescribe something that makes me less drowsy than the Benadryl. I make a mental note to call his office to set up an appointment.

I take their orders and pour them coffee, when out of the blue, Paco starts barking like he's possessed. I've never seen him like this before. I'm about to apologize to the next customer in line when I see that it's Phoebe Van Cleave and her ghost society pals.

Phoebe takes one look at the dog and goes pale.

I should tell her that I'm on to her. How I know all about how she wanted Cornelius, and that she's not fooling anybody. Especially not me.

"It's Cornelius!" Victor crouches down to Paco's eye level. "What are you doing here?"

Paco keeps barking.

"This is the dog that Abby had with her when she passed," I say, trying to gauge everyone's reactions.

No one, not even Gloria seems surprised by this, which is pretty telling.

"Paco," I say, "stop it. You're disturbing the customers."

"Paco?" says Victor.

"I'm calling him that, since it's the name Abby gave him."

Paco barks one more time for good measure, then lets out a final growl and runs up the stairs back to the apartment. Not that I blame him. If I were him, I'd want to get as far away from Phoebe as I could too. "Sorry, I don't think he likes you."

Phoebe sniffs. "I don't understand. He's never reacted like this to me before."

Gloria nods in agreement. "Cornelius, er, that is, Paco and I have done several séances together at Susan's home, and he's always been extremely charming. What do you think got into him?"

"Considering that his owner died, then a few days later he was dognapped, and then he was with poor Abby when she passed, I'd say he might have some trauma going on."

"*Dognapped*!" Gloria says. "Who on earth would do that?"

The hairs on my neck tingle. Gloria isn't as shocked by this information as she wants me to think she is.

"Derrick Delgado. He denies it, but there's a surveillance tape that proves otherwise."

If I thought Phoebe was pale before, then it's nothing compared to now. It's like all the blood has drained from her face. "This is so disturbing," she murmurs.

Victor tsks. "I'll say." He studies me closely. "How have you been, Lucy?"

I mentally sigh because I know what's coming next. "I haven't gotten any messages from Abby if that's what you want to know."

The three of them exchange a look.

"If you'd agree to participate in a séance," says Gloria, "Maybe we could find out why Abby's brother dognapped Paco."

I'm about to ixnay the séance idea when I snap my mouth shut. It occurs to me that I've been looking at this all wrong. Phoebe knows a lot more about this dognapping than she's let on. Gloria and probably Victor do, too. But Phoebe is the only one of them with a motive to get rid of Abby. I'd bet my last mixing bowl that Phoebe is at least partially responsible for fast tracking Abby along to the pearly gates.

Not in a million years do I think a séance trying to communicate with Abby's spirit is going to work, but Phoebe believes in it, and that's what matters. Maybe it will be the catalyst for her to confess everything she knows.

"Now that you mention it, maybe Abby *has* been trying to communicate with me."

"I knew it!" says Gloria.

"Really?" Victor gazes behind me like there's something there. "Do you think she's here now?"

"Sure. At least I think so. I really can't tell because, you know, I'm not trained to look for any of the signs."

"That's it. We absolutely need to do a séance," Gloria persists. "Abby is practically calling to us from the grave."

Victor nods enthusiastically. "I agree."

"Oh, I don't think a séance is necessary," says Phoebe.

Gloria and Victor turn and stare at her. There's only one reason Phoebe wouldn't want to do a séance. And that's because she's afraid of what we'll find out. Which means I want to do this more than ever.

Sarah comes up to the counter to refill the coffee pot. "Did someone just say séance?" She looks like she's trying not to laugh.

"Lucy has agreed to help us talk to Abby," Gloria says.

Sarah's jaw goes slack before she pulls her expression together. "Really?"

"I just want to help," I say trying to sound innocent.

"And of course, Paco will need to be there," says Victor.

"I don't think that's a good idea," Phoebe says. "Didn't you just say that the dog has been through a trauma? To expect him to participate in a séance so soon after all he's been through… no. It's inhumane. Also, Lucy, dear, I couldn't help but overhear part of your conversation with Lanie Miller. It seems like you're looking for a home for the little angel? As I said before, I'll be happy to take him. As a matter of fact, I practically consider it my civic duty."

Gloria puts her arm around Phoebe's shoulder. "I'm sorry to be so blunt, but do you think that's a good idea considering that the dog doesn't like you?"

"Gloria's right," says Victor. "He seems to be fairly aggressive toward you."

Phoebe looks like she's going to cry. "I don't understand why he suddenly doesn't like me."

"Thanks for offering, but Paco has already been adopted," I blurt.

"He has?" Sarah asks.

Oh boy. How am I going to get out of this one?

"Yep. My brother wants him. Yes, that's right, my brother, the priest, wants Paco."

It's been my experience that whenever you add "the priest" in any sort of communication, people back down. It seems to work here too because no one questions me anymore.

"That was fast," Phoebe mutters.

Gloria lowers her voice. "So, about the séance...."

16

GLORIA LAYS DOWN ALL THE CONDITIONS FOR THE "IDEAL" séance environment. They're a bit wacky, but what do I know about talking to the dead? All I know is that to pull this off, I'm going to need help from my best friend.

It kills me to have to wait till The Bistro closes for the day, but I've already left work early twice this week, and it wouldn't be fair to Sarah if I take off again. Once all the customers are gone, and the kitchen is clean I put Paco in my car and head over to Will's.

He's just getting home from the library at the same time I pull into his driveway. He looks exhausted, which doesn't make sense since he took some vacation days this week.

"Big run on Hemingway today?" I ask.

He grins at my joke. "Been cataloguing a new shipment." He unlocks his front door to let us all in. "Hey, little guy," he says, rubbing the top of Paco's head affectionately.

"You wouldn't happen to be in the market for a dog, would you?"

Why didn't I think of this before?

It makes so much sense. Will isn't allergic. He's kind to animals. Paco already likes him. And, he's already offered to take him once, even though it was just for the night. If Will adopts Paco, then I can see Paco all the time. It's a total win-win scenario.

"Lanie Miller wasn't interested?"

"She was. Dharma wasn't. So, how about it?"

"I don't know, Luce. He seems like a great dog, but I'm at work all day. I'm too busy to give him the kind of attention he'll need."

"But he doesn't need much," I protest. "And I'd help."

"What about Sebastian?"

"I already thought about him. He's my last resort, but he's busier than all of us combined."

"I wish I could, but—stop it."

"Stop what?"

"Doing that thing with your eyes."

"What am I doing with my eyes?"

"Making them all sad looking. It's like you have deer eyes."

I giggle. No one has ever told me I have deer eyes before. "Okay, I'll try to look mean."

He sighs. "Look, if you can't find anyone else to take the dog, then I'll do it."

"Really?"

"Sure, why not?"

"Thanks! Hey, by the way, what you do know about an author named J.W. Quicksilver? Apparently, he writes these intense thrillers."

"Never heard of him."

"Really? I thought you were supposed to be a librarian. Anyway, Betty Jean's book club is reading his latest. She promised me lots of big action and hot sex."

He looks at me over the top of his glasses. "You're joining Betty Jean's book club?"

"It's a big honor," I tease. "She says she'll push me to the top of the waiting list if I bring muffins."

Before Will can respond, my cell phone pings. "Yes! It's Travis. I've been waiting all day for this call." Will opens his mouth to say something, but I put a hand up in the air to stop him. "Did the prints match?"

Travis makes a grumpy sound.

"I'll take that as a yes?"

"Don't get all bigheaded, but you were right. Derrick Delgado's fingerprints are on the door knob from the rec center. We already had his prints on file. He was arrested ten years ago for assaulting a guy during a bar fight."

No big surprise there. "You're going to arrest him, right?"

"No. I'm going to bring him in and question him. But you're getting your hopes up for nothing. We don't have any evidence of wrong doing. For all we know he's going to tell us that he was at the rec center during the opening celebration and that's when he touched the door knob."

"Only you know it wouldn't be true."

"And how would I know that exactly?"

If only I could be there when Derrick is questioned, I'd be able to tell Travis if he's lying or not. Except, no, that wouldn't work because it would mean telling Travis about my gift. His dad, I trust. But Travis…it isn't that I don't trust him. And it's not even that I think he won't believe me. But he would definitely think I was strange, and for some unknown reason, I don't want that.

"Is there any way I can be there when you question him?"

"Absolutely not."

"You're no fun."

"Sure I am. You just haven't been around me long enough." The way Travis says this, it sounds almost…flirty. He clears his throat. "So you're not going to like this, but I wanted you to hear it from me first. We're also going to bring your brother in for questioning."

"You're kidding."

"No, Lucy, I'm not. He knows something, and he refuses to cooperate. I have no choice. If he were anyone else, this would have happened three days ago."

Logically, I know that Travis is right. But I still hate that my brother is being dragged into this. I have to find out what went on in that rec center the night Abby died. Which means this séance has to happen.

"Thanks for the heads up," I say grudgingly. When I get off the phone, Will is staring at me as if I've done something wrong. "What?"

"Nothing." But he sounds moody, and that isn't like him.

"So, the reason I came over here is because I need a favor. And you aren't going to like it."

Will opens his refrigerator and takes out two beers. He hands me one. "Why aren't I going to like it?"

I wait till he's taken a sip of the beer and looks relaxed before I say, "Because it's sort of illegal. But totally for a good reason. I need to get a small, *very* small group, into the rec center at midnight so we can have a séance. And since the center is normally closed that means we'll basically have to break in."

Beer comes sputtering out of Will's mouth and spills onto the leather sofa. Paco runs to lick it up. "You want me to help you break into the rec center?" he asks incredulously. "Isn't this the same thing you want Derrick Delgado locked up for?"

"That's different. I'm this close," I say, putting my thumb and index finger up so that they're practically touching, "to finding out what really happened the night Abby died. And I do *not* have PTSD. I just need this séance to help put the pieces of the puzzle together."

"Are you listening to yourself? When did you start believing in this stuff?"

"I don't believe the séance is going to work, silly. But Phoebe does. That's the important part. These people think that Abby is linked to me. So all I have to do is fake it, and once Phoebe thinks she's talking to Abby, I'll get her to confess everything she knows."

Will closes his eyes for a moment like he's trying to absorb all this. "Let's say I thought this was a good idea, which I don't, why does the séance have to be in the rec center? Why can't it be in someone's spooky old house? Or better yet, in a graveyard?"

"Right? The rec center is Gloria's stipulation. She says we need to do the séance in the rec center because that's where Abby died, and we need to do it as close to the time of her death as possible. Which means we need to do it around one in the morning. Oh, and Paco needs to be there too because you know, they think he sees dead people, and that could really come in handy."

"And you don't think this all sounds crazy?"

"Maybe. A little." He glares at me. "Okay, maybe more than a little. All I know is that my gut is telling me Phoebe had something to do with Abby's death. And now the cops want to bring Sebastian in for questioning. And you know him. He'll never tell them anything that he thinks might be breaking some sort of sacred confidence. Even if the cops go easy on him, there will always be a cloud of suspicion hanging over his head unless we can figure out what he and Abby were doing in the rec center."

Will sighs wearily. "What do you need from me?"

"You're the head librarian, which makes you an important public employee, right? Isn't there some kind of master key to all the city owned buildings?"

"No."

"Okay, well, Gus had a set of keys to the building during the celebration. Who usually has those?"

"I would imagine that the rec center director has those. And probably some of the class instructors."

"Like Viola?"

"Yeah, she might have a set of keys. If she ever opens or locks up the building. But..." Will shakes his head in disbelief. "I can't believe I'm about to say this. I think I know who might have a set of keys."

"Really? Who?"

"Brittany. She teaches the evening Pilates class. She said something about having to lock up after class the other day."

Fate must be laughing in my face right now because the last person I want to be indebted to is Brittany Kelly. "Do you think she'll help?"

"I don't know, Lucy. She could get in a lot of trouble. We all could."

"Not if we don't get caught."

He snorts.

"Please. Will you ask her?" I decide to play my ace again. "For Sebastian?"

"Let me think about it."

"Thanks, Will!"

"I said I'd think about it. I was going to call her later this evening to solidify our plans for Friday night. I'll throw some feelers out and see if I can gauge her reaction. If she shuts it down even a little, which she probably will, then I'm not going to pursue it. Understand?"

Since this is the best I can hope for, I nod eagerly. "Sure, thanks. Speaking of Brittany, where are you taking her on the big date?"

"I was thinking of that steak place in Seaside. Then maybe a walk along the beach afterward. What do you think? Too lame?"

There's no such thing as too lame for Brittany.

"Sounds perfect."

Neither of us say anything for a few beats.

My cell phone rings. It's too soon for it be Travis again, so I'm about to decline the call when I notice the area code. "Oh my God. It's the Cooking Channel!" I'm too excited and shocked to move.

Will's eyes light up. "Lucy, you're on the show."

"What if they're calling to turn me down?"

"They'd do that in an email. Go on," he urges. "Answer the phone."

I take a deep breath and press the accept button. "Hello," I croak.

"Is this Lucy McGuffin?" asks a female voice.

"Yes, that's me."

"This is Tara Bell from The Cooking Channel. How are you today?" She sounds upbeat, which is a positive sign. Right?

"I'm good. I think."

She chuckles, but it sounds more practiced than sincere. "I've had a chance to go over your application, and I've seen your audition tape. You're fabulous, by the way. A complete natural."

"I am?"

"The camera loves you, Lucy, and the camera doesn't love everyone. I'm *thrilled* to tell you that we're moving you on to the next phase of the auditions."

"There's another phase?"

"Oh yes. We'll be sending a camera crew to your kitchen. To get a feel for the locale, that kind of thing. You'll receive an email with an attachment that explains everything." I can hear her shuffling some papers around. "Let's see...your café is called The Bistro by the Beach, and you own it along with a Sarah Powers?"

"That's right."

"Fabulous. Of course, we'll need Sarah to agree to the filming, and she'll need to sign all the waivers."

"Sure! She's just as excited about this as I am."

"Marvelous. We'll be in touch soon. Ciao!"

I click the disconnect button in a daze.

"Are you on the show?" Will asks eagerly.

"Not yet. There's one more phase to the auditions."

"Lucy, that's awesome."

"It is, isn't?"

And then because it feels natural, I reach out and hug him and he gives me a quick sisterly hug back. I wish he didn't feel so solid or smell so good. My life would be a whole lot easier if Will and I were on the same page here.

"Do they go to all the contestant's hometowns before they decide to put them on the show?" he asks.

"I don't know. Maybe this is part of the intro package. You know, when they're telling the audience about the contestants. Only you'd think they'd only film those with the people they've already picked."

"Seems to me that you're a shoo-in."

"Thanks. But you have to say that because you're my best friend, which reminds me if I win *Muffin Wars*, I'll be able to pay you back the money you loaned me for the down payment on The Bistro."

"No worries. Pay me back whenever you can."

"No worries? Ten grand had to have put a big dent in your savings."

"It's a great investment," he says sounding uncomfortable the way he always does whenever I mention the loan. "Have you thought about how you're going to fake like you're talking to Abby Delgado's spirit?"

"That's the easy part. I just have to watch *Ghost* again and get my Whoopi on."

"That'll make, what? The hundredth time you've seen it?"

Will knows that *Ghost* is one of my favorite movies. The pottery wheel scene between Patrick Swayze and Demi Moore always makes my heart do flip flops. I've made him watch it at least three times. He pretends that he hates it, but deep down, I know he gets a big kick out of the whole who's-good-and-who's-bad theme.

"So I'll make it a hundred and one. Your job is to convince Brittany to let us use her key to get into the building."

"That's if she even has a key."

"I have every confidence in your abilities to persuade her."

He shakes his head. "Sometimes being your best friend is a lot of work, Lucy."

"But you wouldn't want it any other way. Right?"

He hesitates just a fraction of a second too long before he answers. "Right."

17

AFTER I LEAVE WILL'S HOUSE, I TAKE PACO TO THE PARK, WHERE he behaves like a perfect little gentleman. Every five minutes I check my phone to see if either Will or Travis has called to update me on their respective assignments.

When a good hour goes by, and I don't hear from either of them, I decide to take matters into my own hands. I'm about to dial Travis when my cell rings.

"Hello?"

"Lucy? It's Aurelia Finch, Susan Van Dyke's cook."

"Oh! Hi, Aurelia."

"Anthony and I were wondering how Cornelius was faring. Have you found a permanent home for him yet?"

"I'm pretty confident I can talk my best friend Will into taking him. He'd be terrific with the dog."

"The sweet little thing has been through so much. I feel better knowing that you're looking out for his welfare."

Now that I have Aurelia on the phone, I realize she's the perfect person to give me some intel. "When Susan was alive, you said that she used to host séances in her home? And that Cornelius assisted?"

"Oh, yes. She couldn't have done them without him. He's a very gifted medium."

"Good to know because he's going to be participating in another séance soon. Maybe even as soon as tomorrow night. Is there anything I should know about how to prep him? Any special foods or anything?"

"No special prep is needed, but I should warn you. Talking to the dead isn't a trifling thing. This has to be done correctly, or who knows what might happen. If the environment isn't carefully monitored, it can turn dangerous for Cornelius."

Dangerous? It occurs to me that I'm clueless here. "Exactly how does Cornelius whisper to the dead?"

"Cornelius makes contact with the spirit we're calling to. Then the human medium picks up on Cornelius's vibrations and communicates those vibrations back to the other members of the séance. If the human medium isn't talented enough to sense what Cornelius is feeling, then all those thoughts can be trapped inside him and create an unhealthy chi."

Just as I thought. It's all a big bunch of hooey. "Got it."

Aurelia tsks. "I'd already pegged you as a non-believer, but I didn't know you were also a cynic."

Oops. "Sorry, I didn't mean to sound skeptical."

"It's all right. Anthony and I are used to it. Who's in charge of this séance?"

"The Sunshine Ghost Society, so Madame Gloria will be the, um, human medium."

"I see."

It's not hard to figure out what Aurelia thinks of that. "I know you're not crazy about Phoebe Van Cleave, but the rest of the group isn't so bad."

"Whose spirit will they be talking to?"

"Hopefully, Abby Delgado's."

"You know, Lucy, Anthony and I were an integral part of the séances that Susan used to host. Since this is the first séance that Cornelius will be doing without Susan, perhaps we should be there too. For moral support."

"Sure. Why not? Except.... I have to tell you, we're using a building without permission."

"Oh dear."

I tell her about the conditions Gloria put down for the séance.

"She's correct. The spirit does tend to linger in places where he or she was last alive."

"So I've been told. I'm really hoping that we can get to the bottom of why Abby's brother stole Cornelius." *Among other things.*

"I take it the brother didn't confess?"

"Hardly. And since Deborah doesn't want to press charges there's nothing the Whispering Bay police can do about it."

"Nothing?"

"Well, I did manage to get the brother's fingerprints without him knowing it." I can't help but brag. "They matched a set of prints on the door knob to the rec center where his sister was found. Travis Fontaine, that's the police officer in charge of Abby's case, is bringing him in for questioning. They might not be able to get him for dognapping, but there's a possibility they could charge him for trespassing, which is better than nothing."

"How clever you are," she muses.

"Thanks, not that it will do much good. Even though I think he had something to do with his sister's death he has an alibi."

"The police checked it out?"

"Yep. Derrick was at home in Mexico Beach playing cards till two in the morning. It's an hour away so even if he left right at two he couldn't have gotten to Whispering Bay till three a.m. earliest, which puts it a little too far off from the time Abby died."

"Mexico Beach? Anthony and I have been there. It's an adorable little town."

"Yeah, well, he lives in the not so adorable part. Almost in the boonies, really."

"To the east?" she asks.

I still as Aurelia's words sink in.

Holy wow. Why didn't I think of this before?

Mexico Beach sits directly on the line between the eastern and central time zones. I'm pretty sure that Derrick's house lies in what the north Florida natives refer to as "fast time" or Eastern Standard Time. Whispering Bay, on the other hand, sits in "slow time" or Central Standard Time. Which means that two in the morning at Derrick's place was one in the morning in Whispering Bay, giving him plenty of time to get to the rec center during the time period that the coroner placed her death.

I need to get this information to Travis ASAP.

The Whispering Bay Police Department is located on the gulf right next to the city municipal building. Since there isn't a sign on the door that explicitly says no dogs allowed, I bring Paco inside. "Better to ask forgiveness than permission." Paco wags his tail like he agrees.

Cindy, the receptionist, looks up from her computer screen. She and Rusty have been dating for about a year now. She's another good customer of mine, although she hasn't been to The Bistro in over a week which can only mean that she's dieting again. Her favorite muffin is cranberry. Maybe I can come up with a low-fat version.

"Hey, Cindy. Is there any way I can see Travis Fontaine? It's kind of an emergency."

She shakes her head. "You too, Lucy?"

"What do you mean?"

"Just that every single woman under the age of forty has come by in the last week on some pretext or another to see Travis."

A part of me finds this amusing. Another part finds it…irritating. "I guess there's no accounting for taste."

Paco whimpers, drawing attention to himself.

"Oh! I didn't see your dog." Cindy leans over her desk and pats him on the head. "When did you get him? What's his name?"

"I'm watching him temporarily. His name is Paco."

"Hey, little guy," Cindy croons.

He makes a big show of wagging his tail and looking utterly adorable like he's trying to win her over, only I'm pretty sure he's already done that.

"I could just die you're so cute!" Cindy reaches into the top drawer of her desk and pulls out a granola bar. "Is it okay if I give him a piece?"

Paco barks as if to say *yes, please*!

"Sure, why not?"

She ends up giving him the entire granola bar, and even though I fed him just a couple of hours ago he gobbles it down like he's starving,

"So, Cindy, Travis told me that he was bringing Derrick Delgado in for questioning. Do you know how that went? Is it still going on?"

And more importantly, is Derrick in handcuffs yet?

"Well, I'm not supposed to say, since it's official police business and all."

Paco nudges me with his nose like he's urging me to try another tactic. If I didn't know better, I'd think that he understood what we were saying. "Did you know that I was the one who found Abby Delgado?"

"Rusty told me. Bless your heart. That must have been awful! Did you have to do CPR?"

"No, but it was still traumatic," I say playing it up.

"I know what you mean. Rusty and I were at The Harbor House a couple of weeks ago to celebrate our one-year anniversary, and the man in the table next to us started to choke. It was horrible. His face turned red as a tomato. Rusty was a real hero," she adds proudly.

"Did he have to do the Heimlich maneuver?"

"No, but he was the one who dialed 911."

"And they saved the guy?"

"Actually…by the time the paramedics got there, one of the waiters had done the Heimlich." She shrugs like that part of the story is inconsequential.

I lean in closer to her desk. "Cindy, did you know that Officer Fontaine is planning to bring my brother in for questioning?"

She squirms in her chair. "Rusty mentioned something about that."

"How did Officer Fontaine get put in charge of this case? I mean, doesn't Rusty have seniority over him?"

"Yes, but Zeke thinks that Travis practically walks on water. Rusty has been with the department for twenty years. Then this hot shot swoops in and just because he's from Dallas everyone thinks he knows so much more."

"That's so unfair."

"Tell me about it."

I sigh dramatically. "I bet if Rusty were in charge, we'd already know what happened to Abby."

Even though there's no one else in the room, she lowers her voice. "I guess it won't hurt to tell you that Derrick Delgado is in the interrogation room as we speak."

My heart speeds up. "Really?"

She nods. "Rusty and Travis are in there with him now. You should have seen him strut in here like he owned the place! I've worked here a long time, and I can always tell when someone's guilty. It's the eyes. His are shifty as hell."

"Oh, believe me, I've had the displeasure of speaking to the man twice, and I totally agree." *If I could just get into that interrogation room somehow…* "Cindy, Officer Fontaine mentioned that there was surveillance footage that showed both Abby and my brother Sebastian entering the rec center the night she died."

"Oh, yeah, I've seen it."

"You have?" I can barely contain my excitement. "Do you think it would be okay if I took a look at it? I mean, maybe I can pick up something that *Officer* Fontaine didn't." I made sure to add a snarky tone to my voice whenever I say Travis's name.

"Golly, Lucy, I wish I could show it to you, but I don't think Zeke would like that."

"I understand. It's just…Officer Fontaine hinted that he was going to use the tape to press charges against Sebastian. For trespassing into the rec center."

Okay, so this isn't *exactly* true, but it works because Cindy looks mortified. "*Arrest* Father McGuffin? I can't believe it! He's going too far now."

"I agree. But what can we do?"

She thinks this over. "I don't see how it would hurt for you to take a look at the footage."

"Really? You're a complete doll!"

Cindy pulls an empty chair up to her desk. I place Paco on my lap, and we both look on as she taps on her computer screen. "It should come up any minute."

A series of black and white footage appears. "See," she says pointing to the top of the screen, "here's the date and time." The date reads November 3 and the time is set at 11:55 pm. We watch for the next five minutes as nothing happens. Then there's a shot of Abby walking along the side of the building. She stops at the door, jiggles the lock and walks in.

"So the door was already open," I say to myself.

Cindy fast forwards to twelve-thirty when Sebastian shows up. He stands in front of the door, and even though the camera angle doesn't show his face clearly, I can tell by his body language that he's hesitant to walk inside. After a few seconds, he opens the door and enters the building.

Nothing else happens for the next few minutes or so. At precisely twelve thirty-five, Sebastian walks out the building through the same door.

"That's all there is to see," Cindy says.

Something here isn't right. Only I'm not sure what it is.

"What about earlier? How far back has anyone looked?"

"I just told you. That's all there is."

I still. "You mean, that's *all* the security footage that's available? From any of the doors?"

Cindy nods. "The system was getting revamped, and the cameras weren't fully operational until just a few days ago."

I remember now that during the rec center celebration Gus said something along those lines.

"So there could be lots of people who came and went at some other time or through other doors, but they weren't caught on camera?"

"Sure. I mean, yeah, who knows?"

Except the footage doesn't show anyone else entering or leaving the building. Which means that Sebastian is the last person who saw Abby alive.

Ha! No wonder I thought Travis was lying to me. He purposely mislead me about the security footage because he wanted me to get Sebastian to tell him what he and Abby were doing in the building. That sneaky…

I begrudgingly have to admire his tactics.

"Can I see the footage one more time?"

We rewatch the film. This time I'm on super alert for any little thing. Only nothing stands out.

Paco nudges me with his nose.

"Not now, sweetie."

He nudges harder.

"Paco, what do you—" I glance down at him. He looks back at me with those sweet brown eyes, and I swear he's trying to tell me something. If I've learned anything over the past week, it's that I should listen to this little dog. "Do you mind if we watch it again?"

Cindy shrugs. "Why not?" She sets the recording back. Five minutes later, we watch once more as Abby goes through the motion of trying the lock and walking through the door.

"Holy wow," I mutter. "Can you freeze that?"

"What? Do you see something?" Cindy pushes the pause button.

I turn to look at her. "When I found Abby, Paco was with her."

"Poor tyke. It must have been traumatic for him."

"Yeah, but don't you see? According to the footage, Abby goes into the rec center, but she's alone. The dog wasn't with her. Which means Paco must have *already* been in the rec center when she got there."

"Are you sure about that?"

"Positive. Sebastian specifically told me when he saw Abby she had the dog with her."

"So someone else brought the dog into the rec center?

"Yep. And I'd bet a dozen of my best apple walnut cream cheese muffins that it's the same person who unlocked the door. If we can find out who had the key, then we'll know… well, we'll know something important, that's for sure."

"Golly." She glances nervously off to the side. "And you think maybe it was the brother?"

"He has a pretty good motive for wanting to get rid of Abby. She left him everything. And he certainly likes to wave a gun around. Plus, Officer Fontaine told me Derrick's been arrested before. For assault."

Cindy shudders. "I get so worried when Rusty has to deal with these criminal types."

Considering that Rusty is a cop, I'm not sure what to say here.

"Rusty and Travis have been interrogating Derrick for a while now, huh?"

She nods. "At least thirty minutes."

"I sure would love to know what's going on in there."

Cindy doesn't say anything.

"You know, on T.V. they always show those interrogations taking place in one room while another cop is in the next room looking through one of those two-way mirrors and listening in through a speaker."

"Oh yeah, isn't that cool?"

"The Whispering Bay police department wouldn't happen to have one of those rooms, would they?"

"Nah. We're not big enough for anything that fancy."

"Oh." I can't hide my disappointment.

"But we have an intercom system."

"Really?"

"Sure. That way if someone in the room needs something they just have to call out for it. And vice versa. If I need to speak to the cop in the room, then I just call in."

"So, you could also use the intercom to listen in?"

Cindy's cheeks go red. "Technically, I suppose I could do that."

Technically, my butt. Cindy has listened in before. And not just once or twice either.

"Thirty minutes seems like a long time to be interrogating someone about a simple trespassing case, doesn't it?" I let that sink in. "You know, I would never tell anyone if you accidentally hit the intercom button."

She wets her bottom lip. "If we make any noise, then they'll know we're listening."

"I promise, I'll be quiet as a mouse."

She smiles coyly. "Okay." She hits a button next to her phone.

Derrick's voice is the first one we hear. "So I took the dog. Sue me."

Well, this at least is the truth.

At the sound of Derrick's voice, Paco's body goes tense. Using my eyes, I plead with him to stay silent. Luckily, he seems to understand.

"The dog was being abused," Derrick continues. "Left out in the yard with no food or water. The way I see it, I was doing the mutt a favor. You said no one was pressin' charges so draggin' me down here today is total crap."

"What about your fingerprints on the door knob at the rec center?" Travis asks.

"Didn't know it was a crime to touch a door."

"It isn't. But it is a crime to trespass into a city building after hours."

"Look. I told you already. I took the dog because Abby asked me to. She gave me a couple of hundred bucks for my trouble, which I appreciated, you know? You try living on social security. But that was it. End of story. I probably touched the door knob during that big…what was it? Celebration? Yeah, that's when it must have happened."

"You were at the opening day celebration?" Rusty asks.

"Sure. I promised Abby I'd meet her, but she never showed so I went home."

This is such a big lie that I can hardly catch a breath.

"Okay," says Travis.

"So I can go home now?"

"Yeah."

The sound of chairs scraping against the floor makes Cindy snap off the intercom button. "I think they're coming out now," she whispers.

A minute later, Derrick Delgado emerges from the hallway, followed by Rusty and Travis. Paco goes wild barking. I scoop him up in my arms.

The look on Derrick's face when he spots me is priceless. Like I'm some pesky wad of gum he's tossed out the window that's come back to hit him in the face. "What are *you* doing here?"

"This is a public building. I have every right to be here."

Paco bares his teeth at Derrick.

"Keep that mongrel away from me. Or I'll have animal control put him down."

This is entirely the *wrong* thing to say to me.

"Funny how he seems not to like you. Oh, wait. I guess that since you *dognapped* him, he's a little sensitive around you. Deborah Van Dyke might not have wanted to press charges before, but when I tell her that you've also been arrested for assault, she just might change her mind. She might consider it her civic duty to put you away."

"Can't you make her shut up?" Derrick says to Travis.

"Lucy," Travis warns. "Leave it alone."

"How many times are you going to let this guy get away with who knows what?" I ask. "He wasn't at the rec center celebration that's for sure. Oh, and ask him about his alibi! He might have been playing cards till two in the morning, but it was two in the morning *eastern* time. Which means he had plenty of time to drive over here, get inside the building, and—"

"And what?" Derrick sneers. He turns to Travis. "Are you gonna let her talk to me like this? I'm a grieving brother, and this crazy lady is harassing me."

"He's right, Lucy. You need to cut it out."

"But he was lying about how his fingerprints got on the door knob! He was never at the rec center celebration. And if he's lying about that, then he could be lying about everything else too."

Travis frowns. "How do you know he told us he was at the rec center celebration?"

Oops. I can't very well tell Travis how I know that without getting Cindy into trouble.

"It was a lucky guess."

Everyone is looking at me like I've gone bananas. Except Cindy who won't meet my gaze.

Derrick jabs a finger at me. "I want her arrested, and that damn dog put down! He's a menace. Look at him! She's probably trained him to attack me!"

I'm about to open my mouth when Travis puts a hand up in the air, stopping me.

"Mr. Delgado," he says, "Thank you for coming down here today to answer our questions. You're free to go home."

As he's leaving out the door, he brushes past me on purpose and leers. "I better not catch you trying to break into my place again. You or that damn little dog you like so much."

How I manage to hold my tongue is beyond me, but I do.

A full minute goes by before anyone says anything.

"Wow," says Rusty. "That sure was intense."

Travis motions me toward the back of the hallway. "Can I have a word with you? In private?" The way he says it doesn't sound like a request. More like an order.

Cindy and Rusty immediately go to work appearing busy. She starts typing on her computer and Rusty rifles through a stack of papers on his desk, but I can tell they're both dying to know whatever it is Travis is going to say to me.

Unfortunately, I have a pretty good idea already.

Paco, who's calmed down considerably since Derrick left, nudges to be let down. We follow Travis to the alcove.

"Before you say anything, I know I was a little out of line—"

"A *little*? How about a lot?"

"I can't believe you're going to let Derrick get away with… everything he's done."

"What's he done? Other than taking the dog? Which, I might add, we've already established we can't do anything about."

"That's just it, we don't know, because there's no video evidence, is there?"

He looks taken aback. "What do you mean?"

"You didn't lie when you said that the footage only showed Abby and Sebastian going into the rec center because that's the only footage that exists. The truth is, you have *no* idea who went into that building the night Abby died because most of the cameras weren't operational until the day after the rec center officially opened."

"It doesn't matter anyway, because this case is closed. The autopsy report just came in a few minutes ago. Abby died of a heart attack with no evidence of any foul play, and no trespassing charges are going to be filed. Against *anyone*. I just left your brother a message telling him not to bother coming down for questioning."

"A heart attack?"

Travis nods wearily.

"But what about the fall? Didn't she hit her head?"

"The coroner can't tell which came first, the heart attack or the fall. There's a pretty good chance that the fall was caused by her heart attack."

"And that's *it*?"

"Yeah, that's it." He frowns. "I thought you'd be happy that Sebastian is off the hook."

"Of course I'm happy. But...don't you still want to know what Abby was doing in the rec center in the first place?"

"No, I don't. Right now there are two cops out with the flu, and the chief has his hands full at home so I'd appreciate it if you stop trying to make more work for the department. In the future, I suggest you stick to doing what you do best. Stay away from my crime scenes, and I'll stay out of your kitchen."

"So, you admit it was a crime scene."

He rakes a hand through his hair. "That was a figure of speech. I mean it, Lucy, the next time you interfere with an official police investigation I'm not going to be so easy going about the whole thing. Now if you don't mind? I have work to do." He stomps off down the hall leaving Paco and me to stare after him.

18

So much for getting the new information to Travis. And to think, I was just beginning to like him. Well, not like *like* him, but he was almost tolerable.

It's as if he doesn't want to listen to reason. Or maybe, I'm the one who doesn't want to listen. Maybe Abby's death was just like Travis said—completely natural with no sign of foul play.

Only my gut tells me that something sinister happened in that rec center. I'll never rest until I know what Abby and my brother were doing there in the middle of the night, and there's only one person who can tell me that. Since it's Wednesday afternoon, I know exactly where to find him. St. Perpetua's Catholic Church holds weekly reconciliations *aka* confessions every Wednesday from four to six p.m. There's no way Sebastian can avoid me there.

I hastily drop Paco off at The Bistro then head over to see my brother. The church is quiet. Only a handful of parishioners wait in line to partake of my least favorite of all the sacraments. Sebastian was right when he accused me of never going to confession.

I hang around till the last person comes out of the confessional. I open the door and kneel inside the cubicle. The partition opens. It's so dark I can barely make out Sebastian's silhouette. "Whenever you're ready," he says quietly.

"Bless me, Father, for I have sinned, but right now we need to talk about you and Abby Delgado."

"*Lucy*?" He swings back the door flooding the tiny area with light. "What are you doing here?"

"I know you told me to leave this to the police, but something happened to Abby Delgado, and I can't let it go. I keep thinking about the last time I saw her, and…you were right. She didn't have any real friends. Even her own brother didn't like her. I feel like I owe it to her to find out the truth."

He silently walks to the front of the church where he sits in the first pew. I follow and sit next to him.

"Does this have anything to do with…you know, your ability to tell when someone's lying?"

"Sort of. But not really. I mean, yeah, there's that, but I have this niggling sense that her death wasn't just the case of a simple heart attack. There are too many weird things surrounding it all."

"I think you're right," he says softly.

I sigh in relief. Finally! "So, are you going to tell me everything you know?"

"It's not much, but yeah, I'll tell you what I can." He looks up at the large wooden crucifix looming over the altar then gazes back at me. "A few days before she died, Abby came to me with some concerns about a parishioner here at the church."

"Let me guess? Phoebe Van Cleave?"

He nods.

"I didn't know Phoebe was Catholic."

"Lapsed, but still a registered parishioner."

"Okay. So Phoebe was who Abby wanted you to do the exorcism on, right?"

The corner of his mouth twitches up in a very un-Sebastian like way. "No. Phoebe wasn't her intended...victim."

I cross my arms over my chest. "Maybe you should start at the beginning."

I drive to the library, and it's perfect timing because Will is locking up for the day. "I was wondering when you were going to show up," he says.

"Does that mean you had a chance to talk to Brittany about the keys to the rec center?"

"She said she'd think about it."

"Really?" I have to admit, I'm surprised. I figured Brittany would have the vapors at the idea of using her key in some illicit fashion. "I guess that's better than a flat-out no."

Will adjusts his backpack over his shoulder. "I rode my bike here. Want to meet me back at my house, and we can make dinner?" When I hesitate, he turns to study my face. "What?"

"What do you mean what?"

"You look like you just won the lottery."

"I have some new intel on the case."

Will moans. "You're going to be the death of me, Lucy. Between this séance and running around confronting strange men with shotguns—"

"Shut up and get in my car. We can have dinner at my place. Sarah made some of her excellent mac and cheese. I'll fill you in on everything on the ride over."

He secures his bike on the rear rack of my car. I barely wait till he's buckled into his seat before I start. "Abby wanted Sebastian to perform an exorcism on Paco."

"The *dog*?"

"Yep, and there's a whole lot more." I put my car in drive and head to The Bistro. "According to Sebastian, Abby came to him a few days before she died. Apparently, she and Phoebe Van Cleave were in this huge power struggle over their positions in the Sunshine Ghost Society."

"We already knew that."

"Yeah, but after Susan Van Dyke's death the conflict escalated because both of them wanted Paco."

"The Ghost Whisperer." Will struggles not to laugh.

"It's not funny. I think Phoebe might have killed Abby over Paco."

Will's smile disappears. "Seriously? What proof do you have?"

"None. For now. According to the autopsy report, Abby died of a heart attack, but hear me out. Susan Van Dyke used to host all these séances in her home and Paco was a huge part of the show. Aurelia and Anthony—"

"The cook and the butler?"

"I know, it's all so Agatha Christie-ish, isn't it? Anyhoo, Aurelia and Anthony said that Phoebe and Abby argued about the dog. I guess they figured that whoever had Paco would have an advantage since he has special powers."

"Since they *think* he has special powers."

"A few days after Susan died, Paco was dognapped by Derrick, which you know about. He gave the dog to Abby, but now she was in a bind. Since she'd gotten the dog illegally, she couldn't very well run around town with him openly, hence her weird behavior last Friday at The Bistro."

"Okay. But how did Sebastian get involved?"

"Initially, she wanted him to do the exorcism on Paco. Abby told Sebastian that Paco bit someone, which is totally out of character, by the way. She thought maybe he accidentally picked up an evil spirit during his last séance."

"Ah, the old *the-evil-spirit-made-me-do-it* excuse?"

"Be serious."

"You want me to be serious about a dog that's possessed?"

"Pay attention. He's not possessed. Abby just thought he was."

Will blows out a breath. "How do you know it's out of character? You've only had the dog for a few days. Maybe he bites people all the time."

"Believe me, if Paco didn't bite Derrick Delgado this afternoon, then he'd only bite someone to defend himself. Or maybe to defend someone he really cared about."

I tell Will about my trip to the police department, how Cindy let me see the security footage and about my repeat run in with Derrick. "I can't wait to find out what really happened to Abby and show up that...*Neanderthal* Texas Ranger. He practically told me that my place was in the kitchen!"

"I thought this was about getting justice for Abby Delgado."

"That too. Showing up Travis Fontaine is just for bonus points."

We pull into the parking lot behind The Bistro's kitchen. I turn in my seat to face Will. "This is what I think happened. Even though Abby was trying to hide Paco, somehow, Phoebe found out that she had him and I think Phoebe stole the dog from Abby."

"This is one popular dog."

"Sebastian said that Abby wanted him to go the rec center to solve a problem between her and Phoebe. She thought that Phoebe would listen to Sebastian because he's her parish priest. But when Sebastian got there, Abby told him everything was okay. Paco was with her, and she seemed happy. Since the security footage shows Abby going into the rec center without Paco, we know for sure that someone else brought the dog. I think Phoebe had the dog, brought him to the rec center and she and Abby made up. Phoebe went to leave, but then she changed her mind and hid somewhere in the building waiting for Sebastian to come and go. After he left, she told Abby she wanted the dog back. Somehow, Abby must have fallen, and the stress of everything made her have a heart attack."

"I don't know, Lucy, that's pretty farfetched."

"Phoebe lied to me about Paco, and it wasn't just a casual lie. There was a lot of stress and anguish behind it. She's hiding something big, Will. I just know it."

"Let's say you're right about what happened between Phoebe and Abby. Then how did Derrick's fingerprints get on the doorknob? Unless he was telling the truth about being at the celebration?"

"Oh no. That was a big lie. I'm not sure how Derrick ties into all this, but he does. That's why it's so important that we do this séance. It's the only way we can get Phoebe to tell us what really went down between her and Abby."

"I feel like my brain is going to explode."

"Mac and cheese to the rescue?"

He's already out the car door. "You got it."

We go in through the back way that leads into The Bistro kitchen, only I don't have to use my key to get inside.

"You left the door unlocked?" Will snaps on the kitchen light. Everything looks in order.

"I was in such a hurry to go see Sebastian I must have forgotten to lock the door. No worries. I've never had a problem before. Besides, I have a watch dog now." Speaking of which, it's strange that Paco hasn't run to greet me. "Paco!" I yell.

I open the stainless steel industrial refrigerator door and pull out a tub of macaroni and cheese. "We can eat it down here or take it up to my apartment. And if you're a good boy, I might even let you see *Ghost* again."

Will moans, but he's also grinning, so I know he really doesn't mind. As we climb the stairs, I turn on the lights to my apartment. "Paco, we have mac and cheese," I say, trying to bribe him out from wherever he's hiding.

I place the container on my kitchen counter and glance around my apartment. "That's weird. Where do you think he is?"

"I'll find him." Will goes into my bedroom. "Paco," he calls.

I pull two plates down from my cupboard.

"Lucy! Come here quick. In the bathroom."

The tone in Will's voice makes me drop the ceramic plates. They shatter into a thousand pieces as they hit the floor, but I don't care. I run to the bathroom.

Paco is lying on the floor, just as still as Abby was only a few days ago.

19

"HE's STILL BREATHING." WILL RUBS PACO's BACK FIRMLY. "C'mon, boy, that's it." He looks up at me. "We need to take him to the vet. *Now.*"

I'm so shocked I can't move. But hearing Will's commanding voice propels me into action. I grab a towel off the rack and toss it to him. "Here wrap him up in this."

Will drapes the towel around Paco and gently lifts him up into his arms. That's when we both see the open bottle of Benadryl on the floor.

"He must have gotten into my medication." I think I'm going to throw up.

Will looks me steadily in the eye. "Get the bottle, Lucy. We'll need to show it to the vet."

We're dashing to the car when I realize that I have no idea where to take Paco. "He doesn't have a vet…that is…"

"Call Lanie. She'll know where to take him."

Lanie directs me to an emergency vet's office. "I'll call ahead and explain what's happened. I'll meet you there, Lucy."

An hour later, Will, Lanie, and I are huddled in a small waiting room at the Gulfside Veterinary Clinic. The door opens. A woman in her forties with kind brown eyes greets us. *Dr. Julia Brooks* is monogrammed in teal over the right breast pocket of her lab coat. She searches our gazes. "Which of you is the dog's owner?"

I stand up to face the music. "That would be me.

She smiles tightly. "He's going to be all right."

A wave of relief washes over me like a tsunami. If anything had happened to Paco, I'd never forgive myself. "Thank you," I croak. "Thank you so much."

"You got him here just in the nick of time. He was too lethargic to induce vomiting, but we were able to pump his stomach. He's on IV fluids now." She pulls the empty Benadryl bottle from her lab coat pocket. "Do you know how many pills he might have ingested?"

I appreciate her professional tone, but I still wince at the unspoken implication that this is my fault. I could have sworn the pills were in my medicine cabinet, but I've been so tired lately… I must have left the bottle on the counter top. But with the cap open as well?

"There was at least half a bottle in there. Maybe twenty or so pills? I…I'm allergic to dogs with fur, so I've been taking Benadryl to keep from itching."

She pulls out a clipboard. "Now that he's stabilized, I'm going to need some more information. Does he have any allergies? How about his previous medical history?"

"I'm not sure."

"How old is he? What did he eat today?"

"I don't know how old he is. And he ate the usual. His dog food, which is something that Lanie recommended, and um, well, maybe he also had a blueberry muffin and a granola bar."

Dr. Brooks stares at me.

A trickle of sweat runs down my back.

I'm the worst dog mother ever.

"She's only had the dog a few days," Will says in my defense. He goes on to explain the situation to Dr. Brooks.

"I see." Her tone is friendlier now. "The dog looks familiar. Has he been here before?"

"I have no idea. Maybe. His name used to be Cornelius. Does that ring a bell?"

"I'd definitely remember a dog with the name Cornelius." Her forehead scrunches up like she's thinking hard. "Still, he looks really familiar."

"He's kind of famous," Lanie says. "He's a ghost whisperer. Has a huge Facebook following?"

Dr. Brooks makes a face. "*That* I would definitely remember too. Oh well, it'll come to me eventually. Is there anyone who might be able to fill in his history?"

I pull out my cell phone and redial the last number on my log, but instead of getting Anthony or Aurelia, Deborah Van Dyke answers.

I tell her what happened to Paco and reassure her that he's going to be all right,

"Oh, I don't blame you a bit for trying to calm him down with medication. What a little beast. I have no idea why Susan took him in. He was always getting into things."

I don't bother to correct her assumption that I'd purposely given Paco the Benadryl. I'm more interested in her last statement. "You mean, he's gotten into pills before?"

"Not pills, but the dog was always getting into mischief. One time he chewed through the strap on my Louis Vuitton bag." I can hear her shudder over the line. "Thank God, I don't have to worry about that anymore. He's nothing more than a rude little mutt. My poor sister. I'm sure it was all his barking and carrying on that caused her heart attack."

"Heart attack? I thought Susan had cancer."

"She did, but it was in remission. Strangely enough, she died of a massive heart attack." For the first time, I hear empathy in Deborah's voice. "It was actually a blessing. Fast and quick. In her sleep. Susan was terribly afraid of lingering for weeks in pain. At least she was spared that."

I'm still processing this information when I glance up and see Dr. Brooks waiting patiently.

"Deborah, the vet needs Cornelius's health history. Is there any way—"

"Let me get you Aurelia. She'll know the information you need."

Aurelia gets on the line. I hand the phone over to Dr. Brooks who asks her the same questions she asked me earlier, only Aurelia can actually answer them.

Dr. Brooks echoes Aurelia's answers for confirmation which gives me a chance to find out more about Paco. He's about four years old, has no known allergies or significant health history, and surprisingly, Susan Van Dyke wasn't his first owner. She found him walking down the street a couple of years ago and took him in.

Dr. Brooks finishes up her conversation then hands me back the phone.

"Thank you," I say to Aurelia.

"Oh, Lucy! Poor little Cornelius. I'm just grateful that he's all right." I can hear Anthony in the background, shooting off a barrage of questions.

The next voice I hear on the line is his. "Lucy, it's Anthony here. Aurelia told me what happened. Is there anything we can do?"

"Not really, I mean, I'm just so grateful that Aurelia was able to provide a health history for the doctor."

"I don't understand. Cornelius has been naughty before, but never like this."

I gulp. "I must have left the pill bottle out by accident."

"That must be it. Aurelia had all of Susan's medication locked up tightly, so Cornelius was never tempted by them."

Talk about pouring salt over the wound.

"Susan was on a lot of meds, huh?"

"Oh yes. She was on all sorts of pain killers for her cancer. Aurelia was a wonderful nurse," he adds proudly. "She handled all of Susan's home regimen."

"Aurelia has nurse's training?"

"She was a certified nurse's assistant for ten years before she came to work for Susan as her cook. All that experience came in very handy when Susan became ill."

Dr. Brooks motions like she wants to speak to me again. "Anthony, I need to get off the phone. Please thank Aurelia again for the information."

"Certainly. And...you'll let us know about the séance?"

"Sure."

I hang up. "Sorry," I say to Dr. Brooks.

"No problem. So, let me fill you in on the plan of care. We'll need to keep Paco for at least twenty-four hours." She glances at her wristwatch. "It's already past ten. How about you plan to pick him up Friday morning? That will give us plenty of time to make sure his labs all come back normal. Barring any complications, which I have to warn you, could still happen, we should be able to give him a clean bill of health by then."

Complications. "Okay, sure, whatever is best for Paco."

"Can I ask, what you plan to do with the dog?"

Before I can answer, Will pipes up. "I'm taking the dog."

I whip around to face him. "For sure?"

He nods.

"Oh, Will! Thank you!"

Lanie claps her hands. "Yay for a happy ending!"

My happy ending glow is ruined when I see the preliminary vet bill. Will takes the paper from my hands. "He's going to be my dog, so I'll pay for his treatment."

I snatch the paper back. "That wouldn't be fair. I'm the one who messed up by leaving the pills out."

"Luce—"

"*Please*, Will, this is all my fault. I need to do this. Okay?" The urgency in my voice stops him from protesting again.

The door to the vet office opens. Brittany rushes in. "How's little Paco?" she asks breathlessly. "I came as soon as I heard the news."

I look at Will who shrugs. "She called my cell while we were waiting to hear from the doctor, so I left her a text explaining why I couldn't talk."

"Is he all right?" she asks again. "I've been so worried! What happened?"

"He accidentally got into a bottle of Benadryl," Lanie says, "but he's going to be okay."

"Thank God!"

"I didn't know you were so into dogs," I say.

"Oh, it's not just dogs. I love *all* animals."

"Brittany is this year's chairperson for the annual shelter fundraiser," says Lanie. "She's doing a terrific job, by the way.

I give up. Not only is Brittany giving away her prize money to feed the poor, but she's also a modern-day St. Francis of Assisi. Let's just go ahead and give her the Nobel Peace Prize while we're at it.

"Now that the crisis is over, I'm heading out," Lanie says. "If you need anything, Lucy, just let me know."

I give Lanie a big hug. "Thank you for all your help. You've been awesome."

"No worries." She waves goodbye to Brittany and Will before heading out the door.

Which leaves the three of us alone in the waiting room.

"Lucy," says Brittany, "Will told me all about your special project."

"My special—oh, you mean the séance?"

"Shh," she admonishes me, keeping her voice low. "We don't want the whole town to find out. Will told me what you need, and after some careful deliberation, I've decided to help you."

"You're going to give me the key to the rec center?" I can hardly believe my own ears. "That's great—"

"No need to give you the key, silly. Not when I'll be there to let you in and lock up later."

"You mean—"

"There's absolutely no way I'm going to let you have all the fun!" Her brown eyes glow with excitement. "I'm going to be there too. A real honest to goodness séance," she whisper-giggles. "I can hardly wait!"

20

THE WAY I SEE IT I HAVE THREE CHOICES:

A) I could cancel the séance.

B) I could go ahead with Brittany's plan and include her.

C) I could kill Brittany for her key and do the séance without her.

I'm *sooooo* tempted to pick C or at least some version of it that wouldn't actually include murder. Maybe I could just steal her key. But then I'd be no better than her (let's not forget the kindergarten paintbrush incident).

If I want to find out what really happened to Abby Delgado, then I have no choice but to go with B.

After we make plans to meet up tomorrow night at the rec center, we say goodbye to Brittany. I drop Will off at his place then head back home. My apartment that I love so much feels empty and sad without Paco.

Before we left the veterinary clinic, Dr. Brooks let me see him. He was hooked up to an IV, and he looked so small and pitiful. He stared up at me with his big brown eyes, his tail wagging furiously like he was happy to see me. Obviously, he has no idea what a loser I am. At least he doesn't blame me for his current predicament but then I'm blaming myself enough for the two of us.

After a fitful night, I wake up groggy, but with a clear plan in mind. I have to get my two suspects, Phoebe and Derrick, to let their guards down and confess to everything they know.

Phoebe won't be a problem. As head of the Sunshine Ghost Society, she'll be at the séance. But Derrick? I'm going to have to convince him to participate. Considering that he's threatened to have me arrested if I go near him again, it won't be easy.

It occurs to me that I might have an ally in all this. I fish out the business card that Gloria gave me and call her. We agree to meet me at The Bistro after the lunch crowd has waned. I take her up to my apartment, so we can have some privacy.

"What a great view," she says looking out my living room window.

"Isn't it? I was pretty lucky to score this place."

After spending the morning on my feet, I'm exhausted, so I flop down on my couch and motion for her to join me.

"I was sorry to hear about Paco," she says. "I'm glad he's going to be all right, but it will be a huge loss for tonight."

"Yeah, I was looking forward to seeing him in action." As in, running around trying to get everyone to pet him.

"Oh, he's *very* talented."

"But you'll be able to, you know, tap into Abby's spirit?"

"With your help, I believe so." She smiles and once again I'm reminded of how much younger she is than the rest of her crowd. It occurs to me that I don't know much about Gloria. Does she work? Or does she actually make a living off of being a medium?

"Do you mind if I ask a question? How did you get involved in the ghost business?"

"It's a long story."

"I've got time if you do."

She shifts around in the couch so that she's facing me. "My father died when I was a baby, so growing up, it was just my mother and me. She was wonderful. Very caring and supportive of everything I wanted to do."

"Like what, join the circus?"

Gloria laughs. "Hardly. I enlisted in the military."

"Oh wow. That's awesome."

"It's a good way to grow up fast. I spent four years in the army and earned enough money with the GI Bill to put me through college. Unfortunately, while I was away, my mother got sick. I was able to get home in time to spend her last days together."

An intense feeling of sorrow is behind her words. I've never been able to pick up so much emotion from another person before. It makes me feel sad as well.

"I'm so sorry."

She stares out the window. "It must be quite peaceful, sitting here in the evenings after a long day of work."

"It is rather spectacular."

"Still, I imagine it's hard to get away from your job what with the restaurant just downstairs. Deliveries at all hours, that kind of thing." She blinks, then smiles at me.

"It's not too bad."

"I know you'll find this hard to believe, Lucy, but after my mother died, she started talking to me. It was such a...balm to my soul. I knew I had to help other people connect to their loved ones as well."

She's right. I am finding this hard to believe. But *she* believes it, and that's what's important.

"After she passed, I got my degree in I.T. and came out to Florida to take a job with a local company."

"You...work?"

She laughs. "I'm just like most people. I work, pay taxes, that sort of thing. I'm fortunate that at this point in my career I'm able to work from home, so it gives me an opportunity to indulge my passion."

"Ever been married? Any children?"

She heaves a big sigh. "No to both of those. I've tried online dating, but most men aren't looking for someone who spends their free time communing with the dead."

"I guess not."

She pats me on the knee. "Now, you didn't invite me over here to talk about my love life. Did you?"

"Not exactly. Here's the thing, Gloria." I start off by explaining how the only way we're going to get inside the rec center is with Brittany's help.

"Actually, she could prove very useful besides just her willingness to provide the key. She was also present shortly after you found Abby's body, correct?"

"Yes, along with Sarah and Will."

"You should definitely invite them too. We really have no idea who Abby might have imprinted upon or who she might feel a kinship with."

The idea that Abby's ghost might be making herself at home inside Brittany makes me smile. "The more the merrier, huh?"

"In this case, yes."

"Then you don't mind if Aurelia and Anthony Finch come as well? Anthony called me this morning. Even though Paco won't be participating, they'd still like to come."

"I have no objection to that. They're a lovely couple."

"The thing is… I really think that Abby's brother should be there too. He was Abby's closest relative, and like you said, you never know who her spirit might gravitate to."

She frowns. "I don't know why I didn't think of that earlier. Yes, please invite him."

I hate deceiving Gloria about my intentions, but it's the only way that I can get Derrick to the séance. "I'm afraid that

Derrick and I got off on the wrong foot. But if you were to ask him maybe?" I hand her a slip of paper with Derrick's number.

"Of course. I'll give him a call. Like I said, the whole group is looking forward to talking to Abby again."

"Even Phoebe?" I ask, testing the waters. I wonder if Gloria suspects that Phoebe isn't as innocent in all this as she'd like everyone to think.

"Poor Phoebe. She's so insecure! Victor and I tried telling her over and over that Abby wasn't a threat to her position in the society, but she had trouble believing it. I'm sure she's not looking forward to whatever Abby has to tell her now."

Yeah, I bet.

Gloria gets up to leave. "So I'll see you tonight? Around midnight, outside the building?"

"I'll be there. And…you won't forget about calling Derrick?"

"Don't worry, Lucy. I'll make sure Derrick is there. Tonight, we'll talk to Abby. And all will be revealed."

21

_____

After Gloria leaves, I head over to the veterinary clinic to check on Paco.

"He's doing much better," Dr. Brooks assures me. "He's off the IV fluids, and we began introducing solid foods. Just a little chicken and rice." She hands me a pamphlet. "Here's a list of some dog food brands that I recommend. This breed is very susceptible to spinal cord problems, so you have to be careful to keep him at a healthy weight. Carrots are a wonderful treat. Most dogs really love them."

I glance at the list, noting that blueberry muffins and granola bars are definitely not included. "Thanks. I'll make sure to give this to Will."

I visit with Paco for about thirty minutes. He's back to his usual happy self, but I don't want to take him home before Dr. Brooks gives him the green light. "I'll come get you first thing in the morning," I say to him, stroking his back lightly. My throat tightens up. "And...we'll spend another night together before you go to live with Will. Okay? No worries. We'll see each other all the time. I promise."

Paco's tail stops wagging. He nudges me with his wet nose and once again I'm hit with the feeling that he knows exactly what I'm saying. I always knew I'd have to give him up eventually, and there's no one better to take him than Will, but I'm still torn up about the whole thing.

I hug him tightly and try not to let him see how wet my eyes are.

Since I'm expecting a long night, once I'm back home, I attempt to take a nap, but I'm too wired, so I go down to the kitchen to prep for tomorrow morning's breakfast. When I open the pantry, I realize that I'm almost out of flour. We're low on other essentials as well. Armandi's, our primary supplier, has never been so late with his deliveries. I call Sarah to ask if she knows anything about it, but she doesn't.

"I'll call Tony first thing tomorrow," Sarah says. Per Gloria's suggestion, I invite her to the séance, but she politely declines.

Will, who up to now has basically laughed at the idea, agrees to join us. "There's no way I'm letting you and Brittany do this without me."

I'm not sure what's motivating him. The opportunity to see what I predict will be the world's best acting job by yours truly or spending more time with Brittany. I have a strong feeling that it's the latter.

At exactly eleven-thirty p.m. Will's car pulls into the parking lot. I grab my sweater and tote and head out to meet him.

Ugh.

Brittany is with him. She's dressed in black yoga pants, a sleek black turtleneck sweater, and black sneakers. It's like she just stepped off the set of *Mission Impossible*.

"I wasn't sure what to wear to a séance, but this seemed the most appropriate," she says, eyeing my outfit of jeans and a baggy maroon and gold Florida State T-shirt.

Since Brittany is in the front with Will, I get into the backseat of the car. "Thanks again, Brittany. For helping us out here."

"This is pretty exciting, isn't it? Sneaking into a building in the middle of the night. It's like we're all…friends and we're on some kind of big adventure."

Something about her tone makes me uneasy. It's just occurred to me that I never see Brittany with anyone her own age. She's always either by herself or with her mother.

I catch Will's gaze in the rearview mirror. He raises a brow at me as if to say, *see what I mean?*

Maybe Will and Sebastian are right. Maybe Brittany isn't so bad after all. The two of us will never be real friends, but it wouldn't hurt for me to be more openminded about her.

Will parks his car a few blocks from the rec center. He hands us flashlights, and we begin the short trek.

"Isn't this fun?" Brittany whispers.

"Let's just hope no one gets in trouble here," Will mutters.

"Don't worry," I say. "I have a master plan."

We approach the building from the same side that I entered the day of the rec center celebration. "Hold on. We need to make sure the cameras don't catch us." I take out a towel from my tote and hand it to Will. "Toss this over the security camera in the corner over there."

"Why me?"

"Because you're the tallest. You're always bragging about how you're the best three-point shot maker on your basketball league. Here's a chance to prove it."

He grudgingly takes the towel, rolls it into a tight ball then tosses it high in the air. The towel falls perfectly over the camera, draping it completely.

"Yes!" Brittany looks up at Will adoringly. "That was awesome!"

"Not bad," I say, glancing at my watch. "It's T minus fifteen minutes, the rest of the gang should be here soon."

Brittany pulls out her key. "I'll go ahead and open up the room." She unlocks the door and steps inside.

"Remember, no lights," I warn.

I told everyone coming tonight to park anywhere but the rec center parking lot and to bring their own flashlights. The last thing we need is for some Good Samaritan to see the building lit up from the road and to report it to the police. Gloria said she would pass the info along to Derrick. I really hope she was able to convince him to come. Otherwise, this might all be for nothing.

Brittany and Will head into the building and I hang out by the door. Gloria is the first to arrive. She's dressed simply and has a small bag with her.

"Were you able to get ahold of Derrick?" I ask.

"Yes, and he said he'd be here."

"What did you say to get him to come?" Not that it matters, but I'm curious.

"I told him that tonight we'd be speaking to Abby's spirit and that if there was anything he needed to say to her, then this was his chance." She shrugs. "I might have also mentioned something about how we were going to ask Abby if she wanted to leave the Sunshine Ghost Society anything in her will. Even if Abby does tell us that she wants to leave the society some money, the authorities won't honor that. But Derrick seemed very motivated to make sure nothing slowed down getting his inheritance."

"That's *brilliant*."

She smiles. "You know, Lucy, you and I could be good friends. You should think of coming to one of our meetings."

Me? A member of the Sunshine Ghost Society? The idea is ridiculous, but I don't want to insult Gloria, especially not when she's been so helpful.

"Darn. I just joined a book club. Between that and The Bistro, I won't have enough time for anything else."

"What book club is that?" asks a voice from the dark.

I whip around to find Victor and Phoebe. "Oh, hey, Victor. Betty Jean Collins told me about it. Not sure if they have a name or anything." I really hope they don't have one of those cutesy book club names likes Babes and Books or something equally goofy.

"I'm in that book club," says Victor. "Betty Jean said she asked someone new to join, but I didn't know it was you, Lucy! Have you started reading the J. W. Quicksilver thriller? I think it's his best one yet."

"Yeah, um, I haven't started, but I'm really looking forward to it."

Oh boy. I guess now I'll have to go to the book club meeting next Thursday. I'll go to one meeting then drop out gracefully, citing a work conflict or something.

"Will you be bringing muffins?" Victor asks hopefully.

"I pretty much think that's a requirement."

"Can we get this séance over with?" Phoebe asks gloomily. She brushes past me to go inside the building.

Victor makes a face like he doesn't know what's wrong with Phoebe and follows her through the door.

Aurelia and Anthony show up next.

"How is dear sweet little Cornelius?" Aurelia asks.

"The vet says I can take him home in the morning."

"Thanks again for inviting us," Anthony says. "This might be our last chance to be around like-minded people for a while."

Aurelia nods. "We'll be leaving in a few days for our cruise. Who knows when our next séance might be?"

A figure emerges from the shadows. "Okay, so I'm here," Derrick says. "Now what?"

"Mr. Delgado," Gloria says pleasantly, "I'm so glad you were able to join us."

Derrick takes one look at me and freezes. "You didn't say she was coming."

"Lucy is the one who put the séance together. Without her presence, I'm not sure we'll be able to speak to Abby."

"I thought you said *I* was the one Abby wanted to speak to."

"It's a community effort." She links her arm through his. "Now that we're all here, why don't we join the others inside?"

22

———

THE ROOM IS SMALLER THAN I REMEMBERED. SINCE THIS IS A Pilates classroom there aren't any chairs, so we pull some mats from a closet and arrange them on the floor. Gloria instructs us all to sit in a circle.

She lights several candles and sets them in the middle of the circle, then takes her place across from me. I'm sitting cross legged between Victor and Brittany. It's dark and eerily quiet.

"Let's all hold hands, shall we?" Gloria's voice echoes off the walls adding to the spooky ambience, but all I can think is, thank God I'm not sitting next to Derrick because I would really hate to have to hold his nasty old hand. Plus, I have no idea if he even washes regularly. Who knows what kind of germs he could be spreading?

I gaze around the room. Phoebe avoids my eyes. Derrick glares at me, but that's okay. I expect by the end of the night he won't be looking quite so smug.

In Gloria's infamous words, *all will be revealed*.

I certainly hope so.

A few minutes go by. No one says anything.

Am I supposed to talk?

Is Gloria?

Just when I'm beginning to get antsy, Gloria begins. "Abby, dear friend, sister, and faithful colleague, we're gathered here tonight in hopes that you will speak to us from the Great Beyond. Come, Abby, be with us once more as you were in life. We beseech you to come out from the shadows and join us."

Silence.

O-kay. This is my cue to—

"Derrick?" a female voice asks hesitantly. "It's me, Abby."

Chills shoot up my spine, but not because we've made contact with Abby. It's Gloria disguising her voice, pretending to be Abby.

I don't know why I'm so disappointed in Gloria, but I am. I knew this séance was a sham, but I figured that at least she believed in it, but no. She knows *exactly* what she's doing. I can hear the lie in her fake voice.

"Abby?" Derrick asks gruffly. "Is that really you?"

"Yes, brother. It's me."

I'm surprised that Derrick is so gullible. I figured he would be a tough nut to convince. Maybe his guilty conscience is making him extra stupid.

"We've just made contact with Abby," says Gloria, using her own voice again. "Her spirit is willing to speak to us, but the connection is weak. I need everyone to keep their eyes closed and to concentrate on Abby. Those of you who were present when they discovered her mortal remains, think of that moment. Draw her spirit into yours."

Brittany squeezes my hand. Her eyes are shut tight like she's trying hard to do what Gloria wants.

"Derrick," says Gloria, using the fake Abby voice again, "I'm so glad you're here. We have a lot of unfinished business between us."

"We do?"

"I want you to know that despite our differences, I've always cared about you. I've always loved you."

"Same here, Abby." Derrick's voice trembles like he's on the verge of tears.

Gloria is good at this fake talking to the dead thing if she can bring a hardened character like Derrick Delgado to tears.

"And Phoebe?"

Yes, Abby?" There's fear in Phoebe's voice, which can only mean one thing. Just like I've suspected this whole time, she's guilty of something.

"I forgive you."

"Oh, Abby! Thank you! Thank you so much!"

Hold on a minute.

As entertaining as all this is, it isn't going the way I intended. I'm the one who called for this séance. It's *my* spirit Abby is supposed to be linked to. Not Gloria's. I can't very well have "Abby" forgive Phoebe for something until I know what it is and how it might have caused her death.

I think back to the last time I saw *Ghost*. How did Whoopi do it again? Oh, yeah. She just jumped right in.

"Derrick," I say, trying to sound trancelike. "It's Abby again. I've decided to talk to you through Lucy McGuffin, who, as everyone knows, makes the best muffins in town. Lucy, thank you for finding my body. I didn't like being left alone on this cold hard floor for so long."

A collective gasp sweeps through the room.

"What…what do you want, Abby?" Derrick asks.

"I want to thank you for stealing Cornelius for me. He's such a sweet little dog. I miss him."

"Er, yeah, we already went through that when you were alive. You're welcome."

"But, Derrick, remember. Cornelius is a special dog. He knows what *really* happened."

"So?" Derrick says defensively. "What's that supposed to mean?"

Not the reaction I expected.

"Oh, Abby, I'm so sorry!" Phoebe breaks in sobbing.

Aha. Here we go.

"You should be sorry, Phoebe. This is all your fault."

"Wait," Anthony whispers loudly, "I thought Abby just forgave her."

"Maybe she changed her mind," Aurelia mutters.

"I never meant…that is, it wasn't supposed to happen this way," Phoebe says. "You're right. It's my fault. You said you forgave me. Did you mean it?"

"On one condition. You have to tell everyone what you did to me. It's the only way your soul can be saved."

Brittany clutches my hand so tight I think it's going to fall off. She doesn't really believe this, does she? I must be better at this than I thought.

"Yes, yes, I'll confess to everything. I'm so sorry, Abby, I never meant for us to get in that big fight. I was just so jealous because you had Cornelius."

"Go on. Tell everyone what happened. It's the only way I'll ever be at peace. Otherwise, I might have to…haunt you forever. You wouldn't want that, would you?"

"No, no," Phoebe says. She takes a big breath. "After Derrick took Cornelius for Abby, I couldn't stand it. I just had to have him for my own. So…that Friday evening, I broke into Abby's house and stole him for myself."

I knew it!

"Abby was furious," continues Phoebe. "Not that I blame you, Abby, not one bit."

"Tell them the rest of the story," I command. I have to admit, this is kind of fun. No wonder Gloria is so into this.

"Abby called me and said she knew I'd taken the dog. We got in a huge fight, and she threatened to sic her pyscho brother on me if I didn't return him."

"Hey!" says Derrick, "Who's calling who a psycho here?"

"Silence!" I say in my best Abby-dead voice. "I want the truth and nothing but the truth! You're leaving out the important details. Like what happened when Cornelius bit you, and we had to get Father McGuffin involved for the exorcism."

"*Bit me*?" Phoebe sounds confused. "Cornelius never bit me, and that exorcism was *your* crazy idea."

Now I'm confused as well. If Phoebe wasn't the bite victim, then who was? Derrick?

"Forget about the bite for now. Continue."

"First, I need to know." Phoebe clears her throat. "Is it…very horrible where you are, Abby?"

"Yes," says Victor, "We need to know that you're all right."

Horrible?

Oh. I see what they're getting at.

"I'm in a wonderful place. Very quiet and lovely. And not hot at all. It's like…Florida, but in the winter. And I get to eat all the ice cream I want."

Phoebe lets out a huge sigh of relief. "Oh, Abby, I'm so happy for you!"

"Now, back to the business at hand. Everyone must know what really happened to me. For *their* sakes," I add ominously.

Phoebe nods. "So, Abby and me made a deal. Cornelius should be with the person he felt the strongest connection with. We decided to put him to the test and try to resurrect the old ghost haunting this place. Earlier Friday afternoon, I was here to help some of the Gray Flamingos with the pre-tour preparations, and I stole a key off of Gus Pappas. Abby and I agreed to meet here at midnight. I...oh, Abby I'm so sorry. I *cheated*. I came a couple of hours early with Cornelius, and I tried to get him to commune with the ghost, but nothing happened. All he did was run around the building and bark."

So that's how Paco got in the building. That part makes sense now.

"Tell the rest," I say.

"There's not much else. Abby met me at the prescribed time. I told her that Cornelius didn't respond to me so she could have him. You were so happy, Abby. Remember? We made up."

"Yes, I remember, Phoebe."

"Then Abby told me that she'd called Father McGuffin to come and act as an intermediary between us, but since I'd decided to give her Cornelius, there wasn't any need. I was... ashamed of what I'd done, stealing the dog and being so petty about the whole thing. I didn't want Father McGuffin to find out, so I left through the back door before he got here. In the end, I confessed it all to him anyway the next day at the grand opening celebration. I just didn't want all that hanging over me." She sniffles. "I'm so sorry, Abby. It all must have been too much for you. If I'd known you were going to have a heart attack, I would have stayed. I would have done CPR. Maybe I could have saved you."

No one says anything for a few minutes.

Everything Phoebe has said is the truth.

I feel awful making her relive all this. But at least now I know she didn't do anything to cause Abby's death.

Which leaves Derick.

"Thank you, Phoebe," I say in my Abby voice. "Derrick, it's time you told the truth now too."

"Me? But I haven't done nothin'."

"That's not exactly true, is it?"

"I already confessed to stealing the dog for you. What else do you want me to say?"

"You told the police you were at a poker game at your house till two in the morning and then you went to bed. You also told them that you were here at the opening day celebration and that's how your fingerprints got on the door knob. We both know those are lies. Come on, brother, tell them everything. Tell them how I looked the last time you saw me."

A strained hush descends over the room.

"Oh my God…" Derrick whispers hoarsely, "it *really* is you."

Now we're getting somewhere! It's hard to hide my smile of satisfaction, but I do my best to stay in Abby mode. I pause dramatically and glance around the circle to gauge everyone's reactions. Brittany, Victor, Phoebe, and Anthony all seem riveted. Derrick, too, now.

Will knows I'm faking it, so he's avoiding my gaze. Probably because he doesn't want to laugh and give me away. Gloria catches my eye, and there's a gleam of...admiration? No, it's more like resignation because I've stolen her little show away from her and she knows there's nothing she can do about it without exposing herself.

Aurelia is looking at me oddly. As if she's seeing me for the first time. It's eerie, actually. I stare back at her and blink, trancelike, and she quickly looks away.

"Of course it's me," I say to Derrick. "Go on. Let's finish this."

I can practically hear him sweating. "After Phoebe over there stole the dog away from Abby, my sister was pretty upset. Not that I blame her. What's the point of stealin' a dog just to have him stole out from under you? So she called me and told me all about their little arrangement. Said she didn't trust Phoebe to stick to her end of the bargain and she wanted me to come here as back up. Just in case things didn't go the way she planned."

"What?" Phoebe sputters. "Abby! You didn't trust me?"

"Didn't you just admit to cheating by coming here early that night?" I say in the Abby voice.

"I would never have—" She shakes her head like she can't believe it.

Oh boy. Talk about a complicated relationship. But back to Derrick and how he got his fingerprints on the door knob. "And you did come and help me, didn't you, brother?"

"Well, golly, Abby, you know if you'd still been alive, I would have done that CPT on you. But seein' as how you were dead, there wasn't much I could do."

The silence in the room is deafening.

Did Derrick just admit to seeing Abby's dead body?

"You mean CPR?" Victor asks.

"Yeah, sure, that too. Look, I know I should have called the police, but what good would that have done? I'm sorry, Abby, I really am."

I'm stunned, but I manage to squeak out a response. "It's all right."

"Does that mean I'm still in your will?"

Just as I'm about to respond, the door crashes open. The overhead lights flood the room, causing me to blink.

"What's going on in here?" We all look up to see Travis standing in the doorway. He slowly takes in the scene.

"Officer Fontaine, is the building secure?" asks a female voice over his radio. "Do you need back up?"

Everyone starts talking at once.

Travis puts a hand up in the air demanding silence.

He unclips the radio from his belt. "The building is secure. No back up needed. It was just a bunch of squirrels creating trouble."

Squirrels? I automatically shudder. Why did he have to bring them into the picture?

He and the dispatcher exchange a few more words, then he clips his radio back onto his belt. "I'd ask who's in charge here, but I have a pretty good idea." He turns and looks directly at me.

I swallow hard. "I can explain everything."

Phoebe looks around the now brightly lit room like she's just lost her best friend. "Abby, are you gone? Abby, please come back."

"Abby was never here," Aurelia says tightly. She stands and points a finger at me. "This one. She was faking it." The accusation in her voice makes me wince.

"Lucy!" Victor says, clearly shocked. "Is it true? Were you *faking* being Abby?"

Everyone turns to look at me, except Gloria, who can't very well throw stones here, can she? And Will, who knew my plan from the beginning. Everyone else looks at me with varying degrees of suspicion and disbelief, except for Brittany.

She crosses her arms over her chest. "Lucy would *never* lie to us like that. She's the most honest person I know. Right, Lucy?"

"Well...um—"

"You really are despicable," Aurelia sneers. "First your carelessness almost got poor Cornelius killed, and now you mock the very sanctity of the séance! What kind of person are you?"

Anthony wraps a protective arm around his wife's shoulder. "I don't know how we could have been so wrong about her."

"Okay, Okay, I admit, that was me pretending to be Abby, but I did it because it was the only way to get to the truth. I really thought...that is, I just wanted to make sure there wasn't any kind of foul play behind Abby's death. I did this for her." Sort of.

Brittany looks as if I've just told her there's no Santa Claus.

"You mean you thought I killed Abby?" Phoebe looks hurt, and that's worse than any shock or disbelief.

"Not *killed* exactly." Even though it's chilly, sweat trickles down my back.

"I knew all along it wasn't Abby we was talkin' to," Derrick says. "She never fooled me one bit."

"Not true," I say. "Otherwise you would have never told everyone how you found your sister dead already."

This gets Travis's attention. "People," he says, "Listen up. I don't know what you're all doing here, and frankly, I don't want to find out. But you're all guilty of trespassing. So if you don't want to spend the night in jail, then I suggest we break up this little campfire sing-a-long."

"Oh!" Brittany says, "Officer Fontaine, we weren't doing anything wrong. I promise. I have every right to be here. See?" She reaches into a secret pocket in her snug yoga pants and produces a key. "I teach a Pilates class here on Tuesday and Thursday nights."

"This is a Pilates class?" he asks incredulously.

"Not exactly," she admits.

"You all have five minutes to get out of here. Starting now." The restrained fury in his voice puts everyone into motion.

Gloria snuffs out the candles and begins putting away the mats. Victor and Phoebe woodenly follow her lead.

"We need to talk," Travis says to Derrick.

I follow Derrick over to listen to whatever Travis has to say. "Not you, Lucy," Travis says.

"But I'm the reason he admitted to finding his sister dead!"

Travis turns away to block me from the conversation, but no way am I going to miss out on this. So I hang back to listen.

"What's this about finding Abby dead?" he asks.

"You already know I took the dog," Derrick says in a whiny voice.

Travis nods curtly.

"So, I promised Abby I'd do whatever she needed to keep him. She'd paid me two hundred bucks, and she promised me another hundred if I just showed up that night. Kind of like back up. Not that I would have done anything to that other lady."

"What other lady are we talking about?"

Derrick points to Phoebe. "That one. She wanted the dog too. So they were meeting here that night to duke it out. Abby just wanted strength in numbers, you know? But I got to playin' poker and forgot about the time. After I finished playing, I got here as fast as I could. Abby had told me the side door was going to be open. When I got inside, she was already dead."

His voice falters. "I swear on my life. I would never do anything to hurt my sister."

"What time was this?" Travis asks.

"About two fifteen in slow time, I reckon."

"Why didn't you call the police the minute you found her?"

He groans. "You know why. I got a record. I didn't want anyone thinkin' the wrong thing. I swear, there wasn't nothin' I could do for her. She was stone cold dead. Besides, I knew they'd find her the next morning when they opened up the place."

Travis gives him a hard stare. "Against my better judgment, I believe you."

"So I can go now?"

"As fast as you can before I change my mind."

Derrick takes Travis's advice and hightails it out the door.

Gloria and the rest of her group brush past me without a word.

I get it. They feel deceived.

Anthony and Aurelia stop on their way out to confront me. Anthony looks down at me coldly. "We'd appreciate it if you never call us again. Any communication regarding Cornelius's welfare can be made through Susan's attorney."

"I'm sorry. I never meant to make anyone feel as if I was—"

"What?" Aurelia spits. "Poking fun at our beliefs?"

"No! That's not it at all."

She grabs Anthony by the hand, and they storm away.

This leaves just the four us, Brittany, Will, Travis, and me looking at one another.

"Sorry, man," Will says to Travis.

"I can't believe she talked you into this."

Will shrugs.

"But you have to admit, it worked, sort of," I say. "Now we know how Paco got into the building before Abby, and how Derrick's fingerprints got on the door knob."

"Which in the long run, doesn't change squat," says Travis. "Abby died of a heart attack. Case closed. You got all these people riled up for nothing."

Brittany spins around to face me. "I hope you enjoyed making me look like a fool. I thought you were my *friend*. You could have told me your plan. I would have gone along with it. But instead… I even stood up for you! I have no idea why you dislike me so much, Lucy. Ever since kindergarten you've had it out for me. Well, I'm through trying." She sniffs like she's holding back tears, then runs out the door.

Will gives me a look that makes my heart break. He wants to follow her, but he doesn't want to hurt my feelings. I don't want him to have to choose between Brittany and me, so I'll choose for him.

"It's okay. Go find her. I'll get my own ride home."

"I'll make sure Miss Misdemeanor gets home safely," Travis says.

"Thanks." Before Will leaves he turns to give me the *we'll talk later* look. I can practically feel the disappointment dripping off him.

I feel awful. Everyone is mad at me. It's like the day Mrs. Jackson accused me of taking the paintbrushes. All I wanted to do was help, but now I'm suddenly the bad guy.

Travis makes that growly sound in his throat that I'm beginning to get way too familiar with. "I know I'm going to regret this, but can you tell me what in hell you thought you were going to accomplish here tonight?"

"I thought I could get to the bottom of how Abby really died, so I had Gloria, and the rest of the Sunshine Ghost Society arrange a séance to bring Abby back. And it worked. Sort of."

We stand there staring at each other. It occurs to me that we're alone.

"You're dangerous, you know that?" His dragon green eyes bore into me. Right now, he feels kind of dangerous too, but in a totally delicious way.

For one crazy second, I swear Travis is going to kiss me.

Instead, he clears his throat and reaches over to turn off the lights. "C'mon. I'll take you home. I got a city to patrol."

23

It's Friday morning. Exactly one week ago today, I was happily serving customers, talking up the big rec center celebration and thinking about my Annette Funicello costume. The biggest worry on my mind was how high to tease up my hair and perfecting my mango coconut muffin recipe.

Boy. What a difference a week makes.

In *Beach Blanket Bingo*, the bad guys get their due, the surfers win the day, and Frankie and Annette end up together. But this isn't a Hollywood sixties beach flick. It's real life, and even though it's barely been ten hours since the séance broke up, just about everyone in Whispering Bay has heard about last night's debacle.

The whole town hates me.

Well, except Betty Jean, who thinks I'm a hoot.

"I knew you were the right person to invite to join our book club!" She leans into the counter. "Everyone in the club wanted to black ball you after they heard about how you tricked Victor, but personally, I think we need your kind of spunky blood! Yep. I can't wait to hear your take on the latest book. Have you gotten to chapter fourteen yet? It's my favorite. If you know what I mean," she says with a wink.

This is another way that my life has changed. Last week, the thought of joining Betty Jean's book club would have made me giggle. Now, all I can do is humbly nod and be grateful that at least someone in town wants my company. Someone besides Sarah that is. But she's my partner, so she has to like me.

The old Lucy might have lied and told Betty Jean that she'd already read the book or fake her way through the book club discussion, but I've changed my ways. No more lies for me. From now on, I'm going to be one hundred percent honest with everyone. No matter the consequences.

"I'm sorry, I haven't had a chance to read the book yet, Betty Jean, but I promise, I will."

"Okay," she warns, "But make sure you do. I can always tell when someone hasn't read the book. Oh, and bring muffins. Lots of them."

"Sure thing." I fill her order and look up to see the next person in line.

Yikes. It's Gloria and Phoebe and Victor.

Sarah comes out from the kitchen and immediately sees my dilemma. "I'll take their orders, Lucy."

"Thanks, but I have to face the music." I turn and give them my biggest smile. "Good morning, how can I help you?"

"Coffee and a breakfast sandwich," Phoebe says stiffly.

"Would you like a muffin with that?"

"No muffins for me. Not now and probably not ever."

My stomach sinks. "Okay. Coming right up."

Victor is equally frosty.

Gloria is a little friendlier, but not much. "We thought about going to Heidi's Bakery. Their biscuits are infinitely superior to the ones here, but why should we deprive ourselves of the view?"

"Look, I never meant to hurt anyone. For what it's worth, I'm really sorry."

They ignore my apology and take their coffees over to their table. I guess I can't blame them. In their minds, I made fun of something they truly believe. Which makes me a bully. Or worse.

"Sorry about that, Lucy," says Sarah. "Is there anything I can do?"

"Not really."

She pats my shoulder. "It'll be okay. People will get over it."

"Eventually?"

"Yeah." She smiles. "The good news is I signed all the waivers you forwarded me from The Cooking Channel. They have to pick you for *Muffin Wars*. Otherwise, why go to all the bother to come out here and film us?"

"It does sound pretty positive, doesn't it?" I don't want to get my hopes up too much, but on the other hand, this *Muffin Wars* gig is all I have to look forward to right now.

"By the way," Sarah says, "We just got a delivery from Armandi's Supplies."

"Thank God. I was down to my last cup of flour." Which is an exaggeration, but still. The Bistro's pantry was getting pretty skimpy. "Did Tony say why he was so late with the delivery?"

"He said he came by a couple of days ago but we were closed, and you weren't here."

"Why does he insist on coming after hours all the time?"

Sarah grins. "I think he's hoping to catch you alone so he can flirt with you."

I laugh. "More like show off pictures of his thirteen grandchildren." Tony Armandi must be at least sixty. He's a total sweetheart, and his prices are the best for top quality items.

"Say, how's Paco doing?"

"I called the clinic this morning. According to the vet, he's good to go. I'm picking him up after the lunch crowd leaves."

"And it's for sure that Will is going to take him?"

"I'm going to have one last night with him then bring him over to Will's in the morning."

"Did I just hear my name?"

I turn around and see Will and Sebastian in line.

"The usual?" I ask.

They both nod.

"I'll get their food ready, Lucy. Why don't you take a break?" says Sarah.

I take her up on her offer, pour myself a cup of coffee and join Will and my brother at a table as far away from the Sunshine Ghost Society as physically possible.

"Get any sleep last night?" Will asks.

"A little." I glance at my brother. "I suppose like the rest of the town you already know all about last night?"

Sebastian smiles in his kindly priest way, which means he must really feel sorry for me. "It'll blow over."

"Eventually." It seems as if that's my word of the day.

"How's Paco?" Will asks.

"Good. I'm picking him up from the clinic in a few hours. Thanks for letting me have one last night."

"He's really your dog, Lucy. I'll just be watching him for you."

"That's not really true." Boy, do I ever sound like a Debbie Downer. I do my best to smile and mean it. "So tonight's the big date with Brittany. Don't forget to put on deodorant."

Instead of laughing, Will makes a pained face. "I'm not sure tonight's going to happen. Brittany is pretty mad at me. She thinks I was in on the fake séance, which I was. I guess I can't blame her for being upset."

"But…that's all on me!"

"No worries, Luce. It's not like I ever really stood a chance with her anyway."

My eyeballs practically explode out of my sockets. "Are you *kidding* me?" I shout. "What do you mean you never stood a chance with her? Will…you're completely *awesome*! You're brilliant and funny and kind and loyal and—"

Sebastian looks at me funny.

And Will looks…embarrassed.

I slowly gaze around. The entire place is gawking at me. My gaze lands on Sarah. Her blue eyes are filled with sympathy.

"And…your breath only stinks half the time," I end woodenly.

Will chuckles uncomfortably, but it's too late. *I've outed myself.*

Sebastian knows it. I know it.

And Will knows it too.

This is turning out to be the worst twenty-four hours of my life.

I jump up from the table. "Don't worry. I can fix it. I'll tell Brittany that last night was all on me."

"Lucy, it's okay," I hear Will say.

But I'm already half way to the kitchen. I tear off my apron and toss it onto the counter. Sarah rushes to follow me. "I need to go," I tell her. "Right now."

"Yes, no worries. Go get Paco. Take the rest of the day off."

"Thanks," I mutter. I plan to do exactly that, but first I have to try and make things right again.

The Whispering Bay Chamber of Commerce is located on Main Street next door to Heidi's Bakery. I open the door and Ginny, the receptionist automatically smiles. Then when she sees it's me, the smile fades.

"Oh, it's you."

Really? Does no one in Whispering Bay have a freakin' sense of humor?

"Is Brittany in?"

"May I ask what this is about?"

Enough is enough. "Tell her that as a local business owner, I need to speak to her pronto."

Ginny falters a moment.

"The Chamber of Commerce still works to promote local businesses, right? Which means you work for me."

She sighs. "She has five minutes before she has to leave for a meeting. I'll let her know you're here." She picks up her phone and almost immediately, Brittany comes out of her office.

Her auburn hair looks sleek and shiny. She's wearing a black linen shift that fits her size two frame perfectly. With every step she takes in her four-inch heels, she exudes confidence and poise. No wonder Will is crazy about her. Who wouldn't be?

"Lucy," she says stiffly. "How can I help you?"

Apparently, we're going to have to do this out here in the waiting room with Ginny as our audience.

"Look, I came over here to tell you that Will had no idea what was going down last night, but that would be a lie. He knew I was going to pretend to be Abby and he went along with it. He didn't do it to make fun of anyone or make anyone look foolish. He did it because I asked him to because he's my best friend. He's the best guy I know, Brittany. He's… everything and more. And he really really likes you. He's liked you forever. If you want to be mad at someone, then be mad at me. But Will doesn't deserve it."

Brittany's bottom lip quivers.

"And for what it's worth, I was never making fun of you. And… I'd like for us to be friends. Maybe. If that's what you want."

"Oh, Lucy!" She grabs me in a hug. "Really? I want that too!"

"So, we're good?" I'm a little dazed by how well this is going.

"Absolutely!"

I can't believe I'm about to say this. "And you'll give Will a chance?"

"Definitely. If you think he's so awesome, then he must be."

Not exactly the answer I'm looking for, but it will have to do.

"Okay, then."

"When can we have lunch?" she asks eagerly.

"Huh?"

"Lunch, silly! All best friends have lunch together." She snaps her fingers at Ginny. "Check my calendar and see what day I have free next week. Oh, Lucy, we have so much to talk about!"

We do?

Ten minutes later, I walk out the door in a daze with plans to meet my new "best friend" for lunch next Wednesday.

Lunch with Brittany on Wednesday and book club with Betty Jean on Thursday. I'm still trying to wrap my head around my new social calendar when Paco comes bounding through the clinic door to greet me. He wags his tail and jumps up and down.

The vet tech goes over Paco's discharge instructions, then I head to the front desk to face the music. It's a good thing my credit card has a healthy limit. Otherwise, I'm not sure how I'd pay the enormous bill waiting for me. The figure at the bottom of the paper makes me queasy. When I hand the receptionist my credit card, she informs me that the bill has already been charged to my card since it's on file and that she's mailed the receipt to my account.

"My account?"

She nods. "I mailed it to the address we had for the dog."

"Oh, okay great. Thanks."

I really hope I hear from The Cooking Channel soon. That ten-thousand-dollar prize money can't come fast enough.

I put Paco in the car, and we head home. After everything that's happened, I just want a quiet night in. My cell phone buzzes. It's Will. I put him on my car speaker phone then I take a deep breath and try to pretend that my little outburst from this morning never happened.

"Hey," I say.

"Hey, yourself."

"I went to see Brittany this afternoon."

"She told me. You didn't have to do that, Lucy."

"Yes, I did. So…everything still on for tonight?"

"Yep."

"Good."

"What about you? How are you doing?"

I glance over at Paco, who's watching me expectantly. It's like he knows what's at stake here with my answer. "I figure the town is going to have to forgive me or else find another way to get their muffin fix."

He laughs, but it sounds off.

I gulp. Have I ruined our friendship forever?

"Seriously, Cunningham, I'm fine. I have Paco sitting next to me, and we're going to order pizza and watch T.V."

"Sounds like fun. I'll swing by tomorrow morning and get him."

"Or I can drop him off. Whatever works for you."

"Sure. And, Lucy? Thanks for making things okay with Brittany."

"Anytime. You know you're like a brother to me."

24

Paco and I swing by Tiny's Pizza and get the anchovy and mushroom special. Will hates anchovies, but since I'm doing pizza night solo this week, I can get whatever I want.

I take a long hot bath, open a bottle of wine and settle in on my living room sofa with Paco and my pizza. I've reheated it in the oven, so it's bubbly hot. This is another thing Will and I disagree on. He thinks nuking pizza is perfectly acceptable, but I prefer to take the extra time to heat it back up the right way (which is *always* the oven).

I flip through the channels.

I've watched just about everything on Netflix, and the Hallmark Channel has already begun its Christmas programming, which I'm totally into, but the movie they're playing is one I've seen three times already.

I scroll back to the main channels and lo and behold, *America's Most Vicious Criminals* is starting. It's a new episode featuring all their unsolved cases, including Will's favorite, The Angel of Death. He's going to kick himself for missing this. I hit the record button on my DVR so that he can watch it later.

I wonder if Jim Fontaine knows about this special episode. I wish I had his number so I could call him. Maybe I should let Travis know so he can call his dad. Except Travis and I didn't exactly part on the best of terms the other night. So, no. Bad idea.

The opening credits begin. I love the theme music to this show. It's so wonderfully eerie that if the subject matter didn't already spook you out, the music alone would do it.

I finish off my first slice of pizza, and only give Paco the teeniest bit of the leftover crust. "Just this one time," I say as he eagerly gobbles it down.

"Welcome to a special edition of *America's Most Vicious Criminals*." The male host's deep somber voice adds another layer of creep to the experience. "Tonight, we'll be revisiting cases involving our most notorious serial killers. The one thing they all have in common? They've never been caught."

Oh, I can already tell this is going to be epic.

A younger Jim Fontaine appears on my screen. "Detective Fontaine, what do you think the Angel's motive was to commit murder?" asks the show's host.

Jim rubs his jaw thoughtfully. "That's a question I've asked myself a lot over the past year, and honestly, the only thing I can come up with is that she or he thinks that what they're doing is for the victim's good. It's what I refer to as a God complex. The Angel thinks that they're helping ease a patient from their suffering, but no one has a right to take anyone's life. Not under any circumstances."

They show some pictures of the Dallas hospitals where the Angel struck.

"Our killer may or may not have been a nurse, but they definitely had enough medical knowledge to know how much morphine to use to overdose a patient, and how to administer it," Jim says.

As I'm watching, something Deborah Van Dyke said flashes through my head. She said she was grateful that her sister died quickly of a heart attack instead of lingering with the pain of cancer. It seems oddly similar to these cases. Only a morphine overdose wouldn't cause a heart attack. Would it?

And then I'm reminded of something else she said right after I told her that Abby had passed.

I had no idea Florida was so dangerous.

At the time I thought it was just a boorish observation, but now...

Both Abby and Susan died of heart attacks less than a week apart. Both women knew each other. And both women had links to Cornelius.

She was on all sorts of pain killers for her cancer. Aurelia was a wonderful nurse. She handled all of Susan's home regimen...

This was never released to the press or featured in the T.V. show, but our Angel left a note each time they struck... R.I.P...

Yes, poor lamb… She makes the sign of the cross… May her soul rest in peace…

Rest in peace?

Could Aurelia be some sort of copycat killer?

Only Jim said that the police never revealed the R.I.P. notes, so that part doesn't jibe.

My mind is whirling with a million possibilities when my cell phone rings. It's the Gulfside Veterinary Clinic. Shouldn't they be closed by now? Then I remember it's a twenty-four-hour emergency facility.

"Hello?"

"Is this Lucy McGuffin?"

"Speaking."

"Hi Lucy, this is Emily, I'm the night receptionist at the veterinary clinic. I was just going over today's charges when I saw that we accidentally sent your receipt to another account. But no worries, your credit card number wasn't on the statement. Just your name and address and the final amount."

"Oh. That's weird."

"Yeah. I'm so sorry. This has never happened before, but since the dog was in just last week, we assumed the account was the same."

I still. "You mean, Paco was at the clinic last week?"

"Yeah, only his name wasn't Paco then. But it's definitely the same dog. Those I.D. chips don't lie."

"His former name was Cornelius."

"Mmmm, according to our records the dog was named Fido."

Fido? "Can I ask who brought the dog in?"

"The name on the account is Jane Smith."

"Let me get this straight. A woman named Jane Smith brought a dog named *Fido* into your clinic. Doesn't that sound strange to you?"

"A little," she admits.

"Can I ask you what he was brought in for?"

"Dog bite."

"He was bitten by another dog?"

"No. He bit his...well, I guess she's not his owner since you have the dog. This is all pretty confusing. It reads here that a woman by the name of Jane Smith brought the dog in last week for a rabies test. She said he'd bit her, and she wanted to make sure that he wasn't rabid. The chip I.D. said that the dog was registered to a woman named Susan Van Dyke and he was current on all his shots, so that was that. But we always open up an account for every client who comes in the door." There's a pause. "Uh-huh."

"What?"

"Whenever a dog bites a human, we're required to report it to the city, in case the dog has a history of aggression. Since the owner, er, this Jane Smith person seemed okay, we let her take the dog home, but there's always a follow up. There's a note at the bottom of the record stating that when animal control went out to the address she'd given, it didn't pan out. It was an abandoned lot."

"Did this Jane Smith pay with a credit card or a check?"

"Cash."

"Which makes her basically untraceable."

"Well, yeah."

"Do you remember what she looked like?"

"Sorry, I wasn't here. But like I said, no worries about your credit card being compromised. Oh, hold on. Dr. Brooks might remember her." In the background I hear Emily and Dr. Brooks exchange a few words.

"Lucy? This is Dr. Brooks. How is Paco doing?"

Paco is currently wolfing down a piece of pizza that he's stolen off my plate, anchovies and all, but I think I'll omit this piece of information. "He's doing great, thanks."

"Emily told me about the mix up with the account. So sorry about that. I knew I remembered seeing Paco, but the circumstances were just so different, it didn't come to me until now."

"Did you see the person who brought him in? This Jane Smith person?"

"I remember she was pretty upset about being bitten, and the dog seemed so *hostile* toward her. He kept barking and snarling. It really worried me at first, but when we got him alone, he was the sweetest little thing. We checked him out, and he was fine. But we still had to report it to the authorities."

"What did Jane Smith look like?"

"Let's see, I'm so bad with faces. I'm much better with dogs, you know? But if my memory serves me right, she was probably in her late thirties, maybe early forties. Long blonde hair with some gray. Yes, that's it. I remember now thinking how much younger she'd look if she washed the gray out."

"Okay, thanks."

I can't get off the phone fast enough. My hands are shaking.

Holy wow.

I'd bet my spot on *Muffin Wars* that Gloria Hightower is the mysterious Jane Smith.

I think back to the morning that she came into The Bistro with Victor and Phoebe and Paco went crazy barking. I'd assumed his hostile demeanor had all been for Phoebe, but now in hindsight, I realize it must have been Gloria he was barking at.

But why on earth would Paco bite Gloria? He's the sweetest dog ever.

Except when someone he cares about is being threatened.

Could *Gloria* have done something to Susan Van Dyke to cause her heart attack?

I have to tell Travis asap. Except, Travis thinks I'm crazy. He's never going to take me seriously. But Jim will. I quickly put on my sneakers and grab a jacket. I might not have his phone number, but I know where he lives.

"I'm going out for a few minutes," I tell Paco. "You be a good boy and stay put. No getting into any of my medication—"

My mind jolts back to something Gloria said to me the other day while she was here.

I imagine it's hard to get away from your job what with the restaurant just downstairs. Deliveries at all hours, that kind of thing.

How does Gloria know that we get deliveries after hours?

Sarah said that Tony was here a couple of days ago to make a delivery, but that no one was home. It was the day that Paco got into the Benadryl. Could Gloria have driven by and seen the delivery truck in our parking lot? Or maybe it was just an innocent comment inspired by the view from my living room window.

Except, the only window from my apartment that looks down on the parking lot is the one in my bathroom, and Gloria was never in my bathroom. Unless…

I didn't leave the Benadryl out! I didn't leave the cap off the bottle.

I'm *not* the worst dog mother ever.

Gloria broke into my apartment (okay, so I made it really easy by leaving the back door unlocked). She then deliberately gave Paco the Benadryl and tried to make it look as if it was due to carelessness on my part.

But why?

My entire body goes cold as the pieces all fall together into a neat little pile.

The first victim was probably someone important to her. A patient or family member she cared about and didn't want to see suffer anymore, so she slipped them a little extra morphine.

I run down the stairs, grab my car keys off the rack near the kitchen door, and—

Whack!

The back of my head explodes.

The last thing I see before everything goes fuzzy is Gloria standing over me with a syringe in her hand.

25

I wake up with a massive headache and a mouth that feels like it's stuffed with cotton.

What am I doing lying on the floor in The Bistro kitchen?

Then I remember that I have to tell Jim about Gloria Hightower. I try to get to my feet, but my hands are bound together tightly at the wrists, making it difficult. I grab the edge of the counter and slowly pull myself up.

"I was beginning to think that frying pan to the head did you in."

I whirl around. *Ugh*. Not a good idea. My stomach feels like a volcano that's about to erupt. Gloria stands just a few feet away, calmly holding a syringe in her hand.

My gaze darts to the kitchen door. I need to make a run for it. Under normal circumstances, I'm pretty confident I could outrun her, but with my hands tied and my head swirling, I'm not so sure.

Does she plan to inject me with that thing?

What's in it anyway?

"I take it you plan to overdose me with morphine? Or something that will make it look like I've had a heart attack?"

"Take a deep breath, Lucy. You're hyperventilating." Her tone is smug and condescending.

"And you're the Angel of Death."

She raises a brow. "All those fancy FBI people and Dallas detectives. None of them could figure it out. But you did. It really is too bad. I'm going to miss you. But I'm going to miss your muffins more."

As far as offhanded compliments from psychotic killers go, I could do worse.

"Sorry to disappoint you, but I'm not going anywhere, Gloria."

"Oh, I'm afraid you are. I can't have you running around telling everyone who I am, can I? And in case you're wondering, it was potassium that I gave Susan and Abby. Too much isn't good for the heart I'm afraid." She lifts the syringe up to the light to admire its contents. "This isn't potassium, though. You're much too young to stage a heart attack. Don't worry, Lucy, I'm not going to let you suffer. I'm not a cruel person. Just the opposite. I made sure there's enough morphine here to put you to sleep. Once you're out, I'll knock you on the head hard enough to do the trick this time. It's really shocking how Whispering Bay has become so dangerous. Someone broke into the kitchen intending to rob the place. You came down and caught them... Use your imagination. Everyone will be terribly sad, but believe it or not, life will go on without you."

The casual way she describes my murder makes my skin crawl.

"How do you get it? The morphine and the potassium? I mean, you just can't walk into a drugstore and get those."

"Didn't I tell you I was in the military? I guess what I didn't tell you was that I was a medic. I stayed in the reserves for almost a decade after getting out. Yes, ma'am, every other weekend I marched myself off to do my duty."

"Gee, thank you for your service."

"Your sarcasm isn't very patriotic." She shrugs. "Oh well. Where was I? The potassium was easy, but the morphine? That was a little harder to pilfer. I've had the vials for almost five years. In case I needed them, which I did. I'm pretty sure this stuff stays potent long after the expiration date. At least I hope so. For your sake." Gloria glances toward the door that leads up to my apartment. "Now, before I put you to sleep, where's Cornelius?"

A chill runs down my spine. She's not going to stop with killing me. She's going to kill Paco too. "He's not here. He's still at the veterinary clinic.

"Bull."

"It's true. You did a good job almost killing him the other night. He's still on IV fluids and medications."

She studies my face like she's trying to figure out if I'm lying or not. Good thing she doesn't have my special gift. Of all the lies I've told in the past week, this one is the most important.

"You don't have to hurt him, Gloria. He's not a threat to you." *Please, Paco. Please stay upstairs and keep quiet.* I chant this over and over in my head. I don't for one minute believe that he's any kind of ghost whisperer, but he does have a strong intuitive nature, and for some reason, he's bonded to me. *Stay upstairs, baby. Save yourself. Hide under the couch.*

"Don't look at me that way. I never meant to hurt Cornelius. He's an exceptional dog. So talented. Unfortunately, that was his downfall. The little minx saw me inject Susan with the potassium and he bit me." She raises her pants leg to show me a red bite mark about an inch above her ankle. "Thank God I didn't need to get a rabies shot. I'm afraid of needles." She laughs like this is funny.

I discreetly try to wiggle my wrists to try to loosen the slack on the rope. I have to keep her distracted, so she doesn't notice what I'm doing. The large heavy frying pan staring at me from the counter is a hell of a motivation.

"You're not just a murderer, you're a crazy murderer and a *faker*. But then I've always known that. You're about as much of a medium as I am."

"I have to admit, you surprised me the other night at the séance. I had no idea you were going to pretend to be Abby. You're clever, just not clever enough. You should have stuck with trying to perfect your mango coconut muffin recipe. As for being crazy? Is it crazy to want to help people? Then guilty as charged. And I don't plan to stop either."

"What? You're going to go around killing more people?"

Her voice hardens. "Don't be so dramatic. I'm not going to kill anyone else, well, besides you. The Angel of Death retired fifteen years ago when she moved here to Whispering Bay. These days I help others by communicating with their deceased loved ones. It's been wonderfully therapeutic for me."

"What about Susan Van Dyke?"

"Susan was an anomaly. She needed my particular kind of help, and I had to give it to her.

"Just like you had to help your mother?"

"Yes. Just like that."

"So Susan *asked* you to kill her?"

"Kill is such a nasty word. I eased her into the next world. She has no idea the pain and suffering I saved her."

"And Abby? You think you helped her too?"

She sighs heavily. "Abby was an unfortunate incident. Just like you. She knew too much, and she had to go. Like I said, you're too clever. You should have let it go, Lucy. Even the police were willing to write off Abby's death. But no. You had to keep pressing, didn't you?"

My head is starting to feel better. Maybe if I keep her talking long enough, it'll stop spinning, and I can make a run for the door.

"So, Abby knew you killed Susan? Or did she figure it out after the dog bit you? That's what happened, right? Abby might not have known what you did to Susan, but she knew that Cornelius had an irrational hate for you. It was only a matter of time before someone else saw it and put two and two together."

"I know what you're doing. I watch T.V. too. This is the part of the plot where the *murderer* has the too-smart-to-let-live busy body tied up and confesses everything while the busy body tries to escape. Sorry, Lucy, but that only happens in really bad James Bond movies." She comes at me with the syringe.

"Wait!" I plead. "Will Cunningham is on his way over. He should be here any minute. Any second now. You'll never get away with this. And...you're right, Gloria. You were only trying to help people. I see that now."

The rope is beginning to loosen, but it's still too tight to allow me any real movement of my hands.

"Good try, but you'll say anything to save yourself. And Will is out on his big date with Brittany tonight."

At the look of surprise on my face, she snickers. "That's the thing about small towns. Everyone knows what everyone else is doing and when they're doing it. Poor Lucy. I've felt so bad for you. In love with your best friend and all this time, he's clueless. But he's a man. We can't expect them to be as astute as we are. I'm afraid that at this point of the night, you're probably the last thing on Will Cunningham's mind."

If I could grab that frying pan and smack the look off Gloria's face, I would.

Which isn't a bad idea...

I inch toward the frying pan. Unfortunately, it also takes me closer to Gloria, but it's my only hope. If I run, she'll overpower me. I know that for sure now.

"You're right," I say trying to sound resigned. "Will isn't coming over here tonight. He wants Brittany. Not me."

"He has wonderful taste in books, but in women?" She shakes her head. "I'm sorry, Lucy."

The knot on the rope seems to be easing. I have to keep her talking so she doesn't realize what I'm doing.

"I know you're not a bad person, Gloria. If you were you'd have killed Cornelius after he bit you. Instead, you took him to the vet. Didn't you?"

"I had to make sure he didn't have rabies. No one even missed him! I thought he would be fine with Anthony and Aurelia and I'd never have to see him again, so I dumped him back off at the house. But then Abby convinced her dimwitted brother to steal the dog. As long as that dog is hanging around, I'll always be in jeopardy."

A movement near the doorway catches my attention.

Oh no. It's Paco.

How he came down the stairs without making noise is a miracle. Usually, his nails make that annoying click-click-click sound. It's like he purposefully snuck down the stairs. He's standing in the doorway, and he's looking at me with his soulful brown eyes. Only there's anger in them.

I know exactly what he's going to do.

Oh. My. God.

I hope it works. Or we'll both be dead.

Gloria uncaps the syringe. "It's all right, Lucy," she says in an eerily soothing voice. "It won't hurt. In a few minutes you'll go to sleep, and it will all be—

Paco leaps from his hiding place near the door and sinks his teeth into Gloria's ankle. Vaguely, it dawns on me that it's the same ankle he bit before. *Way to go, Paco!*

"*What the*—" Gloria howls in pain. "Get off me, you horrible little beast!" The syringe drops from her hand onto the floor.

The frying pan on the counter lies between us. We both reach for it at the same time.

Only I'm faster.

I grab hold of the handle and swing it as hard as I can, hitting Gloria on the side of the head. "Take that, you crazy bitch!" At the same time, the kitchen door crashes open.

We both turn to look.

Will stands there with his mouth open.

Gloria turns to me, blinks like she's in a daze, then crumbles to the floor.

I wiggle out of the ropes around my wrists. Paco lets go of Gloria's ankle and jumps into my arms. "Good boy, Paco!"

"Lucy!" The look of disbelief on Will's face is almost funny. "What in God's name—what the hell happened here?"

I point to Gloria's limp body lying on the floor. "Gloria Hightower is the Angel of Death. She killed Susan Van Dyke and Abby Delgado."

26

Sarah makes another pot of coffee while I struggle to balance a bag of melting frozen peas over the lump on my head. I'm sitting on a chair in The Bistro dining area with my feet propped up while Sebastian scolds me. "Why didn't you call Travis the second you realized who Gloria was?" he demands.

"Well if I'd known a crazed serial killer was waiting for me down in the kitchen I would have."

"Ever heard of locking your door?"

"I lock my door." At least I do now. Ever since the night I came home to find Paco unconscious, I've been careful to double check. I doubt I'll ever forget again. "I can't help it if Gloria knows how to pick a lock."

Will hands me a fresh bag of ice to replace the bag of peas. "Go easy on her, Sebastian. She's had a rough night."

I'll say.

After Will came bursting through the kitchen, he called 911. Travis and Rusty arrived within minutes and took Gloria down to police headquarters. An ambulance came too. The EMTs insisted on taking me to the hospital in Panama City. After they checked me out head to toe, they discharged me with precautions.

The first thing Will did when we got back was to call Sarah and tell her what happened. Sarah's husband Luke called his sister Mimi, the mayor, and despite the late night hour, within thirty minutes half of Whispering Bay either dropped by to check on me or called. Which is really flattering, except I'm not sure whether it's to see if I'm okay, or if they're just worried they might not get their muffins this morning.

"You're right," Sebastian says. "I'm sorry, Lucy. I'm just really thankful that you're all right. But promise me, you'll never do this again."

"Do what? Provoke a crazy killer into coming after me? Okay, I promise."

Paco barks happily. I kiss him on the nose. "Good boy. You saved my life."

"Thank God for the dog," says Sarah.

"He's a special one, all right." I look at Will. "Sorry, but there's no way I can give him up."

Will doesn't look surprised. "What are you going to do about your allergy?"

"I'm sure Dr. Nate can help me with that." I ruffle the top of Paco's head. "What do you say? Want to stay with me?"

He barks again like he approves, and we all laugh. I swear that dog can understand everything going on around him. How else did he know that I needed him? He might not be a ghost whisperer, but he's definitely a hero.

Sarah brings us all coffee. "I just can't believe it. All this time, Gloria Hightower was a killer. And she seemed so normal!" She glances over at Victor and Phoebe who are talking to Viola and lowers her voice. "Well, except for the ghost stuff."

Phoebe picks up on the first part of the conversation. "I always knew there was something off about her."

Victor nods eagerly. "Me too. I never did trust her. No sirree."

Considering that Gloria has been part of their ghost society for the past fifteen years, you'd think they'd have spoken up a little earlier.

Everyone starts trying to one up each other with their most suspicious Gloria stories. Will goes off to the kitchen. I quietly follow him.

"Hey, I haven't had a chance to thank you."

"For what?"

"For showing up in the nick of time."

"I didn't do anything. Except call the cops, and you could have done that all on your own. If anything had happened to you…" He reaches out and grabs me in a fierce hug.

"Listen," I say stroking his back. "I'm okay. Really."

He breaks off the hug, but I can tell he's still shaken by tonight's events. I am too, but I'm trying hard to keep it all together.

"What were you doing here anyway? How was your date with Brittany?"

"The evening ended early," he says meaningfully.

"Oh?"

"Brittany is great. We just…didn't have a lot to talk about."

My heart starts thumping wildly. "Maybe the next date will go better."

He rakes a hand through his hair. "Lucy, about what you said the other morning—"

The kitchen door opens. "Hey," says Sarah. "Travis is here, and he has big news."

Will and I look at one another. The ER doctor told me that someone needed to stay the night with me to make sure I didn't develop a concussion. If I ask Will, he'll do it. We can stay up and watch reruns of *America's Most Vicious Criminals* and eat cold pizza and maybe he'll tell me what he was about to say before Sarah interrupted us.

Travis is surrounded by people, all of whom are showering him with questions about Gloria, including Brittany. She takes one look at me and hugs me almost as tightly as Will did. "Lucy! Daddy just heard the news from one of the city councilmen so of course, I had to rush right over here. Are you all right? Oh my God! I can't believe it. Gloria killed Abby?"

I sigh wearily. "Yep." I appreciate everyone's concern, but I'm getting tired of telling the story over and over. I glance at Travis. "So, what's the news?"

Travis puts his hands up to get the room's attention. "Everyone, simmer down. Gloria Hightower confessed tonight to killing over ten people in Dallas, as well as Susan Van Dyke and Abby Delgado. She's going to be charged here in Florida, but I'm sure the Texas authorities are going to want to have their share of her too."

Everyone starts talking again.

Travis catches my gaze and tilts his head to indicate I follow him. We manage to find a semi-quiet corner of the restaurant. "How's your head?"

"A little sore but still the same Lucy," I joke.

"I don't know if that's a good thing or a bad thing."

"For you? Probably a bad thing."

He fights back a grin. "I stopped by my dad's place on the way over here to tell him the good news. He's ecstatic, by the way."

"I'm glad The Angel of Death case is finally behind him."

"Thanks to you."

I raise a brow. This would be my moment to say I told you so. If I wanted to be snarky, but my head aches too much to gloat right now.

"I'm sorry, Lucy. I should have listened to you."

"Why do I get the feeling that was really hard for you to say?"

"You're about to get a two for one because I was wrong about something else too."

"Really?" I smile. "And what would that be?"

"I think I'm turning into a muffin man."

The deep timbre in his voice makes my girl parts stand up and pay attention.

Holy wow. I think I'm in trouble.

I mean, I love Will. I always have. But I can't deny that there's an attraction here with Travis.

He clears his throat. "By the way, my dad told me to give you a message. He said to tell you that he believes you. Any idea what he means by that?"

I smile. "Yep."

"Care to share it with me?"

"Nope."

He frowns.

"Oh, Lucy!" Brittany shoves Travis off to the side. She's holding a fresh ice bag. "Sarah just told me that you might develop a concussion and that someone needs to spend the night to wake you up every hour to make sure you're okay. I *insist* that you let me do it."

"Really, that's okay. I—"

"Lucy," she says sternly. "No way am I going to let you spend the night all alone. Besides, we have so much to talk about!"

"We do?"

"Didn't you get the email from Tara at The Cooking Channel?"

"The one about wanting to come out and film the café for *Muffin Wars*?"

"*Muffin Wars*? Lucy, you silly! Did you read the whole email? And all the attachments?"

"Most of it." Well, some of it.

"You're not auditioning for *Muffin Wars* anymore. Once I knew The Cooking Channel was interested in you, I had daddy pull some strings. They're vetting you for something a whole lot better! *Battle of the Beach Eats*," she says. "Have you seen it?"

"Is that the show that spotlights a beach town and puts all the restaurants in the town in competition with one another?"

She nods eagerly "It's sooo much better than *Muffin Wars*. Lucy, this is the big time!"

"Hold on just a second. How did this happen again?"

"When I saw your audition tape, I thought, how can *all* of Whispering Bay benefit from this fabulous opportunity? Working for the Chamber of Commerce, that's just the way my mind works. And it came to me. Let's find a way for The Cooking Channel to showcase all of Whispering Bay's fabulous restaurants, and Tara suggested *Battle of the Beach Eats*. Isn't she fabulous?"

"But...so The Bistro is going to be in competition with The Harbor House and Tiny's Pizza and all the other restaurants in town? We're just a coffee house. How can we compete with your father's place?"

"Oh *that*. No worries. Each restaurant will be judged on its own merits. It's all super fair."

My head is throbbing too much for me to protest. I had a better than decent chance of winning *Muffin Wars*. But this other show? The Bistro is great, but there are some awesome restaurants here in town, and I'm not sure how we'll stack up against them.

"Is there a cash prize?" I hate to sound mercenary, but let's face it, I was really hoping for that ten grand. Besides the money I owe Will, I also have a credit card to pay off now.

"Twenty-five thousand dollars, plus the prestige of being proclaimed the Best Beach Eat in Whispering Bay. And the absolute best part? We'll be doing this *together*!" Brittany squeals. "As head of the Chamber of Commerce's PR department, this is totally my baby. I'm pretty nervous, actually. It's my first big project but with you on board to help me, I know it will all go fabulously."

Brittany absolutely believes every word she's saying.

She hugs me again. "Who would have thought way back in kindergarten that you and I would end up being best friends?"

I inwardly moan.

It's going to be a long, long night.

Thank you for reading! If you enjoyed Lucy's antics then you won't want to miss the next book in the series, WHACK THE MOLE.

Joey "The Weasel" Frizzone has been deep undercover with one of the country's largest organized crime families and the time has come for him to testify against them. The trial isn't for a couple of weeks, and the feds need him to lay low, so they hide him in a place no one would ever think to look—a sleepy little town in Florida called Whispering Bay.

Lucy McGuffin bakes the best muffins in town. She's also a human lie detector, a talent that hasn't always been easy to live with, because, C'mon, how many times can a girl hear "It's me, not you," and keep a straight face?

Lucy's ability to sniff out a lie has given her a reputation for solving crime, so when an attempt is made on Joey's life, local police officer, Travis Fontaine reluctantly seeks Lucy's help. But Lucy and Travis have a wobbly relationship. The arrogant cop thinks he's God's gift to womankind and Lucy isn't about to become President of his fan club.

Someone in the FBI must have a big mouth because soon there are enough hitmen in town to make Whispering Bay look like a reunion site for The Sopranos. Then someone starts whacking the hitmen. As the body count begins to rise, Lucy realizes she has to step up to the plate. Travis needs Joey to stay alive long enough to testify, and Lucy wants her quaint little town back, minus the mobsters.

With the help of her best friend, Will, and her rescue dog, Paco, Lucy and Travis set out to discover who's behind all the hits because if they don't, Whispering Bay may never be the same again. *Ba-da-Bing. Ba-da-Boom.*

BOOKS BY MAGGIE MARCH

Lucy McGuffin, Psychic Amateur Detective

Beach Blanket Homicide

Whack The Mole

Murder By Muffin

Stranger Danger

Two Seances and a Funeral

The Great Diamond Caper

Dead and Deader (coming soon!)

ABOUT THE AUTHOR

Maggie March writes cozy mysteries that will make you laugh. Born in Cuba, she was raised on Florida's space coast. She and her husband of thirty-plus years (along with their four dogs) are thrilled to call central Florida home again. She loves the beach, time spent with family, and is always on the lookout for the perfect key lime pie recipe (but not the kind they served on Dexter). Maggie loves hearing from her readers. You can write to her at maggie@maggiemarch.com

Maggie also writes feel-good small-town contemporary romance as her alter ego Maria Geraci.